TRINITY AND RELIGIOUS PLURALISM

The doctrine of the Trinity is one of the most distinguishing marks of Christian faith. This is the first book to present an overview of the role of the Trinity in Christian theology in relation to religious pluralism and other religions.

Approaching the study of the relationship between Christianity and other religions from the perspective of the Trinity, this book surveys all the major contributions to the topic by leading theologians at the international and ecumenical level. Veli-Matti Kärkkäinen points to future challenges and areas in need of development, examining in detail a case study exploring how the Catholic Church has responded to Islam from the perspective of the Trinity. Students of theology and religious studies will find this an invaluable text for courses that discuss religious pluralism and Christianity's relation to other religions. Pastors, other Christian workers, and academics will also find it a handy reference tool for teaching and further study.

Trinity and Religious Pluralism

The Doctrine of the Trinity in Christian Theology of Religions

VELI-MATTI KÄRKKÄINEN

ASHGATE

Published by
Ashgate Publishing Limited
Gower House
Croft Road
Aldershot
Hants GU11 3HR
England

Ashgate Publishing Company
Suite 420
101 Cherry Street
Burlington
VT 05401-4405
USA

Ashgate website: http://www.ashgate.com

British Library Cataloguing in Publication Data
Kärkkäinen, Veli-Matti
   Trinity and religious pluralism : the doctrine of the Trinity in Christian theology of religions
   1.Trinity 2.Religious pluralism – Christianity 3.Theology of religions (Christian theology)
   I.Title
   231'.044

Library of Congress Cataloging-in-Publication Data
Kärkkäinen, Veli-Matti.
   Trinity and religious pluralism : the doctrine of the Trinity in Christian theology of religions / Veli-Matti Kärkkäinen,
      p. cm.
   Includes bibliographical references and index.
   ISBN 0-7546-3645-3 (alk. paper) – ISBN 0-7546-3646-1 (pbk. : alk. paper)
      1. Theology of religions (Christian theology) 2. Trinity. I. Title.

   BT83.85.K375 2003
   231'.044 2003054486–dc22

Reprinted 2008

2003057838

ISBN   0 7546 3645 3 (Hardback)
        0 7546 3646 1 (Paperback)

ISBN 978 0 7546 3645 8 (Hardback)
      978 0 7546 3646 5 (Paperback)

Printed & bound by MPG Books Ltd, Bodmin,Cornwall.

Contents

Acknowledgements

The manuscript was written during the Fall of 2003, my first sabbatical from Fuller Theological Seminary, Pasadena, California. Had there not been this opportunity to concentrate on the study and writing, I probably would have found another excuse to postpone this project, which had already been in the making in my mind for some time. Let this study be another way of thanking the school that provides such an inspiring and fruitful multicultural, ecumenical setting for teaching, research and writing.

Susan Carlson Wood of the School of Theology Faculty Publications Services at Fuller deserves again a big thank you for her meticulous and insightful editorial work; finishing yet another book with her has not only been a joyful experience but a continuous learning experience, too, for a non-native English speaker.

Most importantly, to my dear family, my wife, Anne-Päivi, and daughters, Nelli and Maiju, with whom I have had the unique opportunity to live and work on three different continents – Europe, Asia and North America – I owe most heartfelt thanks. Without their constant loving support and encouraging smiles I would have not been able to finish this writing project.

Introduction: The Doctrine of the Trinity and the Challenge of Religious Pluralism

Trinity and Pluralism in Focus

At the beginning of the millennium there are two significant developments in Christian theology at the ecumenical and international level which continue to give direction to a number of new publications, conferences and debates, namely, the revival of the doctrine of the Trinity and the explosion of inquiries into the theological relationship among religions. The resurgence of the doctrine of the Trinity, beginning with the groundbreaking work of Karl Barth before the mid-twentieth century, has helped revive the relevance of the Christian doctrine of God and its relation to issues such as salvation, community, creation and eschatology. The challenge of religious pluralism has accounted for the unexpected rise to prominence of issues dealing with how Christianity should relate to other religions. This field of inquiry is known technically as the theology of religions.

However, what is most noteworthy and surprising about these two developments is that they have not converged. By and large, the renaissance of the doctrine of the Trinity and the emergence of Christian theology of religions have existed next to each other in time, but thematically there has been little or no connection. This is remarkable in light of the obvious fact that both deal with God! The purpose of both fields is to offer criteria to identify the God of the Bible and God's relationship to us – and to others. It was Barth who claimed that what makes the Christian doctrine of God different from the gods of other religions is the Trinity. Yet he did not work out any kind of trinitarian theology of religions.

With little exaggeration we can say that with the exception of Raimundo Panikkar, who gleans from the rich pluralistic soil of Asia, even those Christian theologians who have laboured in the field of Christianity's relation to other religions have ignored the relevance of the doctrine of the Trinity. Panikkar has been the first to not only highlight the importance of the Trinity for religions in general and Christianity in particular, but also maintain that there is a basic trinitarian structure embedded in several living religions.

Currently things are changing, and the contribution and challenge of the doctrine of Trinity is beginning to be invoked in Christian theology of religions. Before we take a brief survey of those few existing attempts, let us map out briefly the territory of both the trinitarian doctrine and Christian theology of religions.

The Challenge of Pluralism and Theology of Religions

The Western collective memory tends to be especially shortsighted in its search for the ever new and unexpected. Currently one often hears that religious pluralism is a new phenomenon. It is not. Christianity and other living faiths have both emerged from and existed side by side with other religions and varying religious commitments. Certainly both the early church and the patristic church lived in the midst of competing religions. The great Christian novelist John Bunyan had to fight the devil with these daunting questions:

> How can you tell but that the Turks had as good Scriptures to prove their Mahomet the Saviour, as we have to prove our Jesus is; and could I think that so many ten thousands in so many Countreys and Kingdoms, should be without the knowledge of the right way to Heaven ... and that we onely, who live but in a corner of the Earth, should alone be blessed therewith? Everyone doth think his own Religion rightest, both Jews, and Moors, and Pagans; and how if all our Faith, and Christ, and Scriptures, should be but a thinks-so too? (Bunyan, 1962, p. 31)

Nevertheless, there is some truth to the mantra that the challenge of pluralism has never been of such urgency as it is in the beginning of the third millennium. It is not so much the plurality of religions as it is the rapidly spreading mindset according to which plurality should lead to pluralism, the latter meaning something like a rough parity between religions with none having final authority (and certainly not to the exclusion of others). While Christianity has experienced this effect most dramatically, in principle no other religion is immune to it. With the decay of the verbal inspiration of the Bible and the rise of the Enlightenment modernism that has recently given way to postmodernism, any religion that authoritatively proclaims its truth as *the* ultimate truth has to make its case.

Consequently, since the early 1970s, and especially in the 1990s, a flood of books and other publications dealing with issues related to pluralism have appeared and there seems to be no end on the horizon. Pluralism is here to stay, and Christian theology is invited to tackle the issue. Thus the comment by Alan Race (1982, p. xi), one of the first to outline various Christian responses to pluralism, makes the point that

> the future of Christian theology lies in the encounter between Christianity and other faiths. If they are correct in this, then the Christian theology of religions needs present no apologia for adding one more specialism to the Christian theological enterprise as a whole. Rather, it ought to rejoice at being at the frontiers of the next phase in Christian history.

What, then, is theology of religions? Theology of religions is that discipline of theological studies that attempts to account theologically for the meaning and value of other religions. Christian theology of religions attempts to think theologically about what it means for Christians to live with people of other faiths and about the relationship of Christianity to other religions. Recently some authors have proposed the label 'theology of religious pluralism', as is evident in the monumental work of the Roman Catholic Jacques Dupuis, SJ, *Toward a Christian Theology of Religious Pluralism* (1997). The focus on pluralism in defining the content of theology of religions is appropriate in that it highlights the most significant challenge to theology of religions. Nevertheless, the term 'theology of religions' most probably holds the more established status as a general title for this field of study.

This book approaches religious plurality from an unashamedly Christian perspective; thus it represents *Christian* theology of religions. In principle – even though not much work has yet been done – there also could be a theology of religions from the perspective of other religions, such as a Buddhist or Hindu theology of religions. The goal of each of these theologies of religions would be to reflect on the meaning of other religions in relation to its own convictions and underlying foundations. Christian theology of religions is by far the most developed type of theology of religions.

As a separate field of study, theology of religions is a rather recent phenomenon, even though, as mentioned, the plurality of religions and religious pluralism are no new phenomena. Theology of religions emerged first in Catholic circles, beginning with the radical reorientation of Catholic theology as a result of the Second Vatican Council (1962), and soon spread to Protestant spheres as well. In the wake of these dramatic Catholic changes, the World Council of Churches, under the leadership of the Indian Stanley Samartha, published *The Living Faiths and Ultimate Goals* in 1974, followed the next year by *Towards World Community: Resources and Responsibilities for Living Together*.

As a fairly new field, theology of religions is still looking for canons.[1] Even the question of how to classify Christian responses to other religions is in the making and heavily debated. In the beginning stages, the threefold typology – still most widely used, yet seriously criticized – of 'exclusivism', 'inclusivism' and 'pluralism' was taken almost for granted. In the technical senses of these terms, *exclusivists* hold that salvation is available only in Jesus Christ, to the extent that those who have never heard the gospel are eternally lost. Exclusivists claim that salvation can be found only through faith in Christ; a stricter form of exclusivism maintains that salvation is to be found only in the Christian church. In this scheme, non-Christian religions play no role in the history of salvation. For *pluralists*, other religions are legitimate means of salvation. Pluralism involves both a positive and a negative element. Negatively, pluralism categorically rejects exclusivism (and often also inclusivism). Positively, it affirms that people can find salvation in various religions and in many ways. The mediating group, *inclusivists*, hold that while salvation is ontologically founded upon the person of Christ, its benefits have been made universally available by the revelation of God. This is the official teaching of the Roman Catholic Church after the Vatican II Council. This mediating position currently has the largest group of followers and it cuts across confessional and

denominational boundaries; many theologians from Eastern Orthodoxy to Roman
Catholicism to mainline Protestantism to Evangelicalism see it as the most viable
option.

Recently Paul Knitter (2002), the leading Roman Catholic pluralist in North
America, has suggested the following viable typology: The 'Replacement Model'
argues that there is only one true religion. The 'Fulfilment Model' considers
Christianity the 'true' religion as well, but believes that it has the potential for
helping others to reach their proper goal (the Roman Catholic postconciliar view
being the most typical example). 'The Mutuality Model' represents most of the
typical 'pluralist' paradigms and argues for a 'rough parity' between all religions, as
John Hick and many others have done. Finally, there is the newest one, the
'Acceptance Model' – in a sense the most pluralistic – which argues not for the
similarity of religions (notwithstanding phenomenological differences as most
pluralisms do) but rather for real, irreconcilable differences so much so that
eventually religions have the right to envision different 'ends'. In other words,
whereas nirvana may be the legitimate goal for Hindus and Buddhists, heaven is the
goal for Christians. S. Mark Heim is the most vocal proponent of this rather novel
view.

For this book's purposes there is no need – and certainly no space – to solve this
methodological problem. At the end of this introduction, after a look at the rise to
prominence of the doctrine of the Trinity, and subsequently its relation to pluralism
and theology of religions, a heuristic typology is suggested based on the above
considerations. (That typology serves only the purposes of this book's presentation
and is not meant to be a proposal in a more general sense.)

The Revival of the Doctrine of the Trinity in Christian Theology

For the purposes of our book, there is no need to attempt a history of research into
the doctrine of Trinity even in recent decades; interested students may easily find
resources for that (e.g. Peters, 1993). Routinely Karl Barth is hailed as the originator
of the trinitarian renaissance in the latter part of the twentieth century and rightly so.
The assessment of Barth from Ted Peters – himself a prolific writer on the topic –
is shared by many: 'The major contributors to the contemporary rethinking of the
doctrine of the Trinity either extend principles already proffered by Barth or else
follow lines of thought that parallel his *Church Dogmatics*' (Peters, 1993, p. 82).
Barth helped wake up the doctrine of the Trinity from the dormant spirit in which it
had lain since Immanuel Kant, F.D.E. Schleiermacher and Albrecht Ritschl, to all of
whom the Trinity was not only secondary but a useless appendix to Christian
theology, a later nonbiblical development.[2]

Barth's contribution to the revival of the trinitarian doctrine is twofold. First of
all, he made it the structuring principle of his theology. Second, he affirmed that
what happens in history has a bearing on what 'happens' in the triune godhead; thus,

history was introduced to deity. In that enterprise, Barth was echoing much of what G.W.F. Hegel in the nineteenth century had done in his highly speculative system in which, interestingly, history came into account. In fact, for Hegel, truth was not only historical, but history and historical process was a coming into being of ultimate truth. Even though Barth's theology is certainly not Hegelian, this emphasis on history came to play a significant role in his doctrine.

Barth's focus on history was picked up by the Catholic Karl Rahner, who devised the famous 'rule' according to which 'The "economic" Trinity is the "immanent" Trinity and the "immanent" Trinity is the "economic" Trinity' (Rahner, 1997, p. 22). In other words, Rahner maintained that God in Godself is identical to the God who reveals Godself in the 'economy' of salvation history. Even though Rahner's rule has been modified by many (another question beyond the scope of our inquiry), in its foundational meaning it has become an axiom.

Two leading Protestant theologians, Wolfhart Pannenberg and Jürgen Moltmann, have taken Barth's and Rahner's views as the basis of their own thinking about the Trinity. Moltmann has expanded the doctrine of the Trinity in a panentheistic[3] and eschatological direction. The eschatological direction means that God is 'on the way' to becoming the God who finally will be 'all in all' according to the biblical promise (1 Cor. 15:28).[4] Moltmann also has made the cruxifixion an 'event' in the godhead itself. Pannenberg has taken up Barth's suggestion that Trinity is a structuring principle of Christian theology even more seriously than Barth: the only way to come up with a biblically based understanding of the trinitarian God is to study the history of the coming of Jesus and the Spirit in the Bible as distinct from yet related to the Father. Thus, again, history counts. For Pannenberg, the resurrection is more crucial than for Moltmann since the resurrection of Jesus for Pannenberg is the divine confirmation of the Father of the validity of Jesus' claims of his sonship.

Two other significant voices have to be added to finish this brief sketch of the emergence of the trinitarian doctrine in the last part of the second millennium. The Eastern Orthodox John Zizioulas has approached the Trinity from the perspective of personhood and communion. For him, what makes a 'person' – in complete contrast with Western individualism – is being in relationship, in other words, in communion. A person does not first exist and then enter into relationships; rather, to exist is to be in relationship (Zizioulas, 1985).

The late American Catholic theologian Catherine LaCugna has gathered all these various influences into an ambitious program called *God for Us* (1992). Focusing on the second part of Rahner's rule – the economic Trinity is the immanent Trinity – LaCugna has maintained that it is only on the basis of *oikonomia* (salvation history) that we can come to speak of the Trinity, and thus *theologia* and *oikonomia* are inseparably related. What God does in the world and among us is what matters when we think of the Trinity. In this sense, even though ironically also gleaning from Hegel's insistence on history, nothing could be more foreign to LaCugna than an abstract speculation into the self-actualization of the 'Absolute Spirit'! At the same time, LaCugna holds on to the communion theology: since God is to be known as triune only in relation to (in communion with) the world, that is the essence of personhood for us too.

In sum – still focusing our reflections to the limited task of the present book – what has been most characteristic and programmatic about the developments of trinitarian traditions in recent decades can be summarized in these four affirmations:

1   The doctrine of the Trinity is the structuring principle of Christian theology and thus of Christian doctrine of God among others.
2   The triune God is not divorced from history; on the contrary, history counts and is 'included' in the 'history of God' not only with regard to salvation history (incarnation, crucifixion, resurrection, ascension), but also with regard to creation and perhaps the rest of history.
3   The triune God of Christian faith can only be known on the basis of God's dealings with us. Thus, we 'ascend' from salvation history to the inner life of God even though the inner life of God can never be exhausted (the danger of Rahner's rule when not qualified).
4   God as triune is divine communion, and thus the archetype for real personhood is communion, being-in-relation, as opposed to the rampant individualism of much of Western culture and theology.

On the basis of these and related considerations, we have to conclude that to neglect or downplay the importance of the doctrine of the Trinity for the theology of religions is both shortsighted and detrimental. One of the potentials for the future of Christian theology in general and theology of religions in particular is a responsible use of trinitarian resources. To assess the extent to which that has happened and the tasks at hand for us is the assignment for the last section of this introduction.

Trinity and Theology of Religions in a Meeting Place

Karl Barth made the following programmatic statement: 'The doctrine of the Trinity is what basically distinguishes the Christian doctrine of God as Christian, and therefore what already distinguishes the Christian concept of revelation as Christian, in contrast to all other possible doctrines of God or concepts of revelation' (Barth, I:1, p. 301).[5] It is one of the ironies of the history of Christian theology that while most theologians have agreed with the statement, little if any exploration has been done on how to relate the crucial doctrine of Christian faith, the Trinity, to other religions. The reasons may be many; one of the most obvious is that theology of religions has been too narrowly occupied with the question of salvation, evident for example in the way typologies are constructed.[6]

Raimundo Panikkar, a cosmopolitan, Asian-born Catholic theologian and religious scholar, was the first to present the bold suggestion that not only is the

Trinity an appropriate topic to tackle religious pluralism, nor only that it is *the* Christian resource; he went further by claiming that indeed a trinitarian structure can be found in all religions! His small yet highly significant book is called *The Trinity and the Religious Experience of Man*, first published in 1973. In that book Panikkar argues for three different kinds of spiritualities, all of which correspond to different 'persons' of the Trinity in Christian faith and Hinduism (and perhaps in other religions) too.

The next major study on the relationship between the Trinity and religions did not appear until 2000; it was titled *The Meeting of Religions and the Trinity*, by Gavin D'Costa, another Catholic theologian with an intercultural background. D'Costa takes the postconciliar Catholic trinitarianism as a major resource for highlighting the failure of pluralisms – whether Christian, Jewish, Hindu or Buddhist – to deliver their promises. He offers an outline but not yet a full programme of a trinitarian theology of religions. Yet another Catholic theologian, the veteran theologian of religions Jacques Dupuis, in his celebrated magnum opus *Toward a Christian Theology of Religious Pluralism* (1997), incorporates rich trinitarian discussion in his theology of pluralism, but again does not offer a full-scale trinitarian programme. It is significant, nevertheless, that in this book he expands his horizon from the earlier christocentric approach, *Jesus Christ at the Encounter of World Religions* (1991).

The most recent trinitarian theology of religions outside Catholic theology comes from the hand of S. Mark Heim, who originally comes from a rather conservative Evangelicalism. His book *The Depths of the Riches: A Trinitarian Theology of Religious Ends* (2001) is perhaps the 'most' pluralistic theology of religions yet to appear: on the basis of the diversity in the triune God, Heim advances the thesis that not only are religions different, but they also have different 'ends' in terms of salvation goals. Heim's book is undoubtedly the most radical challenge to the task of applying trinitarian resources to world religions.

Still another study that deals in a significant way with our topic should be mentioned, idiosyncratic as it is in its approach and bordering on a 'universal theology', namely, the book by the senior religious scholar Ninian Smart (in collaboration with his student, the Eastern Orthodox Stephen Konstantine) titled *Christian Systematic Theology in a World Context* (1991). In that book, long-time readers of Smart are rewarded by a *summa* of the innovative thinking so characteristic of his prolific career. The reason why the present book does not include a separate discussion of that work is not because I regard it an insignificant work, but because in my reading it does not place itself in the Christian (historical) tradition. (I am not saying that it does not represent Christian theology, but rather that, in contrast to the authors discussed in this study, Smart and Konstantine build their 'trinitarian' doctrine in a mixture of religious traditions which does not easily commend itself to more typical trinitarian approaches.)

A collection of essays by mainly Protestant theologians titled *The Trinity in a Pluralistic Age*, edited by Kevin J. Vanhoozer (1997), based on the proceedings of an international conference, explores various topics and theologians (such as Barth and Rahner) on the relationship between the Trinity and pluralism. Writers represent moderate classical orthodoxy, yet in open-minded, critical dialogue with differing voices. Some occasional contributions to the topic may be found elsewhere, to be highlighted during the discussion.

Topics and Tasks

For the purposes of this book, we have selected the following individual theologians for closer scrutiny in addition to one case study on the Catholic–Muslim dialogue in trinitarian perspective. Before introducing the players, a word about the grouping of these theologians into these broad categories:

In Part I, 'The uniqueness of the Christian trinitarian faith as the end of the dialogue', I discuss Barth's theology, which I see (mainly, but perhaps not exclusively) supporting that kind of approach to the doctrine of the trinitarian God that does not leave much room for dialogue. In my discussion, I will look at some recent attempts to 'open up' Barth for dialogue, but the results of that inquiry will be reserved to a critical assessment later in the book.

Part II deals with 'The potential and critical function of the Christian trinitarian faith in the dialogue with other religions'. In my terminology, this category represents various kinds of 'inclusivistic' attempts to relate the doctrine of the Trinity to dialogue with other religions and to affirmations of their value. Catholic theologians such as Rahner, Dupuis and D'Costa, as well as Protestant mainline theologian Wolfhart Pannenberg and the evangelical Clark Pinnock could be classified in this category. In a sense, this category – in my opinion – is the most open-ended, since it reserves final judgment about the relationship between Christianity and other religions.

Part III discusses 'The Christian trinitarian faith as an embrace of pluralism'. Theologians gathered together in this category represent a wide variety of approaches (so much so that lumping them together must be seen only as a heuristic, pedagogical device), from John Hick's idea of the 'rough parity' of all religions and downplaying of specifically Christian doctrines, including the Trinity, to a highly idiosyncratic fully trinitarian approach of Raimundo Panikkar (concerning whom we may seriously ask if he represents pluralism in the common sense of the term) to the perhaps most pluralistic theologian of all, S. Mark Heim, with his novel idea of the difference of 'religious ends'. It was with great hesitancy that I finally ended up keeping these three theologians in the same category for the simple reason that even though their pluralisms differ widely (and in Hick's and Heim's case immediately contradict each other), they all take pluralism in some form or another as the goal.

In each chapter, I will first offer an exposition of the views of the particular theologian with regard to the relationship between the Trinity and religious pluralism, to be followed by critical comments, questions and tasks for further work. Since I take the liberty of limiting my exposition and discussion to the specific focus of my book (Trinity and religious pluralism), I have no burden to attempt a whole-scale analysis of each one's theology of religions, let alone of their overall theologies. Readers interested in that will be guided to other sources, for example, my new textbook *An Introduction to Theology of Religions: Biblical, Historical, and Contemporary Perspectives* (2003).

Limitations to my selection of theologians are also considerable and should be made explicit to the reader. First of all, I have attempted a balanced survey ecumenically. There are four Roman Catholics (Rahner, Dupuis, D'Costa and Panikkar), which is understandable in light of the prominence of the doctrine of the Trinity in the Catholic tradition. Protestant theologians represent several major traditions such as Reformed (Barth), Lutheran (Pannenberg), Baptist (Pinnock and Heim), and Anglican/Church of England (Hick). The reason there are none from the Eastern Orthodox tradition, to which the doctrine of the Trinity is a household commodity, is simple: Eastern Orthodox theologians have not written on the topic. None of the Eastern trinitarian luminaries, either past (Vladimir Lossky among others) or present (John Zizioulas among others) have touched the topic in any depth.

The theologians selected represent both European and North American traditions, but there is only one Asian (Panikkar, and even he is only partially Asian). Again, the reason is that even though a number of theologians from Asia have written on theology of religions and pluralism (M.M. Thomas and Stanley Samartha being the best known), the doctrine of the Trinity has not played any significant part in their theology. When it comes to Africa and Latin America, there are emerging voices on distinctive trinitarian doctrines, but it is premature to assess their significance.[7]

Finally, there are, of course, Process theologians, most notably John Cobb Jr, but also others, who have written extensively on the topic of religious pluralism, but in their theology of religions – as in their theologies in general – Trinity does not play any significant role. Therefore for the purposes of this study their contribution is omitted.[8]

At the end of my exposition, before venturing to offer more sustained constructive ideas about how I view the relationship between the Trinity and religious pluralism and what I see as the impending tasks for the future, I will offer a case study based on conversations in France between Islamic monotheism and Christian trinitarianism. This is an attempt to make my discussion more concrete and show its relevance to the practice of dialogue.

A final note about the term *pluralism*: those well acquainted with both philosophy- and theology-of-religions discourse on pluralism know how difficult the concept is in itself and that, therefore, it would be more appropriate to talk about pluralisms (in the plural!). That I will not enter that technical discussion is not because I consider it insignificant, but for the simple reason of trying to stay focused on my main task. Thus I take the liberty of using the term *religious pluralism* in its everyday meaning in theology of religions, referring to the mindset that takes a 'rough parity' between religions more or less for granted. To a limited degree I will touch on the issue of pluralism when it becomes an issue with some theologians (such as Panikkar and D'Costa).

Notes

1   For starters, with detailed bibliographical references, see Kärkkäinen (2003a, 'Introduction').
2   For a brief, helpful orientation to what follows, with plenty of bibliographical references to original sources, see Grenz (2001, ch. 1).
3   The term 'panentheistic' – in contrast with 'pantheistic', which equates God and the world, and with 'theistic', which has an in-built tendency to make too great a separation between God and the world – attempts to be a mediating position according to which there is a mutual, interrelated relationship.
4   Rahner's main work on the Trinity is the 1981 *Theological Investigations 17*.
5   References to Barth's *Church Dogmatics* (1956–75) will be given in this form: the Arabic numeral (e.g. I) refers to volume, the Roman numeral (e.g. 1) to the part, to be followed by the page number (e.g. p. 301).
6   Exclusivism: no salvation in other religions; inclusivism: the possibility of salvation in other religions by virtue of Christianity; pluralism: equal chance of salvation in all religions.
7   For Africa, see A. Okechukwu Ogbannaya (1994), and for Latin America, Leonardo Boff (1988).
8   For a recent Process approach to the Trinity, see Bracken & Suchocki (1997).

Part I
The Uniqueness of the Christian Trinitarian Faith as the End of the Dialogue

CHAPTER 1

Karl Barth: The Trinity as the Distinguishing Mark of the Christian God

Prolegomena to Interpreting Barth

Karl Barth's theology of religions – if there is any – poses a daunting challenge to the interpreter for several reasons. The most obvious is the fact that Barth never set out to write a distinctive theology of religions. He of course dealt with the topic of religion extensively, but it is often hard to say how much of that is general critique of religion and how much deals with either specifically Christian religion or other particular religions. Even though rarely noticed, in my opinion, the lack of focus on theology of religions in Barth is far from self-evident in light of the fact that so much of his theology arose out of reaction to Classical Liberalism. It was Liberalism indeed which for the first time on a wider scale, in the aftermath of the Enlightenment, questioned the traditional Christian orthodoxy and Christianity's favoured place. And the fact that so much of Barth's earlier work dealt with topics such as revelation makes one wonder why he was never driven to the interreligious problematic.

Furthermore, his dialectical, often polemic way of writing – to quote Donald W. Dayton's (1990, p. 184) chiding remark: 'What Barth takes away with one hand he gives back with the other' – makes determining his stance extremely complicated. A corollary issue, routinely noticed by interpreters of Barth, is the question of the development of his theology: did he really change his major positions or not?

Ironically, scholarship and popular textbooks especially have added to the confusion: beginning from Hendrik Kraemer's now classic *The Christian Message in a Non-Christian World* (1938), it took selected emphases of Barth's theology as the major backup for an exclusivistic attitude towards other religions; Paul F. Knitter's *No Other Name?* (1985) in a very unfortunate way classifies Barth among 'conservative evangelicals'. Certainly conservatives may find in Barth's theology affirmations that support their views, but there is a wide gulf between Barth's neo-orthodox view of revelation and especially his universalistically oriented soteriology. Surprisingly even Knitter's most recent text (2002) categorically regards Barth as a total denier of the value of other religions.[1]

There is no denying the fact that Barth represents an unabashed restrictivism toward other religions. But what seriously complicates the picture is that, on the other hand, his Christology and thus soteriology seem to lead him eventually to universalism, the idea that (hardly) anybody will perish at the end. There are also other qualifying perspectives, such as Barth's criticism of Christianity among religions questioning the typical textbook view, according to which for Barth Christianity without qualification is the norm.

In what follows I will enter into a critical dialogue with Barth in four movements. First, I will offer a brief exposition of Barth's trinitarian doctrine insofar as it relates to theology of religions. Second, I highlight the dynamic – and in my judgment, somewhat self-contradictory – nature of Barth's trinitarian theology by looking at his 'revelational restrictivism' and 'soteriological universalism'. Third, I will search for resources to negotiate this built-in tension utilizing trinitarian resources. Fourth, I will take a critical look at a recent attempt to 'open up' Barth's exclusivism and make it appear more like a sort of pluralism. The purpose of that dialogue is not to try to make Barth 'fit' the current more pluralistically oriented discourse, but rather to advance our theological quest.

Trinity as the Means of Identifying the Christian God

Not inappropriately, Barth has been hailed as the herald of the 'contemporary revival of theology' in general and trinitarian doctrine in particular (Welch, 1952, p. 45). The starting point for his theology was the anguish over Liberalism's approach in which 'to speak about God meant to speak about humanity, no doubt in elevated tone, but ... about human faith and works.' Thus, in Liberalism 'human beings were magnified at the expense of God—the God who is sovereign Other standing over against humanity', the 'free partner in a history' (Barth, 1989, p. 48). The correction for this malaise was a turn to the Christian God who is identified as the triune God based on God's own revelation.

For Barth, the doctrine of the Trinity is not only the structuring principle of Christian doctrine but also the means of identifying the God of the Bible. 'The doctrine of the Trinity is what basically distinguishes the Christian doctrine of God as Christian, and therefore what already distinguishes the Christian concept of revelation as Christian, in contrast to all other possible doctrines of God or concepts of revelation' (I:1, p. 301). The doctrine of the Trinity is the only possible Christian answer to the question of who the self-revealing God of the Bible talks about.

Changing the course of the writing of systematic theology, Barth begins the whole dogmatics with the doctrine of the Trinity and thus makes it foundational to all other topics. His starting point is the famous formula in the beginning of *Church Dogmatics*: 'God reveals himself. He reveals himself through himself. He reveals himself'(I:1, p. 296). The theological conclusion here is that, for Barth, God's revelation and God's being are identical. God is who God is revealed to be. 'Thus, it is God Himself, it is the same God in unimpaired unity, who according to the biblical understanding of revelation is the revealing God and the event of revelation and its effect on man' (I:1, p. 299). The trinitarian God is the God revealed in and through Jesus Christ. Consequently, Jesus Christ is identical with God, 'the reality of Jesus Christ is that God Himself in person is actively present in the flesh. God Himself in person is the Subject of a real human being and acting' (I:2, p. 151). To the significance of this 'circle of self-revelation' for theology of religions we will return momentarily.

The trinitarian God revealed in Jesus Christ is a God who desires to enter into communion with human beings in his love. God is seen to be trinitarian as he is revealed in the self-giving love of the Father for the Son, which itself corresponds to the self-giving love of God for his creation. The trinitarian love relationships are fundamental to the loving relationship between God and the world (III:1, p. 14, 49; see also Fulljames, 1993, pp. 21–2).

Barth is very concerned about emphasizing the importance of the unity of the triune God, to the point that he does not want to talk about three 'persons' according to the classical trinitarian canons, but rather takes up the somewhat ambiguous term *Seinsweise* ('modes of being') in referring to Father, Son and Spirit (I:1, p. 355). By eschewing the terminology of 'personhood', Barth also seems to distance himself from the kind of individualism so prevalent in Western theology. He also makes the significant statement that were Jesus Christ another personality different from the Father, then he could not be the Father's self-revelation (I:1, p. 350–51; see also Grenz, 2001, p. 37). Furthermore, to posit a threefold subject would make three gods, tritheism (II:1, p. 297).

The use of the term 'modes of being' is another instance in which the shift from German to English has contributed to confusion. I do not think Barth is modalist[2] in adopting the language of 'modes of being'. My assessment seems to be supported by the fact that – against much of earlier tradition – Barth takes history into the being of God, thus giving room for ontological distinctions in the triune God. This is also significant for our purposes in light of the fact that religions do belong to history and are thus not unrelated to who God is in his triune being. The way Barth introduces history into the being of God is instructive. He does it most dramatically in the last volume (part 1) of *Church Dogmatics*. He describes the incarnation as the Son of God's journey into a far land. Acting as the Prodigal Son of Luke 15, the Son of God effects reconciliation since the journey is that of God himself revealed in the Son. 'Barth brought the immanent and economic Trinities together by positing that the Son's journey is God's own journey and that the Son's self-humiliation in birth, life, and death is an expression of God's transcendence. God is exalted in the humility of the Son' (Olson & Hall, 2002, p. 97).

Christocentrism emerges time after time in Barth's trinitarian theology, and we should take a look at it because of its relevance to our topic. Not only revelation and the identification of the triune God, but also creation and God's dealings with the world and humanity (including religions as mediators of the human search for God), are channelled through Christ. There is a Christological origin to the world and humanity. When we ask why God created the world, the answer is simple and profound: Jesus Christ. God 'needs' creatures in order that there shall be the one creature Jesus Christ. 'The reason why God created the world and the purpose for which he created it … is that he was able, willing, and prepared to be one with the creature in Jesus Christ' (II:1, p. 579). And for this purpose, God made a covenant. For Barth, creation is the 'external basis of the covenant', it prepares the sphere in which the life under covenant will take place (III:1, pp. 94–228). The covenant relationship is based on grace and the relationship between God and the world is essentially based on God's love. Creation and incarnation flow out of God's self-willed free decision to let the eternal trinitarian love extend beyond the triune fellowship. This is the God revealed to us in Jesus Christ, and for Barth there is no other God.

Revelational Restrictivism

For Barth, 'Revelation is God's self-offering and self-manifestation. … In revelation God tells man that he is God.' As opposed to Liberalism's idea of 'revelation' as the elevation of human capacities, this is 'something new, something which apart from revelation he does not know and cannot tell either himself or others' (I:2, p. 301).

And where do we find this revelation? Barth's short answer: in Jesus Christ:

> When Holy Scripture speaks of God, it concentrates our attention and thoughts upon one single point. … And if we look closer, and ask: who and what is at this point upon which our attention and thoughts are concentrated, which we are to recognize as God? … then from its beginning to its end the Bible directs us to the name of Jesus Christ. (II:2, pp. 52–4)

Accurately then, the Catholic interpreter of Barth, Hans Urs von Balthasar, described Barth's theology as an intellectual hourglass 'where God and man meet in the center through Jesus Christ. There is no other point of encounter between the top and bottom portions of the glass' (Balthasar, 1979, p. 170).

If God can be known only as God reveals himself – the affirmation that is the core of Barth's trinitarian doctrine – and God has chosen to reveal Godself in Jesus Christ, naturally a question arises of primary interest to our inquiry: what, if any, is then the value of religions in general and specific religions such as Christianity, Judaism or Hinduism, in particular? We wish Barth had been much clearer here. To address the question even tentatively also takes us to the corollary problem of whether Barth changed his opinion or not. In dealing with this issue, two specific passages are usually quoted, and should be, since they highlight the tension present in Barth's corpus. The first one comes from the famous passage dealing with other religions – and in fact, almost the only sustained discussion in Barth of that topic, the famous 'paragraph' 17 (over 80 pages!), titled 'The Revelation of God as the Abolition of Religions'; it is found in the beginning of his *Church Dogmatics* (vol. one, entitled 'The Doctrine of the Word of God', part two):

> From the standpoint of revelation religion is clearly seen to be a human attempt to anticipate what God in His revelation wills to do and does do. It is the attempted replacement of the divine work by a human manufacture. The divine reality offered and manifested to us in revelation is replaced by a concept of God arbitrarily and wilfully evolved by man. 'Arbitrarily and wilfully' means here by his own means, by his own human insight and constructiveness and energy. (I:2, p. 302)

In order to assess the significance of this statement, several points have to be noted. First of all, the title of the paragraph: the original German uses the term *Aufhebung* for the English 'abolition'. Students of Hegel know how notoriously difficult it is to translate the term, the literal meaning of which is 'lifting up'. Thus, ironically, it has the basic meaning of abolishing, but it may also have the related even though largely opposite meaning of lifting up, especially in Barth's dialectical theology in which the 'No' is often said not for its own sake but to lead to 'Yes'. And finally, it has to be noted that neither the passage nor the wider context lets us assume that Barth is excluding Christianity from the religions to be judged apart from the revelation in Christ. Consequently, the passage cannot be read – as it is often done – as a textbook example of Barth's negative attitude *toward other religions*, but rather should be read as a judgment of religions in general apart from special revelation coming from the triune God.

Without being able to address the wider question of the extent to which there is a change taking place in Barth's theology, it is safe to say that with regard to Christianity's relation to other religions, there is a change of tone, if not opinion, as is evident in another passage from a later stage of *Church Dogmatics*, paragraph 69 in volume four (part three) dealing with Christology (the 'prophetic office of Christ'):

> We recognize that the fact that Jesus Christ is the one Word of God does not mean that in the Bible, the Church and the world there are not other words which are quite notable in their way, other lights which are quite clear and other revelations which are quite real. ... Nor does it follow from our statement that every word spoken outside the circle of the Bible and the Church is a word of false prophecy and therefore valueless, empty and corrupt, that all the lights which rise and shine in this outer sphere are misleading and all the revelations are necessarily untrue. (IV:3, p. 97; see also Braaten, 1992, pp. 53–9)

In the same context, Barth also maintains that 'the criticism expressed in the exclusiveness of the statement affects, limits, and relativizes the prophesy of Christians no less than the many other prophecies, lights, and words relativized and replaced by it' (IV:3, p. 91), thus reminding us of the fact that Christianity is not immune to criticism of religion any more than acknowledgment of its relative value – and here the term *relative* has to be taken in its literal sense: 'in relation to' Jesus Christ. We will return to the assessment of these perspectives on theology of religions once we have exposited in more detail Barth's doctrine of the Trinity.

Soteriological Universalism

The key to Barth's soteriological universalism – which, of course, stands in tension with his revelational exclusivism – is the dual role of Christ as the Mediator between the triune God and humankind. Christ serves as the agent of revelation and of reconciliation. By virtue of the incarnation, God and humanity are united. In his divinity, Jesus represents God to us; in his humanity, Jesus represents humankind to God. By virtue of the incarnation, human beings can be made participants in the covenant to which God has obligated himself. In this covenant, God acts on behalf of us, through and in Christ.

In Barth's distinctive terminology, Jesus Christ is both an 'Electing God' and 'Elected Man' (II:2, pp. 105–6). On the basis of the dual agency of Jesus Christ, Barth recasts the whole concept of election. In contrast to the traditional Reformed position, according to which God has elected some for salvation and others for perdition (double predestination), Barth maintains that all God's elective actions are centred on Christ and Christ only. The election of God does not apply to individuals. Barth regards Calvin's Reformed doctrine of election as too static and a misrepresentation of the Bible. The passages in the Bible that talk about election (Rom. 9 and Eph. 1 being the most important ones) have to be read Christologically. When doing so, one formulates a doctrine of election and predestination in light of God's work of revelation and atonement. By sending his Son to be the incarnate God-man, God revealed his will to save men and women, not to reject them. The incarnation is proof that God is for humanity, not against it.

The only person(s) to be elected by God is the person of Jesus Christ. This is Barth's major modification of the traditional view of election. The eternal will of God is realized in the election of Jesus Christ from eternity. There is no other will of God, no other unchangeable 'decree' (a technical term in classical theology to denote God's predetermined will to elect) apart from or beyond Jesus Christ and his election. God is not bound to any kind of deterministic, unchangeable decree of his, but like a king with 'holy mutability', he is absolutely free to fulfil his purpose of saving all. Jesus Christ as the focus of God's election acts not only as an individual but is also the representative of the rest of humanity. In him, the entire human race has been chosen for salvation. But Barth goes further than that. Not only is Jesus Christ the elected man, he is also at the same time the electing God. This is Barth's version of 'double predestination'. As the representative of the whole human race, Christ has freely chosen, not only to become a man, but become a man *for us*; he chose the 'reprobation, perdition, and death' that was ours (II:2, p. 163). Voluntarily, he chose to be rejected by humanity and be crucified on the cross. Thus God elected Christ to bear completely the pain and cost of redemption. God chose to accept the cross and the lot of fallen humanity. Furthermore, God elected Christ to take from us the judgment. Christ was rejected in order that we might not be rejected. The negative side of predestination, which was to be ours, is directed towards Christ.

Thus, rather than speaking about double predestination in the sense of Calvinism, that is, with regard to individual persons, he instead uses the term 'universal election'. All human beings have been included in the election of Jesus Christ by God. After Christ has been condemned on the cross for our sins, no other condemnation follows. Not all are living as elected, and it is the task of the elected community, the church, to proclaim that such a person 'belongs eternally to Jesus Christ and is not rejected, but elected by God in Jesus Christ' and that 'the rejection which he deserves on account of his perverse choice is borne and cancelled by Jesus Christ; and that he is appointed to eternal life with God on the basis of the righteous, divine decision' (II:2, p. 306).

What then is the difference between these two groups of people? Not much. Some know that they are elected while others have not yet realized it; the former are already living in the light of their election, the others as if they were not. What this means in terms of the doctrine of salvation is a disputed issue in Barthian studies and a debate we cannot enter here. It is clear that Barth either is a universalist (the view according to which all will be saved) or at least has strong universalist leanings. The assessment of Barth's view by another neo-orthodox theologian, Emil Brunner (1949, pp. 348–9), does not leave any doubt about the main orientation of his doctrine of election in Christ:

> What does this statement, 'that Jesus is the only really rejected person', mean for the situation of humanity? Evidently this: that there is no possibility of condemnation. ... The decision has already been made in Jesus Christ – for all of humanity. Whether they know it or not, believe it or not, is not so important. They are like people who seem to be perishing in a stormy sea. But in the reality they are not in a sea in which one can drown, but in shallow waters, in which it is impossible to drown. Only they do not know it.

How to Negotiate the Tension

So far, our exposition of Barth's theological themes pertinent to theology of religions has shown us that the doctrine of the Trinity serves as the criterion for distinguishing the Christian God. How this criterion works, however, is less evident. What is clear is that it is through Jesus Christ that the triune God is revealed to us. Furthermore, there is a built-in tension between the revelational restrictivism and the soteriological universalism. My tentative opinion is that Barth never solved the problem and left the question open. There might have been trinitarian resources to deal with the issue, but Barth never really tackled the problem in a way that would cast away this major question mark. Thus the goal of the following discussion is much more modest: in dialogue with some recent commentators on Barth's theology of religions, I look for trinitarian resources to deal with this tension.

Donald W. Dayton (1990) highlights two interrelated issues that need to be taken into consideration when assessing how to negotiate between the revelational restrictivism and soteriological universalism: (1) the extent to which Barth's condemnation of 'religion' includes Christianity and (2) how the statements of the 'later' Barth about other lights relate to the 'Light'. We have already concluded that in his criticism of religion, Barth includes Christianity among the religions. Therefore Barth's restrictivism does not arise so much from the need to place Christianity in contradistinction to other religions, but rather out of his criticism of religions in general, especially the anthropocentric orientation of Classical Liberalism. It is true that Barth finally elevates Christianity as the 'true religion', but that only after the 'justification' of that religion, something like resurrection after death. The reason for regarding Christianity as the true religion is based on the central Reformation doctrine, namely, justification by faith: 'We can speak of "true religion" only in the sense in which we speak of a "justified sinner"' (I:2, p. 325). In religion itself there is nothing valuable; only insofar as the religion allows itself to be taken over by God's judgment and grace can it be true. But that is not the whole picture: eventually there will also be some kind of 'justification' of 'other lights' too, when 'they are taken, lifted, assumed, and integrated into the action of God's self-giving and self-declaring to man and therefore to the world made by him. And in the power of this integration they are instituted, installed, and ordained to the *ministerium Verbi Divini*' (IV:3, p. 164). Here the other meaning of the term *Aufhebung* comes to focus: there will not only be 'abolition' – 'no' to religions, including Christianity – but also 'lifting up', a qualified 'yes' and that by virtue of the revelation in Christ. This is made explicit in the same context:

> This ... is the critical, but also, since it is genuinely critical, the positive relationship of the light of life to the lights which the God whose saving action is revealed by the one light does not withhold from his creatures as such but gives them in His eternal goodness. (IV:3, pp. 164–5)

I believe here we have a fruitful way to negotiate the built-in tension between restrictivism and universalism on the basis of Barth's trinitarian Christology. According to Barth, as the incarnate Word is the eternal Son of God who became flesh, so Jesus the human is none other than the eternal Son of God (I:2, pp. 163–4; see also Chung, 2002, pp. 319–32). Not only that, Barth also affirms that 'In Jesus Christ it is not merely one human, but the *humanum* of all humans, which is posited and exalted as such to unity with God' (IV:2, p. 49). Therefore Barth, while holding on to revelational restrictivism, can also open up his doctrine of incarnation and reconciliation to embrace all humanity: 'Not only Christians, but all persons are included in the realm of Christ's effectiveness. Dogmatically, reversed, this means that the reality of Christ is the framework and realm in which human beings as such are included' (quoted in Chung, 2002, p. 320). Understood in this way, the human species exists *enhypostatically* (a technical Christological term meaning literally 'existence in') in Christ. This opens up a new perspective on human culture, including religions, and Barth noted implications in the same context in his discussion of 'secular parables of the truth'. According to Paul S. Chung,

Barth's concern is to dialectically combine the word of Jesus Christ with various claims to truth in a pluralistic society. According to him, in the world reconciled with God in Jesus Christ, God cannot abandon any secular sphere. Even from the mouth of Balaam we recognize the well-known voice of the Good Shepherd, which should not be ignored despite its sinister origin. Forms of secularism or pluralistic claims to truth ought to be regarded as signs and guideposts pointing to the Word of Christ to whom other cultures and religions are enhypostatically related. (2002, p. 321)

Chung further notes that this is not an exclusive position, but inclusive with radical openness to the strange voices outside the walls of Christianity. This much we can affirm. But then, I believe, Chung makes an overstatement unwarranted in light of Barth's theology: 'Profane words and lights are regarded to be as true as the one Word, because God is active also in other religions and cultures' (ibid., p. 326). Chung qualifies this statement by saying that it is given to the church to scrutinize whether other voices are good. Yet I think it is more true to say that the later Barth has qualified his exclusiveness by opening up to revelationary words outside the church as long as they are measured against the revelation given through Christ. Maybe it is still better to say what Chung mentions later (ibid., p. 326), gleaning from George Hunsinger, the famous interpreter of Barth, namely, that 'True human words or secular parables are conceived as coexistent with Jesus Christ as the one Word of God' (Hunsinger, 1991, p. 263). So, whatever lights are out there, they cannot be totally unrelated to the Absolute Light; nor should they necessarily be exhausted by it since in the final analysis all belongs to Christ.

There are some other resources in Barth's theology that could help make his theology more open to dialogue. I just mention them here with some comments and leave them for further inquiry among Barth students. First of all, that the doctrine of the Trinity also serves as the basis of Barth's doctrine of creation could be significant to his views on theology of religions. Barth seems to set 'nature' (what is there on the basis of creation) and 'grace' (what God has done in Jesus Christ for our salvation) in opposition to each other. But is that necessary for his theology? I do not think so. Creation exists for and by virtue of Jesus Christ, the first creature. There is no divorcing what the triune God has created from what the triune God is doing to recreate and bring about a new creation.

Second, in Jesus Christ, the 'first creature' and the goal of creation, God has obligated himself to an eternal covenant. What would be the significance of the covenant established by the trinitarian God? Barth's idea is not only a 'covenant of grace' in the limited sense of making the incarnation a contingent response to human sin (in the classical terminology, the 'infralapsarian' view), but also the proper goal of and, we may say, 'reason' for creation (the 'supralapsarian' view). Redemption is not an afterthought, a kind of emergency plan: 'Creation is the area of redemption from the beginning' (Dayton, 1990, p. 185).

Third, a corollary conclusion to this is that the triune God has thus bound himself to humankind in an everlasting covenant. This binds humankind into a solidarity rather than an arrogant 'sheep' and 'goats' divide. Thus Barth always annoyed the conservative circles by refusing to categorize people into two camps, 'saved' and 'lost'. Yet I think he did so more by intuition than by a conscious trinitarian reasoning, even if his theology would probably have provided much guidance for doing that.

Barth a Pluralist?

Some contemporary interpreters of Barth have raised the question of whether his theology may contain any orientations to affirm pluralism in any form. At the outset, it has to be admitted that this is a question Barth never seriously posed to himself and so the best we can do is to go beyond Barth's own agenda and see what kind of clues could be found in his system. Even then we need to be cautious in order not to read into Barth something that does not genuinely arise out of his own theological program. With that in mind, let us look at the recent proposal by Trevor Hart to classify Barth as a sort of pluralist.

The point of departure for Trevor Hart's inquiry into potential pluralistic orientations in Barth's theology is the careful distinction between two families of pluralism posed by the late grand old man of Christian theology of religions, Bishop Lesslie Newbigin. Newbigin (1991, pp. 56–7) notes that postmodernism usually makes us choose between an objectivism of either an empiricist or rationalist variety (that is, belief in the possibility of truth either on the basis of 'experience' or rational reasoning) and a pluralism that is essentially relativistic and sceptical, rejecting all possibilities of attaining any objective binding truth at all. Newbigin, also acknowledging that the former option (objectivism) is not feasible in the contemporary intellectual climate, is not happy with that impasse, but makes a significant distinction between 'agnostic' and 'committed' pluralism. What he calls 'sceptical pluralism' is the typical meaning of pluralism as described above. In distinction from that form of pluralism (and of course from objectivism also), he champions the idea of 'committed pluralism'. Gleaning from the work of Michael Polanyi – whose epistemology has greatly influenced Newbigin in general – Newbigin agrees with sceptic pluralists that there is no detached, 'neutral' point from which to view the world, but only a diverse series of perspectives. That acknowledgment, however, does not lead Newbigin to ultimate subjectivism and solipsism, but rather to an approach best described as 'critical realism'. In that approach, reality can be known by placing oneself in the places where reality makes itself known, by viewing it from certain standpoints rather than others. Of course, this kind of knowledge is not something to be 'absolutely validated', but neither is it without any kind of certainty. Polanyi, as is well known, has argued that not only religion, philosophy and the social sciences, but also the so-called hard sciences operate with this kind of epistemology. The 'objectivistic' myth has been left behind definitely and forever.

Hart (1997, p. 128) summarizes Newbigin's approach:

> He [Newbigin] remains, that is to say, committed to the view that pluralism is a
> feature of human knowing rather than of the way things are beyond human
> knowing, and optimistic in the capacity of humans to establish genuine and
> reliable epistemic contact with reality. Truth is there to be known, and may be
> known, if not absolutely or in any 'objective' or universally compelling manner,
> then at least with sufficient certainty and in a mode that compels what Michael
> Polanyi refers to as knowledge-claims bearing 'universal intent'.

Now, back to Barth and Hart's reading of his theology in light of the idea of
committed pluralism. As already mentioned, to Barth the doctrine of the Trinity is
the way to distinguish the Christian God from all other gods and thus a
determinative hermeneutical principle (see also I:1, p. 300). This triune God has
revealed himself in 'a closed circle of knowing'(I:2, p. 280), that is, God in himself
exists as the Great Unknowable; yet this same God objectifies himself as other in
the incarnation of Jesus Christ, 'in such a way that he is over against himself as
revelation over against revealer' (Hart, 1997, p. 135). But if the human person is to
receive such a revelation, then since they possess no common ground to do so, it is
necessary for this self-objectification to be accompanied by another, this time one
in which God indwells us directly and creates in us the subjective conditions for
being open to receiving the revelation, that is the Holy Spirit. As this event happens,
'the veil is lifted and we perceive the Word of God in the flesh of Jesus, the words
of Scripture, and preaching' (Hart, 1997, p. 128), the famous threefold form of the
Word of God. This event – and here the term needs to be taken literally, since
Barth's neo-orthodox view of revelation is focused on revelation as 'event' –
however, is not open to anybody, but only to those to whom it is given. No amount
of apologetics or historical study will open the eyes of others. 'Revelation as such
cannot be grasped, held on to, or controlled by the human knower. We know only
as we are in turn known by a God who draws us into relationship with himself. This
same God it is who determines to whom he will reveal himself' (ibid.).

This is the 'self-enclosed circle', the triune circle of God's self-knowing, into
which humans are drawn in the event of revelation, Hart notes. Thus the revelation
of God is not universally known or knowable, and humans have no natural aptitude
for it. Yet, Hart argues, this state of affairs in no way compromises the universal
intent (cf. Newbigin's and Polanyi's idea of the 'universal intention' of truth) since
it is given to the Christian church to be witnesses to God's self-revelation even
though it has not been given to them to determine who is to believe and who is not.
According to Hart, similar to Newbigin's committed pluralism, Barthianism
champions an epistemology according to which knowledge (of God, in this case)
only comes from a certain perspective, but it is still knowledge with 'universal
intention' to be given testimony to all.

Hart rightly concurs that for Barth, then – as for Newbigin – the central Christian
doctrines such as the Trinity, incarnation and resurrection are not just a matter of

language to be set aside for the purposes of interfaith dialogue as agnostic pluralists (such as Hick) do; they are 'truths' given by God to whom God chooses to give and are thus to be presented to all people. Yet there is no room for arrogance or exclusivistic rejection of others, but rather humility and respect. A Barthian Christian at the dialogue table, as Hart fittingly says, is rather 'a sinner among sinners, who feels that his own glass home is rather too fragile for him to be throwing any stones' (1997, p. 139). The Christian understands that those people whose standpoint does not afford them a view of the truth that has drawn him or her into its sphere of manifestation and influence are not to be blamed (Hart 1997, p. 141). Also, as already mentioned, the Christian knows that his or her own religion is under the judgment of religions and apart from the 'justification' does not have a grasp of revelation. It is only when the triune God reveals himself and thus draws human beings into his own self-knowledge that human persons can know God. Barth calls it 'the sacramental area created by the Holy Spirit, in which the God whose Word became flesh continues to speak through the sign of His revelation' (I:2, p. 359). This is the *Aufhebung* of religion into the life of the triune God himself.

Now what are we to think of Hart's reading of Barth? While I applaud the epistemology of Newbigin and Polanyi with the idea of the possibility of truth, albeit not objective, with universal intention, I fear that Hart reads that idea into Barth. One has to omit too much of Barth's explicit condemnation of religions and 'natural revelation' in order for us to be able to say that Barth concurs with the idea of committed pluralism. It is another thing to say that while Barth's theology is not oriented toward committed pluralism (any more than any other sort of pluralism), his (later) theology could perhaps be developed in that direction. We could also speculate that perhaps Barth in the contemporary intellectual climate would find his standing among those that champion some kind of committed pluralism.

However, I believe the merits of Hart's inquiry lie elsewhere. He has shown – as is also the case with Donald Dayton's reading of Barth alluded to above – that respect and honour rather than outright denial is the attitude that best describes Barth's opinion of Christianity's relation to other religions, and that attitude grows out of his trinitarian doctrine, especially of self-revelation. Also, it is significant in my mind that for Barth respectful and humble attitude is coupled with the insistence on the church's mandate to witness to all people about the triune God and what God has done in Jesus Christ. Even if that kind of attitude may not foster the open-ended dialogue that is in vogue in our age, it does not totally close the doors for a dialogue. Even here there is much similarity to Newbigin's insistence on not only the right of, but also the mandate for, the Christian church to witness to the gospel, which inherently is universal. This in my mind is a challenge to that kind of postmodern pluralism that has left behind all attempts to issue truth claims, let alone try to convince others of their 'universal' validity.

A terminological note is in order here. While personally I do sympathize with Newbigin's idea of committed pluralism, I do not think the term *pluralism* is an appropriate label. The term *pluralism* is already so overused – and as our discussion in what follows will show, there are already not only different but more or less contradictory pluralisms available – that to add yet another layer on it is not helpful. I would be happy to call the Newbigin–Polanyi suggestion 'critical realism', even though I know that this term does not apply exclusively to that idea. But the term 'critical realism' conveys its basic idea: it is critical of the modern (Enlightenment) ideal of objectivism, yet it does not agree with postmodernism's refusal of any kind of 'universal' truth.

Concluding Reflections and Tasks for the Future

So far we have looked at various means to soften the alleged exclusivism of Barth's theology and negotiate the built-in tension between restrictivism and universalism. This tension focuses on Christology, which ironically serves as the backbone for both orientations.

Yet softening Barth's alleged exclusivism does not make him a pluralist. Rather he can be classified as a critical realist on the basis of his trinitarian doctrine of revelation: God, the Unknowable, assumes the form of the Other and reveals himself; the Spirit of God establishes the contact point, missing in humanity, to enable the human person to open up to God's revelation.

Barth claimed that the Trinity is the guiding principle of theology in general and theology of religions in particular: it is the means of identifying the Christian God. Furthermore, it is the key to a humble, respectful attitude to other religions on the basis of his conception of revelation as 'a closed circle of knowing'.

So far so good, but there is one major problem in Barth's theology that I personally consider irreconcilable, and that has to do with his universalism. I am not saying this only because I think universalism carries with it several theological problems: it can hardly be biblically justified; it compromises (as do pluralisms too) any kind of particularity of the Christian God, which classical Christianity is not ready to give up; and (in Barth's case especially) it makes any kind of notion of human freedom an empty word (one cannot but be saved!). While I agree with those criticisms, my concern here focuses only on our task, the relationship between the Trinity and religions. It seems to me that Barth's trinitarianism finally has to be deemed inadequate and internally inconsistent in its ability to describe God's relation to the world and especially to other religions. Let me try to explain briefly my main issues here.

I leave it to Barth specialists to debate exactly what type of universalism Barth represents. In my reading of Barth, however, there is no doubt about the fact that his Christology makes him first an 'anonymous universalist' and later, when the implications are spelled out by Barth himself, a 'reluctant universalist'. I also leave it to Barth specialists to determine what is 'wrong' with his Christology so that it takes him to universalism. I will here only look at the implications for theology of religions. In my opinion, the basic reason for Barth's type of universalism is exactly the lack of a thoroughgoing trinitarianism that results in a disastrous distinction between 'nature' and 'grace' and – most ironically for Barth's theology with its explicit intent on preserving the identity of God immanent and incarnate – between God the Creator and God the Redeemer. Barth begins his system with a fateful dualism of nature and grace; even when, later on, this contradistinction is being softened to some extent, the only way to protect the freedom of God is to build a Christology apart from anthropology. The doctrine of creation, as mentioned earlier, could have come to help here, since it is built on Christological foundations, but – again due to his reluctance to give credit to 'nature' – Barth fails to see the trinitarian connections. In terms of his *attitude* toward 'nature' Barth is becoming more balanced, but not in terms of the *structure* of his theology. For a healthy trinitarian theology, what God does in creation ('nature') cannot be divorced from what God does in salvation ('grace'). Furthermore (and this is a theme we will revisit when discussing Karl Rahner's theology in the next chapter), there is no nature that is not graced. Thus, for example, the knowledge of God (among religions) on the basis of nature cannot be set in such a contradistinction from the knowledge of God through special revelation as Barth seems to do. Even special revelation builds on and can be received on the basis of what is there in nature; special revelation goes beyond and corrects, but it does not nullify general knowledge of God.

Ironically, Barth fails in his trinitarian doctrine exactly in the aim that was its original intention, namely, to provide the criterion for distinguishing the Christian God. Other than affirming the role of the doctrine of the Trinity as *the* criterion, Barth – unlike the Catholic Rahner, as I will argue in what follows – is not able to redeem his promise. Even worse, his insistence on the unity of the triune God to the point of eschewing any kind of terminology of distinct 'persons' (even if the term 'person' in itself is nothing sacred to be preserved just for the sake of its venerated history) makes his doctrine of the Trinity even less relevant with regard to God's relation to the world and certainly other religions. Again, unlike Rahner who insists that we never meet a 'general' God but rather one or another of the trinitarian 'persons', Barth's theology does indicate clearly the mode of the presence of the triune God in the world.

These are the modest results of our discussion concerning the potential and relevance of Barth's theology for Christian theology of religions. Although with regard to the last two major issues (universalism and inconsistent trinitarianism, at least with regard to our topic) we could not advance the discussion much, we were able to offer new light for reading Barth's theology in somewhat more 'open' terms with regard to dialogue with other religions. I find Dayton's (1990, p. 188) final conclusion to his study on potential resources to open up Barth's exclusivism compelling in light of Barth's overall theology:

> The results of this study are modest. We have not challenged directly Barth's own exclusivism. We have merely argued that he is often misunderstood—that his thought is more subtle and dialectical than is often assumed. I am not sure

that Barth himself would have developed his own thought in the direction of dialogue with other religions (indeed, there are signs and incidents that indicate that he did not have much personal interest in these questions), but I do think that it is possible on Barthian premises to have more engagement with other religions than is usually assumed. This is to be sure a modest place, but I believe it to be a valuable place nonetheless.

What about the general title of Part I of our book, 'The uniqueness of the Christian trinitarian faith as the end of the dialogue'? After the survey into Barth's theology, I do not believe we are required to change the title, but perhaps add a question mark and thus leave the topic for further inquiry. Certainly Barth has been read as supporting the title with an exclamation mark. Let the question mark be added to remind us of the need for deeper investigation into this most challenging theological system.

Notes

1   Knitter's doctoral dissertation (1977) is more balanced in its treatment of Barth, placing him in correlation with Paul Althaus, the moderate Lutheran scholar, and Ernst Troeltsch, one of his venerated Liberal teachers.
2   Modalism is an ancient trinitarian heresy according to which Father, Son and Spirit do not represent distinct 'persons' but rather are 'modes' of the same godhead. Modalism is also known as Sabellianism, after its main proponent in the third century, Sabellius.

Part II
The Potential and Critical Function of the Christian Trinitarian Faith in the Dialogue with Other Religions

CHAPTER 2

Karl Rahner: Trinity and 'Anonymous Christianity'

Rahner as the Architect of the Reorientation of Contemporary Catholic Theology

For our dialogue partners in this book we have selected four Catholic theologians, among whom the late Karl Rahner stands as the undisputed mentor and senior colleague. There is no way of understanding contemporary Catholic theology in general, and theology of religions in particular, without at least a passing knowledge of Rahner's contribution. Rahner's enormous theological output is very much related to the most formative church council of the Roman Church, namely, Vatican II (1962–5). With Hans Küng, a theologian still living who subsequently fell into disfavour in the eyes of his superiors, Rahner was the main theological architect of the council. To give needed background not only for the discussion of Rahner's theology but for the rest of our Catholic dialogue partners (Dupuis, D'Costa, Panikkar), a brief introduction to the main insights of Vatican II (with regard to Christianity's relation to other religions) is presented here. D'Costa especially but also Dupuis extensively dialogue and negotiate with Vatican II and subsequent teachings of the magisterium.

Out of the 16 council documents, the two most important are *Nostra Aetate*, the theology of religions document proper, and *Ad Gentes*, the document on the missionary task of the church.[1] The main affirmations of the council relevant to our discussion may be summarized as follows. First, the Council documents open the possibility of salvation to all people with good will and the desire to live according to the light given them. The missionary document *Ad Gentes* (# 7) teaches regarding those who, through no fault of their own, are ignorant of the gospel that God can lead them to that faith without which it is impossible to please him. Significantly, Vatican II was not satisfied with simply stating the possibility of salvation for those without the gospel, but even offered a kind of explanation as to how it happens. The council fathers appealed especially to the universal working of the Spirit in making the paschal mystery of Christ available to all people. The clearest statement comes from *Gaudium et Spes* (# 22), which speaks about Christians coming into contact with the paschal mystery of Christ's cross and resurrection:

> All this holds true not only for Christians but also for all individuals of good will in whose hearts grace is active invisibly. For since Christ died for all, and since all human beings are in fact called to one and the same destiny, which is

divine, we must hold that the Holy Spirit offers to all the possibility of being associated, in a way known to God, with the Paschal Mystery.

Thus it is an axiom of postconciliar Catholic theology that salvation is available to people of good will. What is a hotly debated question, however, is whether other religions *per se* are vehicles of salvation or not. The official interpretation is – and Rahner agrees (1983, pp. 290–91) – that it is not affirmed but rather left open. The conditions for the salvation of non-Christians are that it is through 'no fault of their own' that they are not able to hear the gospel and that they have a sincere striving to live a good life. What constitutes that 'good life' is usually referred to conscience and natural law written in the hearts of all men and women (*GS* # 16).

Second, with regard to the value of other religions, the council offers several related insights.[2] The religions are in various ways related to the church; there is a kind of 'hierarchy of religions'. Judaism is the closest religion to Christianity, then comes Islam with its monotheism. Hinduism, because of its polytheism, is next in the descending order, and then comes Buddhism, a religion without a clear concept of God, and finally 'other religions to be found everywhere' (*NA* # 2). Furthermore, there is a real acknowledgment of all good in other religions: there is a 'ray of that Truth which enlightens all men' (*NA* # 2; see also # 17, *LG* # 17 and *AG* # 9).

There is, then, both continuity and discontinuity between Christianity and other religions. Perhaps the most affirmative passage comes from *Nostra Aetate*:

> The Catholic Church rejects nothing of what is true and holy in these religions. With sincere respect she looks on those ways of conduct and life, those precepts and teachings which, though differing on many points from what she herself holds and teaches, yet not rarely reflect a ray of that Truth which enlightens all men. But she proclaims and must ever proclaim, 'the way, the truth and the life', in whom human beings find the fullness of religious life, and in whom God has reconciled all things to himself. (*NA* # 2)

Clearly, the Thomistic doctrine of nature elevated by the grace of God was still an influential idea behind much of the council's theology of other religions. On the basis of the mystery of incarnation, 'nature' and 'grace', the natural and the supernatural, belong together. The grace of God purifies, liberates and fulfils what is in created nature. 'God has willed to gather together all that was natural, all that was supernatural, into a single whole in Christ' (*AA* # 7).[3]

Third, even with all the acknowledgment of good things in other religions, *Nostra Aetate* clearly holds to the superiority of the Christian faith. It says of the church, 'But she proclaims and must ever proclaim, "the way, the truth and the life", in whom human beings find the fullness of religious life, and in whom God has reconciled all things to himself' (*NA* # 2). Whatever good there is in other religions serves as *preparatio evangelica*, a preparation for the fullness of the gospel. It is in the spirit of appreciation and humility that Christian mission is to be carried on (see *LG* # 11 among others).

It is in light of these foundational postconciliar guidelines that we need to look in more detail at the theology of Karl Rahner and then at the theologies of two younger contemporaries of his. First, I will offer a reading of Rahner's theology of religions[4] based on some key themes in his extensive, nonsystematic corpus (presented mainly in the form of short essays; even his magnum opus, titled *Foundations of Christian Faith*, does not present all of his theology in a systematic fashion). Second, I will present briefly his doctrine of the Trinity and relate it to his theology of religions. Third, I will highlight the positive contributions and thus potential of his theology with regard to Christianity's relation to other relations, and finally point out several inadequacies and challenges to Rahner's trinitarian proposal.

The Presence of God in Human Experience

Rahner's approach to theology of religions is based, perhaps surprisingly, in his theological anthropology. Or, to be more precise, the way people get to know God – even when they are not yet able to recognize God as God – is made possible through their everyday experiences in the world. His basic thesis, therefore, is that God reveals Godself to every human person in the very experience of one's own finite, yet absolutely open-ended, transcendence. God is the Holy Mystery who is the ground and horizon of human subjectivity (Rahner, 1975, pp. 122–32; see also Sachs, 1996, pp. 20–21). As a highly conceptual theologian, Rahner explains this orientation to the divine with his somewhat ambiguous term 'transcendental experience'. Transcendental experiences show that humans are naturally oriented toward the Holy Mystery, called God. The human being is by nature 'spirit', which means being open to receive revelation. God is not alien to human nature but an intrinsic part of it as the necessary condition for human subjectivity.[5] Human beings are not only part of 'nature', they are also oriented toward an infinite, mysterious horizon of being that Christians know as God. In a sense, the human being as such is 'super-natural', oriented to something beyond 'nature'. What is most 'natural' about human beings is that they are oriented beyond that which is just the natural world!

This brings into the picture Rahner's distinctive understanding of grace. Grace is not only – or even primarily – something related to God forgiving our sins, as is often the case in a more typical pietistic Protestantism, but rather God's presence in the finite human existence. God wants to be present to the human subject, and if God wants something, God is able to accomplish it. God prepares the conditions for God's presence – and even for human receptivity to it, in Rahner's technical language:

> not only are humans always by nature open to God *(potentia oboedientalis)*, they are also always supernaturally elevated by God in that transcendental

openness so that such elevation becomes an actual experience of God in every human life. God actually communicates himself to every human person in a gracious offer of free grace, so that God's presence becomes an existential, a constitutive element, in every person's humanity. (Grenz & Olson, 1992, p. 245)

So not only is God present in human experience, but even more: God really communicates himself to human persons, not only to Catholics, nor even just to other Christians, but to all people. Of course, not all people know it, but it is no less a fact for Rahner. Again, using his technical terminology, he says that the human person is 'the event of a free, unmerited and forgiving, and absolute self-communication of God' (Rahner, 1982, p. 116). God's self-communication means that God makes God's very own self the innermost constitutive element of the human person. But how does this happen, one may ask – especially regarding those people who have never heard the name of the Christian God, let alone Jesus Christ. Rahner responds: his is the mystery of the Spirit: 'God ... has already communicated himself in his Holy Spirit always and everywhere and to every person as the innermost center of his existence' (Rahner, 1982, p. 139). It is the Spirit of God who communicates God's presence to every human person, so that paradoxically we may say God is closer to the human person than the human person him or herself! Rahner's theology (of religions) is thus deeply pneumatological, anchored in the ministry of the Spirit, a theme to which we will return shortly.

If so, why do we then need special revelation at all? If God is known in human experience by virtue of God's grace, what does the revelation in Christ bring about? In order to answer this question, Rahner makes another terminological distinction. He speaks of revelation in two related, yet distinct senses: 'transcendental' and 'categorical' revelation. The former is that implicit, unthematic 'sense' or awareness of God on the basis of God's grace, while the latter is the specific revealing of God in history, culminating in Christ. The categorical is needed to fulfil the transcendental. There is continuity, yet there is distinction. The categorical discloses the inner reality of God unknown on the basis of the transcendental revelation. At the same time, the universal, transcendental experience of God in the Spirit does not make void the necessity of historical special revelation. They presuppose each other.

Already it should be evident that Rahner has a trinitarian approach to theology of religions and it brings to focus the dynamic relationship between the universality of the Spirit as evidenced in God's self-communication to the human person and the particularity of Christ in the need for special revelation and faith.

The Particularity of Christ and the Universality of God's Presence in the Spirit

In order for these two premises to hold, revelation and faith must occur at a universal, transcendental level, otherwise it is only about particularity. On the other hand, whatever presence and self-communication of God there is, it cannot be divorced from the special – the 'absolute' – kind of presence in Christ. We need to take a deeper look into Rahner's Christology to be able to converse with other religions. Whereas in much of traditional theology, the 'absoluteness' of Jesus Christ is understood mainly in his substitutionary death (or his salvific role otherwise defined, for example, with the recapitulation theory of some Eastern fathers) and his victorious rising from the dead, for Rahner the role of Jesus Christ as the 'Absolute Saviour' (Rahner's own label) is based rather on Jesus being the goal of humanity and the prime example of God's love. Even the particularity of the Saviour is not unrelated to the universality of God's grace, and thus God's presence in the human person. Therefore the central role of Jesus Christ is his mediation of the 'new and unsurpassable closeness of God' to humanity (Rahner, 1982, p. 279). In his person, Christ is the historical presence of God's disclosure to us. If the human person by virtue of the graced creation of God is open to receiving God's self-communication, how much more is this true with regard to Jesus Christ, the God incarnate.

In Rahner's anthropologically anchored theology, the claim that finite human beings as 'spirit' are also able to transcend themselves in their orientation to God serves as a prolegomena to Christology and the doctrine of the incarnation. It was God who willed this transcendental nature of humanity in order to make room for a genuine self-expression of God in the form of humanity. If God is the aim of humanity, it means that unless humanity is able to participate in God, humanity remains less than perfect. Salvation for Rahner means participation in the divine life to which the whole structure of the human being is naturally oriented, over and above that which human nature is able to ascend on its own. To use Rahner's own expression, humanity is the 'cipher of God' by virtue of being created by God for potential participation in God.

> Theologically, in view of the Incarnation, one must say that our human God-openness is intended by God as the potential for divine self-expression. In other words, the human person is the creature that is incomplete without Incarnation. God is the mystery of humanity, and humanity is the cipher of God. Humanity is the question; God is the answer. Just as the question participates in the answer and the answer participates in the question while transcending it, so God and humanity belong essentially together. God has decided it will be so. (Grenz & Olson, 1992, p. 252)

From this perspective it becomes clear that for Rahner incarnation also means an assumption of part of creation, the human nature, into the inner life of God. Christ is God. As such we could say that for Rahner incarnation in itself is salvific and itself a manifestation of God's grace.[6]

That Jesus Christ is divine is, of course, taken for granted in Rahner's Catholic theology, but that is not a focal point as in much of Christian tradition. It almost looks as if Jesus' divinity is a side effect or presupposition of Rahner's system.

Briefly put, before the crucifixion and resurrection Jesus claimed to be the bearer of this special disclosure and openness to God. In raising him from the dead, God validated his claims. It is in this sense that Christ is the absolute Saviour. If Christ is the absolute Saviour, it follows necessarily that he must be divine. Only a divine Saviour is able to mediate in his own person the self-disclosure of God. Christ's divinity is also accentuated by the larger soteriological vision of Rahner. He maintains that salvation encompasses, not only our 'divinization', but also the beginning of the process of the divinization of the whole world.[7] For this to happen, nothing less than a Saviour who is divine would be needed. How could a figure less than fully divine communicate to us and the world the saving grace of God? How would that idea of divinization – truly a trinitarian insight, God bringing his creation, the culmination of which is *theos-anthropos* (God-man) Jesus Christ, in the power of the Spirit – relate to other religions, say Hinduism or Buddhism? It is left to theologians conversant with those religious traditions to explore that topic and then work back to perhaps revising the traditional nature–grace apparatus.

It is in the light of Rahner's trinitarian, 'transcendental' Christology that the universal ministry of the Spirit comes to focus. How the Spirit ministers in the world of religions and how that is related to the role of Christ are important topics for our purposes.

The Spirit and the Religions in the Economy of Salvation

By now it should come as no surprise that Rahner's approach to the urgent question of theology of religions is distinctively pneumatological in that it is the Spirit who enables human reception of divine grace and the self's experience of existential transcendence (Badcock, 1997, p. 149). Transcendental experience of the Spirit is oriented toward explicit awareness of something beyond. For Rahner, this orientation is expressed in the religious traditions of the world and reaches its apex in the final self-revelation of God in Christ. Other religions also have 'individual moments' of this kind, which makes those people 'anonymous Christians'. However, because of human depravity every such event of revelation remains partial and intermixed with error. The value of religions is in the mediation by these experiences of the Spirit, even when it is less than perfect (see Yong, 2000, pp. 42–4, 72–7).

In that sense, all religious traditions potentially express truth about God's self-communication in the Spirit and therefore are part of the history of revelation. This does not, of course, mean that all religions express equally valid expressions of divine self-revelation: there is error in any religion. Through Christ's death and resurrection, God's gracious self-communication in the Spirit has become manifest in history: the 'world is drawn to its spiritual fulfillment by the Spirit of God, who directs the whole history of the world in all its length and breadth towards its proper goal' (Rahner, 1983, p. 203). In other words, Rahner does not consider other religions as merely 'preparations for the Gospel' in Jesus Christ but also ways of communicating God's revelation, albeit in a mixed form of truth and error.

> Until the moment when the gospel really enters into the historical situation of an individual, a non-Christian religion (even outside the Mosaic religion) does not merely contain elements of a natural knowledge of God, elements, moreover mixed up with human depravity which is the result of original sin and later aberrations. It contains also supernatural elements arising out of grace which is given to men as a gratuitous gift on account of Christ. For this reason, a non-Christian religion can be recognized as a lawful religion (although only in different degrees) without thereby denying the error and depravity contained in it. (Rahner, 1966b, p. 121)

Echoing the views of one of his colleagues, the leading Catholic pneumatologist Yves Congar, Rahner maintains that there is a state of being in which a person can respond positively to the grace of God even before hearing the gospel, which has the purpose of evoking explicit faith. A person in this state qualifies himself or herself as an 'anonymous Christian' insofar as this acceptance of grace is 'present in an implicit form whereby [the] person undertakes and lives the duty of each day in the quiet sincerity of patience, in devotion to his material duties and the demands made upon him by the person under his care' (Rahner, 1969, p. 394). According to Rahner, Christ is present and efficacious in the non-Christian believer (and therefore in the non-Christian religions) through his Spirit (Rahner, 1981, p. 43). And furthermore, anonymous Christians are 'justified by God's grace and possess the Holy Spirit'. In other words, if a non-Christian has responded positively to God's grace, for example, through selfless love for another, then, even though it is not known objectively, that person has accepted the God revealed in Christ. But since salvation cannot be divorced from Christ, the term 'anonymous Christian' is more appropriate than 'anonymous theist' (D'Costa, 2000, p. 87). An interpreter of Rahner, Joseph Wong, adequately summarizes Rahner's pneumatological theology of religions in this perspective:

> Wherever persons surrender themselves to God or the ultimate reality, under whatever name, and dedicate themselves to the cause of justice, peace, fraternity, and solidarity with other people, they have implicitly accepted Christ and, to some degree, entered into this Christic existence. Just as it was through the Spirit that Christ established this new sphere of existence, in the same way, anyone who enters into this Christic existence of love and freedom is acting under the guidance of the Spirit of Christ. (Wong, 1994, p. 630)

How this relates to the need of the Christian church to continue its mission will be discussed below; suffice it to say here that the idea of anonymous Christianity does not make void the proclamation of the name of the triune God to all people.

Now that we have briefly exposited the main orientations of Rahner's theology of religions, before venturing into a more critical dialogue, it is necessary first to take a look at how his theology of religions, heavily trinitarian (and pneumatological), relate to his explicitly formulated doctrine of the Trinity, often known by the name 'Rahner's rule'.

'Rahner's Rule' and Theology of Religions

As mentioned in this book's introduction, Rahner is one of the architects of the contemporary revival of the trinitarian doctrine. What has been called 'Rahner's rule' (Peters, 1993, p. 96) – namely, that 'the "economic" Trinity is the "immanent" Trinity and the "immanent" Trinity is the "economic" Trinity' (Rahner, 1997, p. 22) – is routinely cited as the defining principle of the current trinitarian reorientation (e.g. Kasper, 1984, p. 274). It uses technical terms that refer to God's relationship with the world and our salvation (the economic Trinity) as distinct from, yet related to, the trinitarian relations between Father, Son and Spirit (the immanent Trinity).

But what, in fact, is the importance of this formula? Ted Peters puts Rahner's doctrine of God and Trinity in a proper perspective:

> Rahner proposes this rule in order to advance the thesis that it is God as one or another of the divine persons who relates to the world; it is not God as the unity of the divine being. The way we experience God is through God's saving activity within history—through the economy of salvation—and here we know God as the redeeming word in Christ and as uniting love in the Spirit. We do not know God in general. We experience God first in the economy of salvation, and Rahner believes we can trust this experience. In the economy of salvation, God is communicating Godself. God is internally just the way we experience the divine in relation to us, namely, as Father, Son, and Spirit. (Peters, 1993, p. 96)

What this means is that the way God relates to the world is discovered in terms of each of the three hypostases ('persons'), not in terms of God as a unity. 'Each one of the three divine persons communicates itself to humanity' (Peters, 1993, p. 97). In this view, only Jesus could become incarnated, not the Spirit or the Father. Jesus is not simply God in general, but specifically God as Son. The same applies to the other persons of the Trinity. 'The intended effect of this line of argument is to give us confidence that the divine hypostasis we experience within history corresponds to the same hypostasis within the Godhead proper (Peters, 1993, p. 100). Contra Barth, Rahner is ready to call each of these hypostases 'person', if not for other reasons than for the tradition of one and a half millennia (Rahner, 1997, p. 44).

What Rahner was concerned about was that the theological tradition had speculated into the being of God and God's triunity apart from salvation history, and thus came to emphasize God's unity, which naturally has led to a neglect of the Trinity as well as the relationship between the Christian life and the Trinity. The doctrine of the Trinity easily becomes an appendix to theology as with Schleiermacher, who did not necessarily need it to talk about God. This divorces

God-talk from history and makes it generic in nature; the biblical way of speaking of God is to talk about a particular God, the Old Testament Yahweh who acts as the Father, Son and Spirit in the New Testament.

But one may ask, then, why continue talking about the immanent Trinity at all? In fact, in his main systematic theology, *Foundations of Christian Faith*, Rahner hardly ever ventures into talking about the immanent Trinity. Nevertheless talk about the immanent Trinity – as God is triune in Godself – was needed to protect God's absolute freedom and so not to dissolve God into history. 'Whatever is true of the triune being of God in the economy of salvation must be seen as true of God-in-Himself, and whatever is true of God-in-Himself must be seen as affected by (not constituted by) the incarnation and sending of the Spirit' (Olson & Hall, 2002, p. 98).

So far so good. By now, the reader of Rahner's theology may be ready to applaud the Master and hail him as the first theologian to really make the Trinity speak to theology in general and theology of religions in particular. Unfortunately, that is not the case either for the former or the latter. In a most ironic way, Rahner, who established his fame with the brief yet highly significant work *The Trinity*, in which he lamented the marginal role of the doctrine of the Trinity both to spiritual life and theology, in his *Foundations of Christian Faith*, the only *summa* of his theology, devotes only passing interest to the doctrine of the Trinity and does not, for example, relate it to other religions. Neither do several essays in *Theological Investigations* focusing on theology of religions deal with the relevance of the Trinity. This irony does not necessarily, of course, make his theology or theology of religions 'less trinitarian', but it certainly hinders his drawing all the theological implications that his theology seems to be pregnant with. The ultimate purpose of the present chapter is to advance discussion and in that sense go beyond, but not against, Rahner's own explicit statements.

Let us first register the potential and strong points of Rahner's trinitarian theology of religions and ask the question of how those could be further developed and put into the service of Christianity's dialogue with other religions. Following that, let us highlight the problems and raise some questions.

The Potential of Rahner's Trinitarian Theology of Religions

First, there is a strong universal orientation to Rahner's theology of religions since it is 'primarily a theology of the spiritual life rather than of divine life—to be concerned basically, in short, with our approach to God rather than with God's approach to us' (Badcock, 1997, p. 144). The implications and significance of this perspective cannot be overestimated. For theologies that are intrinsically trinitarian, it is easy to begin 'from above', and indeed, this has been the approach of much of traditional theology, and it has often led to highly speculative musings on the trinitarian life. When, however, as with Rahner, we start with humanity's orientation to God, then both spiritual life and history matter. What happens in human life is not unrelated to the divine sphere. A corollary idea of this anthropological approach is that the presence and indeed the immediacy of God is not limited to Christians, and certainly not to Catholics alone, not even to people of religions, but is open to all. In the first place, even though faith plays a role in Rahner's theology, the presence of God in human life is not even conditioned upon (explicit) faith; rather, it is a deposit given to each and every human being (see further Badcock, 1997, p. 145). Thus the concept of grace, so crucial for most Catholic theologians, is taken out of the confines of 'spiritual' life and certainly of ecclesiastical life and brought to bear on human life as a whole. The implications for dialogue with followers of other religions or people outside of any particular religion are enormous: the first task of the dialogue is to acknowledge the presence of God in the other person. The missionary is not carrying his or her god to the pagan land, but rather, as a Christian, the believer tries to discern the nature of God's presence in the Other and then take him or her to the fullness of the (Catholic) faith.

Second, Rahner's trinitarian theology paradoxically offers criteria for distinguishing the specifically Christian God among the gods in various religions. I say 'paradoxically' for the obvious reason that Rahner never set out to develop a trinitarian theology and anthropology for that purpose. In fact, we could say that his purpose was the opposite: coming from a pre-Vatican II quite narrow mindset, with his theological anthropology he rather wanted to open up Catholic theology to consider the presence of God in wider terms. What he ended up doing, however, was to offer criteria for distinguishing the God of the Bible: we do not encounter a 'general God' of Christianity, of 'philosophers' or of religions, but always a particular person of the trinitarian God. Thus the presence and immediacy of God among religions is not the presence of an unidentified, 'common deity' as in pluralisms, but a God of the Bible.

This insight is further supported by that fact that for Rahner the Trinity serves as a theological criterion also. What I mean is this: there is no separating the ministry of the Spirit from the ministry of the Son or the Father and vice versa. One of the tendencies of 'post-Christological' theologies of religions, especially those based on the 'freedom' of Spirit, is to set the work of the Spirit apart from the other members of the Trinity, as if the Spirit were a sort of itinerant evangelist doing his own business. What the Spirit brings about in Rahner's theology is the presence of God as that has come to light in the 'Absolute Saviour', Jesus Christ. There is no 'presence of the Spirit' apart from the presence of God for Rahner. Therefore, even where the presence and immediacy of God is not yet recognized at all, it still is the presence of the triune God of the Bible. Every human person, created by the Christian God in the image of the Christian God, 'carries' the presence of God within himself or herself. Thus, to make Rahner a pluralist – and this of course was never his intention – is a job that demands a reversal of his theology. Rahner's theology is universally oriented but not pluralist, no more than it is universalist in the technical sense of the term. The last comment brings us to the next noteworthy feature of his theology.

As a further development, we could commend Rahner for being able to set Christology in his trinitarian theology of religions in a way few Christian theologians have ever succeeded in doing. As is well known, Christology has been – and to a large extent continues to be – the critical issue in Christianity's relation to other religions. While pluralists of various persuasions have either ignored the uniqueness of Jesus Christ (Hick and the later Knitter, among others), or focused on theocentrism rather than Christocentrism (the earlier Knitter and Panikkar, among others), and exclusivists made the person and work of Christ the 'stumbling block', Rahner has taken significant steps to avoid both extremes. In the first place, his Christology, unlike most others available (perhaps with the exception of Pannenberg's) is totally anchored in his anthropology: the coming of the God-man, rather than being a miraculous 'mystery' defying the laws of nature, and thus making the *kenosis* finally ineffable and unexplainable, is more or less the logical result of human nature being created as 'spirit', open to God and transcending the 'natural' in its search for God and capacity to have access to God. Furthermore, God's self-communication through the Spirit is such that God becomes the constitutive principle of human nature (not to have God's presence, rather than having it, would be 'unnatural'). On the other hand, human self-transcendence, willed and thus graced by God, is such that it leans toward something that is beyond. This something is Jesus Christ, in whose person the divine self-communication and human self-transcendence meet. God's presence with humanity and humanity's immediate access to God – even apart from conscious faith – has its locus in Jesus Christ, the absolute Saviour. Clearly, God's presence, self-communication (and in Rahner's terminology, God's grace) are present in Jesus Christ in a fuller sense than any other person. Yet to confine God's presence to the particularities of Jesus Christ would not be a right conclusion from Rahner's theology. Rather than setting apart the uniqueness of Jesus Christ from other loci of God's presence, there is a continuum finding its apex in Jesus Christ.[8]

Third, the concept of religion (and thus the value of religions in general as vehicles of God's self-communication) is rehabilitated by Rahner. Even though Rahner himself did not have much first-hand contact with other religions (he was mainly interested in the dialogue between Islam and Christianity), his theology encourages Christians to engage in an open-minded, appreciative study of other religions. Unlike the young Barth, for whom religions represented human unbelief, for Rahner religions are God-willed means of helping people recognize the presence of God. Yet – and this is also significant in light of Christianity's relation to the Other – for Rahner religions with all their resources are not sole possessors of the presence of God. Herein lies yet more evidence for the real universal nature of Rahner's theology: religions are highly valued, but not the only means of carrying God's presence. Social relations, human love, the birth of a child, the beauty of nature – thousands of aspects of life – have the potential of mediating the transcendental experience of the presence of God.

Fourth, I believe Rahner is able to go as far as possible toward a universal offer of the grace of God, yet without ending up being a universalist, even though universalism in a sense would wonderfully serve his cause! There are several facets to this theology (of grace) that prevent him from the kind of necessary universalism that Barth's theology, from a totally different Christological viewpoint, seems to arrive at. Rahner takes human freedom more seriously than Barth and acknowledges the possibility and reality of human resistance to God's gift of grace freely given to all by virtue of being born a human person (see further Badcock, 1997, p. 145). Even though we have to criticize Rahner for not taking seriously enough – and finally, not providing a viable theological explanation for – the phenomenon of human disobedience (a topic to be discussed in what follows), the fact that he does not dismiss that reality is to be commended. Furthermore, Rahner leaves open the chance of those outside the Christian faith being saved, arguing that that is the business of God (Rahner, 1988, p. 250).

A corollary observation is that for Rahner the issue of salvation as such is not the key issue in the dialogue with other religions. Since all people potentially have access to God's presence in the world, a Rahnerian approach to interreligious dialogue is not a business of making distinctions between the saved and the lost. Rather, it is a matter of helping people, at whatever stage they are, to see in clearer terms what they already have. Yet this is no Barthian insistence on the necessity of salvation, but rather a joyful acknowledgment of what God's grace already has done and what is its potential. Where then is the focus here? Paradoxically, its focus is not in the human person, even though theological anthropology is the point of departure; rather, the focus is on how to discern the effects of the grace of the triune God among people who already are oriented to the mystery of God.

> The point of dialogue can therefore be seen to be defined by the need to discern the presence, the love, the voice of God in others, rather than by the need to convince others or to convert them to one's own faith or theology, while such dialogue can be said to become fundamental to the task of Christian theology in general. Since the experience of God is at the heart of everything, including theology, the point of doing theology is simply to enter more deeply into the mystery of his presence. Such must then be the overriding priority in any dialogue with those of other religions. (Badcock, 1997, p. 151)

Finally, and this may sound like something opposite to what has been said above, Rahner is quite successful in maintaining the balance between acknowledging the value of God's presence among all people, whether religious or not, and the need for the church to proclaim Christ. Rahner is a Catholic theologian and in full endorsement of Vatican II pronouncements regarding other religions. The major point of the postconciliar doctrine in that respect is that while salvation is not limited to people who acknowledge the name of Christ, yet all salvation comes through and by virtue of Christ. Thus, for Rahner – as well as for the official Catholic doctrine – it is the task of the church to help people come to the fulfilment of faith, the embrace of the name of the triune God as received by the Catholic

Church. Is that principle in contradistinction to the idea of God's *self*-communication among the people of the world apart from the proclamation of the gospel? No. If it is the self-communication of the triune God of the Bible – rather than a generic, vague notion of the divinity as in various pluralisms, or even a grasp of the 'Ultimate Reality' as in Hick's more recent thinking – it means that the God of the Bible is the only true God. There can be only one true God who has revealed God's self and thus made it possible for all the people of the earth to live in communion with this one true God. That not all people do acknowledge that (yet) is a challenge to the church and its missionaries. In line with the Catholic standpoint, rather than seeing the 'anonymous Christians' thesis as undermining the validity of the church or mission, Rahner argues that the individual should be brought to the fullness of faith by the church obediently carrying out its evangelistic mandate (see further, Rahner, 1974, pp. 161–80). The proclamation of the gospel turns an anonymous Christian 'into someone who also knows about his Christian belief in the depths of his grace-endowed being by objective reflection and in the profession of faith which is given social form in the Church' (Rahner, 1966b, p. 132).

What then are the challenges and problems in Rahner's trinitarian theology of religions?

Questions and Further Tasks

The challenge most often posed to Rahner deals with terminology, focusing on the inappropriateness of the term 'anonymous Christians/Christianity'. Without doubt, it is triumphalist at best and derogatory at worst to impose a name on a follower of another religion or no religion that the person would not accept him or herself. Of course, I agree with this criticism (what would a Christian think of being called an 'anonymous Hindu' or 'anonymous atheist'?), but I think that is to miss the point. First of all, Rahner himself has responded that the name is not intended for interreligious dialogue but rather for an intra-Christian discourse (Rahner, 1976, pp. 280–98). More importantly, at the time Rahner presented this idea, the canons and terminology of theology of religions were not yet available. And he himself, in light of the criticism received, was the first to suggest changing the terminology if offensive. So to write off the whole idea by focusing on the inappropriateness of the term itself is to miss the point completely. We should also mention, in defence of Rahner's idea (and thus also of the term), that in contrast to often very negative assessments of other religions, Rahner was able to affirm the presence of the Christian God among them, an accomplishment of no little significance (see further, Dupuis, 1997, p. 147).

Terminology aside, there are other, more serious, challenges and problems. One is the difference, if any, between Christian faith and the faiths of other religions. Is it only a matter of subjective consciousness or lack thereof, or is there something 'new' about faith in Christ? Rahner is not absolutely clear on this issue. Most interpreters agree that at first his ideas could be interpreted pretty much as the difference being a matter of consciousness, so that the anonymous Christian would be 'a Christian unawares'. Later, especially in his *Foundations of Christian Faith*, he clarifies the issue that between

> anonymous Christianity and explicit Christianity there are indeed ... distinct regimes of salvation and distinct modalities of mediation of the mystery of Jesus Christ. Thus anonymous Christianity remains a fragmentary, incomplete, radically crippled reality. It harbors dynamics that impel it to join with explicit Christianity. Nevertheless, the same mystery of salvation is present on both sides, through distinct mediations. It is the mystery of Jesus Christ, whose operative presence is concealed and unconscious on the one side, reflexive and conscious on the other side. (Dupuis, 1997, p. 146, with references to Rahner's original works)

That question invites another, taken up by some Catholic critics of Rahner, especially Henri de Lubac. He insists that while the expression 'anonymous Christians' is valid, in contrast, 'anonymous Christianity' is not. The reason is that the latter fails to do justice to the newness of Christianity and its singular character as the way to salvation. Some others have agreed with Lubac (see further, Dupuis, 1997, pp. 147–8). While I consider this last point to be well taken, I believe it misinterprets Rahner in two ways. On the one hand, for Rahner these two expressions seem to be totally synonymous since one expression implies the other: 'anonymous Christianity' exists concretely in 'anonymous Christians' (Rahner, 1969, pp. 390–98). On the other hand, for Rahner – unlike for Vatican II documents as mentioned above – religions as such need to be considered as 'salvific', even though not apart from Christ. Lubac and other like-minded critics of Rahner (e.g. Hans Urs von Balthasar) do not see religions as such as salvific, even though as Catholic theologians they acknowledge the possibility of salvation for individuals of other religions. Furthermore, to Rahner, the mediation of salvation is a highly social reality: one's religious life is to a large extent mediated through religious traditions (Rahner, 1966b, pp. 115–34). In sum, we have to conclude that while both the critics' and Rahner's own views concerning the terminology make sense, the terminology is best abandoned as inappropriate. But if it is used, it is best used in the way Rahner himself has suggested.

Back to the issue of 'newness': Rahner has not been able to clarify the extent to which Christianity represents something 'new'. In the biblical sense, faith in Christ represents a transformation that encompasses not only individual life but also the whole creation in anticipation of the coming of the New Creation (2 Cor. 5:17). While Rahner's attempt to build continuity on nature and grace is to be commended to a large extent, I fear he has gone too far. While I do not agree with von Balthasar that Rahner has turned the supernatural into a 'function of nature' (see Dupuis, 1997, p. 148 with references to von Balthasar's works), the way Rahner builds his anthropologically founded theology calls for reassessment. I will approach this issue from two related perspectives: Christology and the concept of sin.

First, his Christology, with all the praise it deserves as discussed above, fails to meet the demands of the 'high Christology' of classical Christian tradition. There is no doubt that for Rahner Christology is normative and constitutive since all salvation comes from Christ and there is no salvation apart from Christ. In this sense, Rahner agrees with tradition, and consequently differs radically from pluralisms that eschew making Christ the critical principle of theology. But still I think that, in light of the trinitarian theology, the way he presents Christ and salvation is not totally satisfactory. There are several issues here. One is the incarnation. It is highly commendable that, in his transcendental anthropology, Rahner has been able to make incarnation consistent with humanity, even a 'predictable' event in a world with human beings created in God's image. But, one may ask, is this the full picture of the biblical tradition? Is there a danger here that incarnation becomes a function of anthropology and the 'newness' of what the incarnation of the Son brought about is lost? If so, are we then really operating within the domain of a genuinely trinitarian theology? In technical Catholic language, we may say that while for Rahner Christ is not the 'efficient cause' of salvation (in the sense, that he would introduce something totally new), Christ is the 'final cause' in that he brings to fulfilment what is there in humanity on the basis of creation.

Furthermore, if the divinity of Jesus Christ is defined, as Rahner does, mainly in terms of the function of mediating God's presence in a unique way and exemplifying God's love in a way no other person has done, can we still speak of God's *self*-revelation as Rahner also does? Is there a danger here that the incarnation comes to function as an 'intermediary', somewhat as in Arianism, which makes Jesus Christ almost divine, but not totally? (I know that a reference to Arianism may sound blasphemous with regard to Rahner's Christology, and I am not of course claiming it is Arian, but rather making my point in a polemical way!) I fully agree with Rahner that for the Christian tradition it has been a real burden to make the incarnation make sense with regard to creation and anthropology. But I also think that the price paid is too high if we go all the way through with his proposal. In the biblical and classical Christian tradition, incarnation brought something radically new, even though it must not be opposite to what the triune God has been doing in creation.

A related issue, still in reference to Rahner's Christology, has to do with the crucifixion and resurrection. There is no doubt about the fact that the classical Christian tradition has focused on the meaning of Christ too one-sidedly in terms of his vicarious death on the cross. Theological criticisms of the limitations of that paradigm are readily available. But if the 'theology of the cross' is nothing more than an example of showing God's love as von Balthasar, among others, has again noted that it seems to be in Rahner, I do not think we are doing full justice to the biblical tradition. I am not willing to go as far as Jürgen Moltmann to whom the crucifixion means the 'death' of God – since dogmatically, it is not right to speak of the death of God, but rather of the death of the Son of God – but neither am I satisfied with what I see as a truncated Rahnerian appraisal of the crucifixion. Furthermore, while Rahner's view of the resurrection seems to go a long way with Pannenberg in that resurrection is the Father's 'amen' to the claims by the earthly Jesus of his unique status as Son, it seems to me that for Rahner resurrection does not serve as critical a function as it seems to serve for Paul (1 Cor. 15 among others) or, say, Pannenberg, who claims that the truth of the Christian message is dependent on the historicity of the resurrection. My reference to Pannenberg does not mean to imply that for Rahner to pass the test of orthodoxy he has to comply with Pannenberg (who certainly has his own critics) but, again, I am just illustrating my point in dialogue with other voices. In my understanding (and here of course I agree with Pannenberg), the crucifixion and resurrection brought something radically new to light in that the deity of the triune God was at stake: had not the Son willingly submitted himself to humbling himself to the point of helpless death on the cross and thus given room to the Father's lordship, and had not the Son been raised by the Father in the power of the Spirit (Rom. 4:25), the coming of the kingdom of God, whose agent the Son served as the Son to whom all power had been given (Matt. 28:18), would have been questioned. Without the kingdom, God would not be God in the world that he had created and over which he claims the rightful reign.

Another issue, noted by many, has to do with Rahner's apparent neglect to tackle the dark side of humanity's nature, namely, disobedience and sin. This is a logical consequence of his Christology. What about the biblical teaching that human beings apart from faith in God seem to be alienated from God, and rather than being drawn to God's presence – let alone possessing God's special presence – they tend to flee away from him? Or what about the fact that even though the Son of God came to his own, he was not received (Jn 1:11)? If it were as obvious as Rahner maintains that the incarnation of the Son is the apex of humanity, a more or less 'necessary' coming to being of a God-man, how then was he rejected and taken to the cross? I do not think Rahner saw the challenge of human rebellion and the effects of the Fall in all its seriousness, and thus his soteriology fails to meet this challenge. A related issue has to do with the concept of grace. I applaud the 'rescuing' of grace from the narrow confines of much of traditional (Protestant) theology, but I again raise the question of whether Rahner has gone too far in equating grace primarily with the presence of God in humanity. Either the presence of God has to be qualified to the point that it becomes just a generic principle with no substance, or the concept of grace has to be reinterpreted in a way that, again, loses the 'newness'. What about the biblical dialectic between God's wrath and grace? Or judgment and grace? Biblical exegesis hardly unanimously supports either Rahner's concept of God's presence or his view of grace.

Still in relation to Rahner's Christology and soteriology, I need to raise a corollary question: what is the relationship between the Spirit and Christ? I do not fully agree with Badcock (1997, p. 153), who questions whether in general Rahner's theology of religions has a clear relationship between the Spirit and Christ. I think it does, and I have tried to give credit to it above. Yet what concerns me (and this is also noted by Badcock) is that Rahner's 'Spirit-Christology' does not seem satisfying in one particular, yet crucial, aspect: how does the crucifixion/resurrection and the giving of the Spirit relate to each other? In other words, how does the presence of God in the world through the Spirit relate to what the crucifixion and resurrection brought about? For any trinitarian theology, this is a crucial issue, and I fear Rahner has not made it explicit. One needs only to refer to the Gospel of John, which connects the giving of the Spirit in a special sense (different from, yet related to, the presence of the Spirit of Yahweh of the Old Testament as the 'Spirit of Creation') to the 'lifting up' of the Son at the cross (Jn 7:39 among others). A further question asks in what way the Spirit of sonship (Rom. 8:15) is different from (even though, of course, not unrelated to) the Spirit of God in creation and humanity.

One further point of uneasiness has to do with Rahner's view of Christianity's relation to other religions. I have commended him above for giving credit to religions as mediators of God's presence and thus participants in the economy of salvation, albeit in a less than perfect way, of course. The other side of the coin is that I fear Rahner's theology leans toward neglecting the real differences among religions. Even though I am happy with the way he looks at religions as a primary way of searching for God, I am open to the possibility that there are radical differences among religions. If so, then their function as mediators of God's presence may vary significantly. It is only through a painstaking phenomenological and theological/religious study that the differences, if any, can be brought to light. Thus assuming an uncritical continuity between religions may not be the most helpful way to further dialogue.

It is only with great appreciation that I dare to express these challenges and questions to Rahner's theology. Wholeheartedly, I agree with Badcock's final assessment:

> Perhaps it is expecting too much of any theology to provide a seamless, watertight web of thought that can hold out indefinitely against all theological storms that may arise. Rahner's theology was not primarily intended to provide a new development of the doctrine of the Trinity, nor to undergird a theology of interreligious dialogue, it was constructed with an express view to the renewal of Roman Catholic theology in the twentieth century. It is clear that to this extent, Rahner achieved a very great deal. ... Rahner has also provided enormous stimulus to the ecumenical enterprise, and ... to those Christians engaged in dialogue with people of other faiths. (1997, pp. 153–4)

Furthermore, I have to agree with the continuation of Badcock's appraisal. He notes that on a number of grounds, Rahner's theology can be found to be wanting, and wanting precisely a more adequately conceived and developed trinitarian structure. 'If in his doctrine of the Trinity Rahner has contributed significantly to the development of modern theology, it is here too, in his doctrine of the Trinity, that his most glaring theological inadequacies can be seen' (Badcock, 1997, p. 154). Therefore, in what follows we will take up two post-Rahnerian Catholic developments of trinitarian theologies of religions, by Jacques Dupuis and Gavin D'Costa. Having exposited in more detail both the background of recent Catholic theology of religions for Vatican II and the views of its most noted originator, Rahner, the following two chapters can be briefer and focus on the question of how they may advance the quest initiated by Rahner and solve the problems evident in his theology. I take up this inquiry as a Protestant theologian acknowledging the enormous ecumenical potential of both Rahner and his colleagues.

Notes

1   Two others should also be noted, namely, *Gaudium et Spes*, which spoke to the challenges of modern life for the church, and *Lumen Gentium*, one of the most significant documents on the doctrine of the church – ecclesiology – ever issued. These documents will be identified by the following abbreviations: *AA = Apostolican Actuositatem*; *AG = Ad Gentes*; *GS = Gaudium et Spes*; *LG = Lumen Gentium*; *NA = Nostra Aetate*; *UR = Unitatis Redintegratio*. Numbers refer to paragraph numbers.
2   For a very helpful summary, see D'Costa (2000, pp. 102–5).
3   The idea of perfection is illustrated, e.g. in *LG* 17 and *AG* 9. See further, Ruokanen (1992, pp. 13ff., 106ff.), with ample bibliographical references.
4   A fine succinct introduction to Rahner's theology of religions can be found in D'Costa (1986, ch. 4).
5   Here Rahner agrees with W. Pannenberg as we will see in due course.
6   Even though Rahner, with Vatican II (unlike the dualism of so much of Protestant theologies), builds on Thomistic theology's continuity between 'nature' and 'grace', he also overcomes the distinction by implying that all nature is graced and that grace is never apart from nature.
7   Rahner himself – at least as far as I am aware – does not notice it, but this brings him close to the emphasis of Eastern Orthodoxy that speaks of divinization as the goal of God's creation. In fact, that concept is not totally unknown to Rahner, who in his Christology envisions Christ's divinity as also accentuated by his larger soteriological vision.
8   For a thoughtful reflection on this and related Christological issues, see Rahner (1965, pp. 149–200 and 1966a, pp. 105–20).

CHAPTER 3

Jacques Dupuis: A Trinitarian Theology of Religious Pluralism

A Christian Theology of Religious Pluralism

Among the living Catholic theologians of religions, Jacques Dupuis of Belgium, who has spent decades in Asia, stands as the senior colleague. His magnum opus, published as recently as 1997, is titled very appropriately in light of his main orientation: *Toward a Christian Theology of Religious Pluralism*. This book brings to maturity the lifelong reflection on other religions by the Jesuit theologian who had already published his widely acclaimed *Jesus Christ at the Encounter of World Religions* (1991). The title for the most recent work is intentional: for Dupuis, it is not enough to develop a theology of religions in general, but more specifically, a Christian theological interpretation of the phenomenon of pluralism. The rationale lies in Dupuis's motive for expanding the concept of the theology of religions beyond the question of salvation to the theological meaning of religious plurality itself. Consequently, it 'searches more deeply, in the light of Christian faith, for the meaning of God's design for humankind of the plurality of living faiths and religious traditions with which we are surrounded. Are all the religious traditions of the world destined, in God's plan, to converge? Where, when, and how?' (Dupuis, 1997, p. 10).

Here we encounter again the intricacies of theology of religions typologies, very much still in the making. Just looking at the title of Dupuis's work, one would suspect him to belong to the camp of pluralists. However, his trinitarian theology of religious pluralism is not pluralistic but firmly anchored in the Catholic trinitarian tradition, even though in the eyes of his superiors (Dupuis was recently invited for a hearing by the Vatican) it seems to cross over the boundaries. In my reading of Dupuis, there is no doubt that most naturally he belongs to the inclusivist category, even though his inclusivism both revises and goes beyond that of Rahner and also challenges the inclusivism of Vatican II as not being inclusive enough. That my assessment seems to be correct is supported by his own words: for Dupuis, 'openness does not gain from syncretism any more than commitment to faith does from isolation' (Dupuis, 1997, p. 203). Like his younger colleague Gavin D'Costa (whose views will be studied in the next chapter), Dupuis claims to go beyond both inclusivist and pluralistic paradigms, yet – at least in my interpretation – represents a type of inclusivism that affirms the salvific role of other religions when interpreted from the perspective of Christian religion and revelation (ibid.). For Dupuis, the task of constructing a viable theology of religions is urgent, since the credibility of the Christian message for the future is at stake (see further, Dupuis, 1999, p. 261).

It is always instructive to pay attention to shifts in the thinking of theologians, since often they serve as a clue to the inner logic and dynamics. The development of Dupuis's theology by and large parallels the paradigm shift of much of the most recent Christian theology of religions. He began his work in the framework of Christology negotiating between the roles of the Father and Son in relation to other religions. At that time, he operated with a somewhat ambiguous concept of a 'theocentric Christocentrism'. The aim was to open up a theological perspective that:

> while holding fast to faith in Jesus Christ as traditionally understood by mainstream Christianity and church tradition, would at the same time integrate, in their differences, the religious experiences of the living religious traditions and assign to those traditions a positive role and significance in the overall plan of God for humankind, as it unfolds through salvation history. (Dupuis, 1997, p. 1)

In his more recent work Dupuis has enlarged his perspective to include pneumatology in its own right, and thus made his approach a more balanced trinitarian one. Dupuis's theology of religions could be called pneumato-Christocentric or even better, if the term were not so complicated, trinitopneumato-Christocentric. Clearly, he has also pushed his inclusivism toward pluralism – many would say, as far as it can ever go without crossing the boundaries. (I understand Dupuis most probably would not sign up to this statement since, in his view, he is going beyond the inclusivism-pluralism paradigm rather than pushing the limits of the former; be that as it may, this is just an observation by an interpreter of his views.)

What lies behind much of Dupuis's work on the theology of religions is the desire to move beyond the 'fulfilment theory', which looks at other religions only as stepping stones to Christianity. Several inadequacies of that model bother Dupuis. First, it places limits on what God may be doing in other religions by using the church as the yardstick. Second, it may end up making the church more important than Christ/God. Third, it builds an obstacle to dialogue by insisting that Christianity represents something 'higher' (Knitter, 2002, pp. 89–90).

Trinitarian Criticism of Existing Models in Theology of Religions

Dupuis enters into a critical assessment of several existing approaches to theology of religions and finds them wanting in their trinitarian orientation. Listening carefully to his criticism, which is targeted at three related problems as he sees them, is a learning experience for anyone searching for a balanced trinitarian approach to religions. The first error puts Christ and God in opposition and wants to downplay the particularity of Christ at the expense of the universality of the Father. Dupuis seriously questions if this dualism is legitimate theologically and biblically.

According to him, the Christocentrism of Christian tradition is, in fact, not opposed to theocentrism, but rather calls for it. Christocentrism

> never places Jesus Christ in the place of God; it merely affirms that God has placed him at the center of his saving plan for humankind, not as the end but the way, not as the goal of every human quest for God but as the universal mediator of God's saving action toward people. (Dupuis, 1997, pp. 191)

Christian theology may not choose either/or, but rather is theocentric by being Christocentric and vice versa.

Dupuis maintains that the theocentrism of Jesus Christ – the fact that Jesus was entirely 'God-centred' – cannot be put in antithesis with the equally valid biblical insistence that Jesus Christ is the way, the truth and the life (Jn 14:6). Therefore, pluralistic theocentrism is one-sided in divorcing the Son from the Father. There is a distinction, yet an integral connection. 'While it is true that Jesus the man is uniquely the Son of God, it is equally true that God stands beyond Jesus' (Dupuis, 1997, p. 206).

The second error rejected by Dupuis champions either 'regnocentrism' (the idea of the kingdom of God at the centre) or 'soteriocentrism' (salvation, rather than a Saviour, at the centre) as the focus at the expense of Christology. The Catholic Paul F. Knitter in his more recent works (1995 and 1996b) has maintained that the main criterion for evaluating religions is the extent to which they contribute to liberation of people and the earth. In Christian parlance, the term denoting a holistic liberation is the reign of God. Dupuis notes that while liberation as the goal of salvation is noble and belongs to the core of Christian faith, in terms of the trinitarian faith it cannot be understood as downplaying the role of the Son (any more than the Father). In biblical tradition, the kingdom of God has broken in through Jesus Christ, and the coming of the kingdom of God is tied to the person of Jesus Christ and to his raising from the dead by the Father in the power of the Spirit (Dupuis, 1997, pp. 193–5).

The third error, quite appealing to a number of more recent theologians of religions, is to champion that kind of pneumatological approach that tends to diminish the role of Jesus Christ as more limited than that of the Spirit. It is argued that while Jesus Christ represents particularity, the Spirit represents universality. But that is true only as far as trinitarian canons are honoured. The freedom of the Spirit, so Dupuis maintains, cannot be set in opposition to the person and ministry of Jesus Christ, any more than that of the Son to the Father. Son and Spirit presuppose each other. The role of the Spirit comes to focus in that Jesus was related to the Spirit. A trinitarian Spirit-Christology 'shows the influence of the Holy Spirit throughout the earthly life of Jesus, from his conception through the power of the Spirit (see Lk. 1:35) to his resurrection at the hands of God by the power of the same Spirit (see Rom. 8:11)' (Dupuis, 1997, p. 206; for his Spirit-Christology, see 1994). Of course, by relating the Spirit to Jesus Christ, Dupuis is not denying the universal sphere of the ministry of the Spirit:

> The Spirit of God has been universally present throughout human history and remains active today outside the boundaries of the Christian fold. He it is who 'inspires' in people belonging to other religious traditions the obedience of saving faith, and in the traditions themselves a word spoken by God to their adherents. (Dupuis, 1997, p. 196)

However, there is no salvation brought about by the Spirit apart from the paschal mystery of Jesus Christ. There are not 'two distinct channels [that of the Son and the Spirit] through which God's saving presence reaches out to people in distinct economies of salvation' (ibid.).

The integral relationship between the Spirit and Son is paralleled in that the universal presence of the Logos cannot be set apart from the Word incarnate. In the Bible, especially in the Prologue to the Gospel of John, Logos, the Word, is depicted in universal terms not unlike the Spirit who blows where he wills (Jn 1:1–4 and 3:6–8, respectively). Similarly, 'this anticipated presence and action of the Logos do not ... prevent the New Testament from seeing in the Word incarnate, ... the universal Savior of humankind' (Jn 1:14). Therefore, 'Logocentrism and Christocentrism are not mutually opposed; they call to each other in a unique dispensation' (Dupuis, 1997, p. 196; 1991, pp. 188–90). Dupuis sees it necessary to offer a theological corrective to all who tend to separate the Spirit-centred approaches from the Christological model. Even in light of the universal ministry of the Spirit, 'Pneumatocentrism and Christocentrism cannot, therefore, be construed as two distinct economies of salvation, one parallel to the other. They constitute two inseparable aspects, or complementary elements, within a unique economy of salvation.' The Spirit is at the same time God's self-communication to human beings and the Spirit of Christ, communicated by him on the basis of his resurrection from the dead. Therefore, the cosmic influence of the Spirit cannot be severed from the universal action of the risen Christ (Dupuis, 1997, pp. 197, 206–8).

There is, however, a still finer theological distinction to Dupuis's understanding of the relationship between the Spirit and Christ, which we will take up below. Now, having looked at his critical appraisal of existing approaches to the theology of religions in light of a truly trinitarian theology, what then specifically is Dupuis's own proposal? Let us look first at how he relates the triune God of the Bible to the god(s) of other religions and at the status of Christ in relation to other salvific figures. That will then give us an opportunity to focus more specifically on the pneumatological aspects of his trinitarian theology of religions. That discussion will then take us to the heart of Dupuis's theology of religious pluralism, namely, how does Christian faith, in the spirit of 'mutual complementarity' relate to other paths and how does all of this relate to salvation, the church and the kingdom?

The Triune God of the Bible and Other Gods

Dupuis takes up the ancient question with which Christian theology has wrestled since the early centuries: is the God of the Bible the same God as the god(s) of other religions? Dupuis distances himself from the pluralistic theocentrism of the earlier Hick, according to which all religious traditions have the same indeterminate God/divine as the ultimate point of reference, and the later Hick who instead speaks of the 'Ultimate Reality', the 'Real' beyond the 'personae' and the 'impersonae'. In both versions of pluralism, God 'in itself' lies beyond human apprehension, yet the same Ultimate Reality is differently but equivalently manifested in various strands, personalist or impersonalist, of religions. In response to Hick, Dupuis argues that from the standpoint of Christian trinitarianism, it seems necessary to hold not only that the Ultimate Reality differently manifested to humankind is a personal God, but also, further, that the Christian trinitarian God represents the Ultimate Reality 'in itself'. In other words, it is not a penultimate sign of the Real 'in itself', but rather the Ultimate Reality itself (Dupuis, 1997, pp. 259, 263). This is, of course, not to say that Christian tradition claims a comprehensive knowledge of God. 'But it does mean that the mystery of the triune God – Father, Son, Spirit – corresponds objectively to the inner reality of God, even though only analogically.' What can be said about this Christian God? Dupuis explains: 'The Ultimate Reality is personal; it is interpersonal. It consists in total interpersonal communion and sharing between three who are one-without-a-second: Father/Mother; Son/Word/Wisdom; Spirit/Love' (Dupuis, 1997, p. 259).

Furthermore, Dupuis maintains that the God of the monotheistic religions (Judaism, Islam and Christianity) is the same and only God, notwithstanding vastly different doctrinal formulations, and that the Ultimate Reality of the mystical Eastern traditions can also be interpreted, 'in a Trinitarian key, as potentially tending toward the unfolding of the Trinitarian God in Jesus Christ' (ibid.).

With regard to the first affirmation, the origin of the concept of God in monotheistic traditions goes back to Abraham. Even Islam traces its historical origins to the faith of Abraham as truly as do Israel and Christianity (Dupuis, 1997, p. 255; see also p. 260). In light of radically differing doctrinal formulations, Dupuis makes an interesting move by referring to the faith of the mystics in whose experience there can be seen convergence. Mystics in all three traditions search for union with God, in Dupuis's understanding, the one and same God (Dupuis, 1997, pp. 261–2).

On what basis, then, can Christian faith claim to represent the Ultimate Reality 'in itself'? And what about the status of the Christian trinitarian doctrine? Dupuis responds that, speaking of the content of Christian faith in the Divine Absolute, we should distinguish between primordial affirmations and derived assertions. The foundation of the Christian doctrine of the triune God can be found in the history of the man Jesus who called the God of Israel his Father, and Jesus' relation to the Spirit whom he promised to communicate to his own, the church (Jn 14:16–17, 26;

16:7). However, the way Christian tradition has formulated its faith in the triune God, according to Dupuis, is open to further elaborations and clarifications. And yet this is not necessarily to be regarded as 'doctrinal relativism', as it has been interpreted by the Roman curia. Neither does this mean that the role of the doctrine of the Trinity as the hermeneutical key for an interpretation of the experience of the Absolute Reality would be undermined (Dupuis, 1997, pp. 263–4).

Are there any stepping stones to be found in Judaism and Islam, or in the Eastern traditions, to point to the doctrine of the Trinity? While Dupuis freely acknowledges the existence of such 'trinitarian traces' (and here the work of his Catholic colleague Raimundo Panikkar has been groundbreaking, to be shown in due time), he thinks it takes much more work to be able to determine their value. Dupuis himself takes an interesting case study by comparing potential trinitarian parallels between Hindu mysticism and Christian mystery (Dupuis, 1997, pp. 268–78). Whatever the precise form of these trinitarian traditions either in monotheistic or Asian traditions, for Christian faith the ultimate mystery is being 'decisively, yet still incompletely, disclosed and manifested in Jesus Christ' (Dupuis, 1997, p. 268).

What about the relation of Jesus Christ to other saviour figures of the religions? And how does that further relate to the Spirit?

Jesus, Salvific Figures of Other Religions and the Spirit

In his earlier book *Jesus Christ at the Encounter of World Religions*, Dupuis argued for the uniqueness of Jesus Christ that would not negate the principle of universality. Echoing the Rahnerian approach, he wrote:

> Christ as mystery is God turning toward men and women in self-manifestation and self-revelation. The Christic mystery, therefore, is present wherever God enters into the life of human beings in an experience of the divine presence. Nevertheless, this mystery remains anonymous in a certain sense for whoever has not been enabled, thanks to the Christian revelation, to recognize it in the human condition of Jesus of Nazareth. All have the experience of the Christic mystery, but Christians alone are in a position to give it its name. (Dupuis, 1991, p. 92)

In other words, Dupuis maintained that Jesus Christ is clearly asserted as God's definitive revelation and the absolute Saviour (like Rahner), yet the door is open to a sincere acknowledgement of divine manifestations in the history of religions (Dupuis, 1991, p. 108). His later work argues along the same lines: a Christian claim for the oneness and universality of Jesus Christ leaves room for an open theology of religious pluralism.

In determining the role of Jesus Christ among religions, Dupuis takes stock of how other religions view their salvific figures. Since other saviour figures are claimed to be 'absolute', the inquiry has direct bearing upon our topic. Indeed, not only monotheistic faiths such as Islam but also others like Hinduism, with all their alleged inclusiveness, argue for their own superiority. In response, Dupuis first mentions that all talk of the 'absolute claims of Christianity' about Jesus Christ should be discontinued. Not because Jesus Christ is not unique and universal, but, as Dupuis has shown, 'absolute' is an attribute of the Ultimate Real; 'only the Absolute is absolutely' (Dupuis, 1997, p. 292). 'The "constitutive" uniqueness of Jesus Christ will stand as an affirmation of Christian faith, but it will not be absolutized by relying merely on the unilateral foundation of a few isolated texts' (Dupuis, 1997, p. 294). In the final analysis, the constitutive uniqueness and universality of Jesus Christ must rest on his personal identity as the Son of God. No other consideration seems to provide such an adequate theological foundation, Dupuis maintains:

> The 'Gospel' values which Jesus upholds, the Reign of God which he announces, the human project or 'program' which he puts forward, his option for the poor and the marginalized, his denouncing of injustice, his message of universal love: all these, no doubt, contribute to the difference and specificity of Jesus' personality; none of them, however, would be decisive for making him or recognizing him as 'constitutively unique'. (Dupuis, 1997, p. 297; see also 1991, pp. 192–7)

Clearly, Dupuis holds to a 'high Christology' and opposes severing a 'universal Christ' from the 'particular Christ'. 'A Universal Christ, severed from the particular Jesus, would no longer be the Christ of Christian revelation' (Dupuis, 1997, p. 297). So there is particularity to Jesus, but – and this is very crucial to Dupuis's approach – the particularity is of an inclusive, not exclusive, nature. How can one hold on to this dynamic? Here Dupuis suggests two theological principles. First, no more than could the human consciousness of Jesus the incarnate Son exhaust the mystery of God – and therefore 'left his revelation of God incomplete' – can the 'Christ-event exhaust God's saving power. God remains beyond the man Jesus as the ultimate source of both revelation and salvation'. Second, the universal sphere of the nonincarnate Logos of the Prologue to the Gospel of John still continues after the incarnation, parallel to the universal ministry of the Spirit. Thus, while Jesus is Christ and Son of God, other 'saving figures' may be 'enlightened' by the Word/Logos or 'inspired' by the Spirit, 'to become pointers to salvation to their followers, in accordance with God's overall design for humankind' (Dupuis, 1997, p. 298). So the unique mystery of the incarnation of God in Jesus Christ, rather than speaking for exclusivism, for Dupuis helps Christian faith to appraise all the more positively the personal advances of God toward men and women in their own religions (Dupuis, 1997, p. 301).

How does the Spirit relate to all of this? Above, we mentioned that while Dupuis opposes that kind of pneumatological approach to religions that sets the Spirit 'over' or apart from Christ, there is a finer theological distinction that we are now ready to take up. While all Catholics agree that the Spirit is alive and active throughout history, what Dupuis suggests is quite novel: the Spirit may be doing something genuinely different from what one finds in God's Word in Jesus, yet never contradictory to it (as that would water down the criticism he expressed above concerning setting Word and Spirit apart from each other). In other words, God may have – and indeed seems to have – more to say to humanity than what God has said in Jesus (Dupuis, 1997, p. 388). That is exactly what was hinted above in saying that Jesus does not exhaust the revelation of God. How can Dupuis say this and still be fully trinitarian? Dupuis goes back to classical theological canons that speak of 'hypostatic distinctions' among the three trinitarian persons. They mean that while trinitarian persons can never be divorced from each other, neither can they be subordinated to or equated with one another. Dupuis wants to walk a very thin line here. On the one hand, as already mentioned, this distinction cannot be made to establish two different 'economies' in God's salvation history, as if that of the Son would be different from that of the Spirit (as the ancient rule of Irenaeus has sometimes been interpreted). On the other hand, the unity among trinitarian persons cannot be such that distinctions do not apply; that would mean compromising the *trinitarian* nature of the Christian God – and would mean the complete identity of the ministries of the Spirit and Son.

So, finally, what is the fine-tuned understanding of Dupuis regarding the relationship between the Spirit and the Word/Jesus Christ? While the Spirit is given more 'freedom' than in most Catholic theologies, eventually there is a kind of 'subordination' of the Spirit to Jesus. 'Christ, not the Spirit, is at the center as the way to God', and thus whatever God has to say in the Spirit through other religions has to be understood 'in view of' Christ (Dupuis, 1997, p. 197).

Dupuis takes a further step on the basis of his pneumatological-trinitarian orientation. If the Spirit is able to give revelation that is different from that received through Jesus, it means that other religions have a 'lasting role' and a 'specific meaning' both with regard to the followers of those religions and Christians; Christians also can learn something they never knew by relating to the Other. Clearly, other religions (cf. the Fulfilment theory) are not stepping stones but actually serve as mediators of God's saving purposes, albeit incomplete and less perfect than revelation in Christ (Dupuis, 1997, p. 211). Therefore – and here Dupuis is going in the same direction as S. Mark Heim (to be studied in what follows), whom he otherwise criticizes for his pluralism – we need to recognize 'squarely that distinct religious communities actually propose distinct aims for human life, as well as the legitimacy of such claims from the point of view of their faith' (Dupuis, 1997, p. 201). This is a bold statement, but it is in consonance with Dupuis's trinitarian approach.

Now we are ready to take a closer look at how Dupuis envisions the relationship between Christian faith and other faiths in his trinitarian theology of pluralism.

'One God—One Christ—Divergent Paths'

The way Dupuis titles part two of his *Toward a Christian Theology of Religious Pluralism* explicates the nature of his trinitarian approach. Every phrase in that title is significant and should be taken literally. 'One God' refers to the Absolute Mystery of the Divine as it has been made known to us in Jesus Christ: Father, Son and Holy Spirit, in the interpersonal communion of the Godhead, a communion of love. 'One Christ' refers to Jesus-the-Christ of the Christian *kerygma* (proclamation) as witnessed to in the New Testament (Acts 2:36), not to a mythical Christ divested of the earthly Jesus. These two, one God and one Christ, belong together as preface to Dupuis's recognition of 'Divergent Paths'. And both of these 'ones' have to be read in light of what we have exposited with regard to god(s) and saviour figures of other religions.

If Dupuis's label read 'One God—Convergent Paths', it would lead to the kind of pluralistic theocentrism of John Hick and others according to which the various traditions revolve around the one Divine Absolute, the 'Ultimate Reality'. If, on the other hand, the title of part two read only 'One God—One Christ', that would end up with the exclusivism that recognizes the possibility of salvation only in explicit Christian faith in Jesus Christ. In Dupuis's estimation, both of these extremes are not theologically adequate and fail to fulfil the promise of a trinitarian theology.

Dupuis wants to hold on to the high Christology of the tradition and to the principle of God's self-manifestation in a way that would not devalue the self-revelation of God among the religions.

> [It] evokes at once the foundational character of the Christ-event as the guarantee of God's manifold way of self-manifestation, self-revelation, and self-gift to humankind in a multifaceted yet organically structured economy of salvation through which the diverse paths tend toward a mutual convergence in the absolute Divine Mystery which constitutes the common final end of them all. (Dupuis, 1997, p. 209)

Consequently, Dupuis is convinced that the affirmation of Christian identity is compatible with a genuine recognition of the identity of other faith communities as representing in their own right distinct facets of the 'self-disclosure of the Absolute Mystery in a single, but complex and articulated divine economy' (Dupuis, 1997, p. 210).

Dupuis's own vision is to work for a theology built on the idea of a 'complementarity' that is not understood in the sense of the fulfilment theory, 'according to which Christian truth "brings to completion"—in a one-sided process —the fragmentary truths it finds sown outside', but rather a 'mutual complementarity', a 'mutual enrichment and transformation' (Dupuis, 1997, p. 326). The ultimate goal for this kind of process is not to convert the Other to one's own side, but rather 'a more profound conversion of each to God' (Dupuis, 1997, p. 383).

If so, then it is quite natural to conclude that 'elements of truth' originating in divine revelation must be found in the various religious traditions of the world (Dupuis, 1997, p. 239). Again, drawing from the trinitarian structure of his theology, Dupuis notes that wherever there is a personal communication of God, it is always necessarily the God of Jesus Christ who engages in self-revelation and self-bestowal, that is, the triune God: Father, Son and Spirit. Notwithstanding all the errors and limitations, the sacred books and other religious traditions of the world participate in the Word of God. 'Seen in its historical context, Muhammad's monotheistic message indeed appears as divine revelation mediated by the prophet. This revelation is not perfect or complete; but it is no less real for all that' (Dupuis, 1997, p. 245). Evoking pneumatological resources in a trinitarian framework, Dupuis also maintains that 'the religious experience of the sages and *rishis* (seers) of the nations is guided and directed by the Spirit. Their experience of God is an experience in God's Spirit' (Dupuis, 1997, p. 247). Furthermore, in the dialogue encounter, the Spirit works on both sides of the table (Dupuis, 1997, p. 382). Yet this does not nullify the fullness of revelation in Jesus Christ. This 'qualitative fullness' of revelation in Jesus, as Dupuis calls it, is no obstacle to a continuing divine self-revelation through others (Dupuis, 1997, pp. 249–50).

Dupuis summarizes his theology of religious pluralism in a way that merits a longer quote. As a way of introduction he notes that it is possible to go beyond both the exclusivist and inclusivist paradigms without recourse to the pluralist one, since the latter would negate the constitutive salvation in Jesus Christ:

> The Trinitarian Christology model, the universal enlightenment of the Word of God, and the enlivening by his Spirit make it possible to discover, in other saving figures and traditions, truth and grace not brought out with the same vigor and clarity in God's revelation and manifestation in Jesus Christ. Truth and grace found elsewhere must not be reduced to 'seeds' or 'stepping-stones' simply to be nurtured or used and then superseded in Christian revelation. They represent additional and autonomous benefits. More divine truth and grace are found operative in the entire history of God's dealings with humankind than are available simply in the Christian tradition. As the 'human face' or 'icon' of God, Jesus Christ gives to Christianity its specific and singular character. But, while he is constitutive of salvation for all, he neither excludes nor includes other saving figures or traditions. If he brings salvation history to a climax, it is by way not of substitution or supersession but of confirmation and accomplishment. (Dupuis, 1997, p. 388)

Especially with regard to the last point, Dupuis points out an important parallel he finds in salvation history. The way Judaism relates to Christianity is for Dupuis an important clue as to how the 'Divergent Paths' relate to Christianity:

> What applies in the first instance holds good, analogically, in the other. … Even as the Mosaic covenant has not been suppressed by the coming to its fullness in Jesus Christ, neither has the cosmic covenant in Noah with the nations been obliterated by reaching in the Christ-event the goal for which it was ordained by

> God. The implication is that the distinction between the general and special history of salvation must not be taken too rigidly: extrabiblical traditions ... cannot be excluded a priori from belonging to special salvation history. To include them in it would presuppose ... events in the history of peoples which, in function of a prophetic charism, are interpreted as divine interventions. (Dupuis, 1997, p. 233)

Consequently, dialogue becomes not so much a way of converting each other or even convincing another of the supremacy of one's own way, but rather a learning experience. Christians will win an enrichment of their own faith:

> Through the experience and testimony of the other, they will be able to discover at greater depths certain aspects, certain dimensions, of the Divine Mystery that they had perceived less clearly and that have been communicated less clearly by Christian tradition. At the same time they will gain a purification of their faith. (Dupuis, 1997, p. 382)

But how does this translate into the doctrine of salvation and Christ's role as Saviour? Even though Dupuis, with many others, has expanded the theology of religions to encompass other issues than salvation, the issues of how salvation comes and what its form is are not topics to be easily dismissed.

Salvation, the Kingdom of God and the Church

The way Dupuis conceives of salvation can be summarized with two terms: the uniqueness of Jesus Christ is neither absolute nor relative, but 'constitutive' and 'relational'. *Constitutive* means that,

> for Christian faith, the paschal mystery of the death-resurrection of Jesus Christ, has according to God's saving design for humankind, a universal significance: it seals between the Godhead and the human race a bond of union that can never be broken; it constitutes the privileged channel through which God has chosen to share the divine life with human beings. (Dupuis, 1997, p. 305)

Relational refers to the universal significance of the Christ-event in the overall plan of God for humankind and to the manner in which it unfolds in salvation history. In particular, it emphasizes the reciprocal relationship that exists between Christian and other religions' paths of salvation.

Acknowledging the necessary difference between various religions' concepts of salvation, Dupuis suggests that what Christians call salvation has to do with the search for and attainment of fullness of life, wholeness, self-realization and integration. For Christianity, that is the triune God. Yet the Christian tradition has always held that God wills the salvation of all human beings (1 Tim. 2:4). Dupuis differentiates himself from the proponents of the 'orientational pluralism' of S.

Mark Heim, according to which a genuine pluralism must account for the possibility of various religious ends in different religions. Rather, in Dupuis's view there are divergent paths to one common destiny (Dupuis, 1997, pp. 307–16).

So far it has become clear that, while the 'faces of the divine mystery' are to be found in other religions, the triune God is the goal of Christianity and all other religions. But a further question then has to be asked: how does this relate to the kingdom of God, his reign? A corollary question asks: what about the church? Dupuis argues for the universality of the reign of God. Not only does the reign transcend the church – gone are the times when the church and the reign of God were identified – but also Christianity, in the sense that followers of other religions also participate in God's reign. It is in this qualified sense that they are comembers and cobuilders of the reign of God:

> The universality of the Reign of God consists in that Christians and the 'others' share the same mystery of salvation in Jesus Christ, even if the mystery reaches to them through different ways. To recognize that the Reign of God in history is not confined to the boundaries of the Church but extends to those of the world is not without interest and bearing on a Christian theology of religions. ... [T]he 'others' have access to the Kingdom of God in history through obedience in faith and conversion to the God of the Kingdom.... [T]he Reign is present in the world wherever the 'values of the Reign' are lived and promoted. (Dupuis, 1997, p. 344)

Therefore, we have to conclude that Dupuis champions a kingdom-centred model, though different from the one supported by Knitter, who does not relate it to the Christian God (and certainly not to Jesus Christ) in the way Dupuis does. Through sharing in the mystery of salvation, the followers of other religious traditions are thus members of the kingdom of God already present as a historic reality. Not only that, but other religions as such contribute to the construction of the reign of God. Referring to Rahner, Dupuis notes that those other traditions contain 'supernatural, grace-filled elements' (Dupuis, 1997, pp. 345–6, quoting Rahner, 1966b, p. 121). This can be seen both as a legitimate implication of Rahner's theology and as also going beyond it, in that not only are the followers of other religions 'anonymous Christians' (Dupuis himself does not use that term), but they are also cosharers of the kingdom. This naturally has grave implications for interfaith dialogue. Dialogue takes place between persons who already belong together to the reign of God. 'In spite of their different religious allegiance, such persons are already in communion in the reality of the mystery of salvation.' Communion in the reality is more foundational than differences in the sacramental structure and elsewhere (Dupuis, 1997, p. 346; see further ch. 14 in that book).

Going back to the role of the church, we need to ask how Dupuis is able to negotiate the subordinate role of the church in light of his otherwise affirmative position regarding Vatican II views. In Vatican II teaching, the church is not only a kind of sacrament of communion with God and of unity among all human beings

(*Lumen Gentium* # 1) and the instrument for the salvation of all (# 9), but also 'necessary for salvation' (# 14). Certainly, there is a difference of opinion here. Dupuis, however, does his best to soften the tension between the conciliar views and his own understanding. The way he does it is a quite ingenious idea (even though in my mind, as I will indicate below, not theologically sound). Dupuis reasons that to elevate the church too much would mean giving the church the same status attributed to Jesus Christ as the Saviour. Dupuis makes the Vatican II idea of the necessity of the church, rather than appearing exclusive, speak for an opposite tendency, namely, that it is through the church that gifts of God are mediated, especially through its sacraments, its intercession and the preaching of the Word. This is the 'proper' way of mediating salvation, if you will, but for Dupuis it does not necessarily nullify the 'substitutive mediations' of other religions. Nevertheless, the Christian church remains the 'sacrament of salvation'. The followers of other religions can be members of the kingdom of God without being part of the church and without recourse to its mediation, he maintains (Dupuis, 1997, pp. 347–52).

Critical Reflections

We have sought to exposit as carefully as possible Dupuis's quite nuanced and multifaceted trinitarian theology of religions. The reason is twofold. In my assessment, it is the first full-scale trinitarian theology of religions. Second, even with some limitations, it takes up most, if not all, the major issues related to that kind of enterprise and as such is a wonderful learning experience. Whatever one finally thinks of the conclusions presented by Dupuis, it deserves a special hearing and acknowledgement. The contributions of his enterprise are enormous, and even persons like the present writer, critical of some aspects of his theology, can hail Dupuis as one of the forerunners of a truly trinitarian Christian approach to other religions. Furthermore, Dupuis gleans from his extensive encounter with Asian (Indian) religions even though his major work operates within the confines of Western academic discourse (with a brief excursus to Hindu mysticism as noted above). In my assessment, the following points seem most praiseworthy (without repeating what I have already said concerning Rahner where Dupuis agrees).

First, Dupuis has offered a needed trinitarian corrective to several less than satisfactory approaches, theologies that succumb to either subordinationism of Christ in its various forms, whether to God (the theocentrism of Hick) or to kingdom (the regnocentrism of Knitter) or to Spirit (pneumatological theologies of religions of several persuasions) or, conversely, elevate one person of the Trinity above the others, usually at the expense of the Son. Thus Dupuis has raised the trinitarian theology of religions discourse to a new level.

Second, Dupuis's approach is a highly dynamic attempt on the one hand to elevate the doctrine of the Trinity as *the* theological criterion for distinguishing the Christian God from other gods (in the Spirit of Barth) and, on the other hand, to open up that specifically Christian doctrine to speak to and even be enriched by the encounter with others. Even though later on I have to raise some critical questions regarding the way Dupuis relates the God of Christianity to other gods, I applaud his desire to hold on to this dynamic.

Third, Dupuis's pneumatological orientation is undoubtedly the most nuanced theological analysis available (at least among theologies of religions) concerning the mutual relationship between the Spirit and Son. Even if, again, I feel compelled to voice some critiques, I think what he does in trying to pay full attention to biblical and historical traditions in Christian theology is admirable. Without doubt, Dupuis also elevates the currently widely debated pneumatological theology of religions to a new level by avoiding the cheap either–or dilemma so prevalent in the earlier approaches.

Fourth, Dupuis works hard, really hard, to avoid the perils of pluralisms' neglect of the 'uniqueness' (that is not his chosen word) of Jesus Christ and his constitutive role in salvation and the exclusive orientation of most nonpluralist theologies, including that of many inclusivists. Whatever shortcomings there might be in that endeavour – and criticize we must, alas! – I think Dupuis's desire not to give up the tension is a most healthy one in the climate of postmodernism, relativism and pluralisms of various sorts.

Fifth, Dupuis makes dialogue count! In fact, the concept of dialogue – so widely debated currently especially in Catholic theology – is faced with new potentials, again negotiating between pluralism that eventually could easily ignore the whole concept of dialogue as if differences between religions do not really matter and that kind of exclusivism that has decided the results of the dialogue beforehand! In addition to Pannenberg's highly unique approach to dialogue (to be noted below), Dupuis's work has to be considered as one of the most groundbreaking.

My criticism, that again I present respectfully and with a learning spirit, has to do with several points in Dupuis's proposal. Let us begin with terminology, even if I do not regard that as extremely important. Dupuis claims to write a 'Christian theology of religious pluralism'. I fear the title for his project is both inaccurate and misleading. To be more precise, he has not written a theology of *pluralism*, but rather opened up some crucial trinitarian theological perspectives on how to deal with *plurality* of religions and differences among them. I am not stressing this almost self-evident point in order to play teacher to the senior scholar in the field (as if he did not know the difference between these two English words). What I want to say is that anyone who makes Christ constitutive for salvation and takes traditional Christian trinitarian faith as the leading principle (even with all the qualifications Dupuis suggests) is not writing a *theology* of pluralism. I say this not only because I personally believe that it is impossible to write a theology of pluralism (I will come back to this issue at the end of the book), but more importantly since Dupuis's explicit intention is to criticize pluralism. I do not think it is a service to pluralism(s) to expand the meaning of the term so much that in the end even its criticism can be called by the same name. Undoubtedly, Dupuis's (what

I call here) inclusivism comes as close as possible to pluralism (especially to the one championed by Heim and his like), but his Christology and trinitarian views definitely hinder us calling him a pluralist. That his ecclesiastical superiors – in my mind, mistakenly – make him appear to be a 'pluralist' or even worse a 'relativist' is no good theological reason for our doing so.

As already mentioned, Dupuis's treatment of the relationship between Christology and pneumatology in a trinitarian perspective is highly nuanced. Yet, in the final analysis, it seems to betray subordinationist traits. In my assessment, the reason is that Dupuis is so enthusiastic in stretching the boundaries of the ministry of the Spirit that he almost ends up going with those he otherwise criticizes for divorcing the Spirit from the Christ. Maybe he also feels the need to be apologetic towards those who think his pneumatology is too open-ended. In fact, I do not have much quarrel with the idea itself that he is trying to defend, namely, the fact that there could be 'something' more to the revelation than what we have received in Christian revelation. But why bother making this a pneumatological – and thus trinitarian – problem in the way Dupuis seems to be doing when he maintains that in the final analysis it is Christ who stands at the centre, not the Spirit? Why could we not say it in a more biblical way? Following Paul, we could just say that in Christ dwells all the wisdom in bodily form (Col. 2:9). Now, I know this verse bothers Dupuis since he does not want to equate the preincarnate Logos totally with the incarnate Word. Let us leave this aside for a while and just look at the problem at hand. If the Spirit of God is the Spirit of Christ (Rom. 8:9) and if the task of the Spirit, the Spirit of truth, is to take from what is Christ's and make it known to us (Jn 16:15) – as the biblical tradition affirms and Dupuis surely agrees with – then whatever truth will be found in other religions or outside religions, it still belongs to Christ. I am not sure if Dupuis would agree with this formulation of mine, since he might feel that it would limit other religions too much, but I see it as a more satisfying way to approach the 'extra' revelation found among religions.

While my sympathies go with Dupuis's enthusiasm for relating the Christian God to the gods of other religions – and in principle I agree with the goal, while not the specific method of Dupuis (my own view is akin to Pannenberg's) – I find there are several problems and challenges that need to be addressed. The way Dupuis avoids the danger of Hick's pluralism, which posits the Ultimate Reality beyond any specific religion's conception of God, is to be endorsed, as well as Dupuis's argument that the triune God of the Bible is not a penultimate sign but the Reality 'in itself'. However, having said as much, I am surprised that Dupuis still – in my estimation, quite uncritically – takes the leap according to which the Christian God is to be identified not only with the God of two other monotheisms (of course, as a Christian theologian, I endorse the identification of the Old Testament Yahweh with the God of Jesus Christ) but also with Eastern conceptions of God. Even with regard to the god of the Islamic faith, I am not so sure if the identification can be made, but to claim the same for polytheisms of the East is for me a totally unwarranted opinion. In my criticism here, I am not yet even thinking of my personal conviction that, with Pannenberg, understands the history of religions as an arena of conflicting truth claims among religions and their gods, but am here only making the negative claim that the Christian doctrine of the Trinity can hardly be stretched that much, and even if it could be, I do not easily see the rationale. The problems arising out that orientation are too many and serious, the personal nature of the triune God being one of the most obvious.

One of the reasons why Dupuis is led to his view is that, in recognizing the difference between primordial affirmations and derived assertions concerning the Trinity, Dupuis takes too much liberty in changing the derived assertions. The distinction between the two, of course, has to be affirmed, otherwise we claim an absolute status for our own theological assertions. Yet the purpose of doctrinal formulations, especially regarding the doctrine of the Trinity, which is upheld as the criterion for distinguishing the Christian God from other gods, is to set forth that kind of linguistic boundary that is so closely related to the Ultimate Reality that it cannot be easily changed. If we take too much liberty we run the danger of lacking all criteria for distinguishing the God of the Bible. In case my view seems to sanctify too readily (early) trinitarian formulations, clothed as they are in Greco-Roman philosophical attire, I hasten to add that it is for this reason that we need to go back to the *history* of Jesus Christ in the New Testament to be able to speak of the triune God of the Bible who is no other than Yahweh of the Old Testament. Of course, there is no absolutely fixed way of defining the essence of the biblical revelation in the history of Jesus Christ and the giving of the Spirit, following the raising from the dead of the Messiah by the Father in the power of the Spirit. Yet the New Testament revelation serves as *norma normans* (the norming norm). What is most helpful in recent trinitarian approaches, noted in the introduction of this book, is that the doctrine is based on the New Testament salvation history rather than on philosophical speculations. What I say next may sound presumptuous: I believe Dupuis basically agrees with my argumentation here; the reason that I am insisting on it here is that the way Dupuis has presented his case leans toward a view which seems to divorce the Christian doctrine of the Trinity, as endorsed by the ecumenical creeds (with all their limitations and perhaps even shortcomings), too easily from the 'primordial reality'. Notwithstanding my reluctance to go with Dupuis's suggestion, I still believe that for the purpose of dialogue there are resources for negotiating between the monotheism of Judaism (and perhaps even Islam) and the trinitarian faith of Christianity[1] – and I am ready to admit that the doctrine of the Trinity can more easily than monotheism deal with polytheistic traditions.

With regard to Dupuis's desire to soften the uniqueness of Jesus Christ in relation to other saviour figures, apart from his avoidance of the term *absolute* (which I do not see as necessary, since the term *absolute* can also be interpreted in a way different from what Dupuis fears), I have a hard time in grasping how Jesus Christ can be at the same time both 'constitutive' for salvation and 'relative'. Furthermore, the fact that other religions also claim uniqueness (or an absolute status) for their saviour figures must not necessarily lead Christian faith to abandon its claims;

rather, one could argue (as I will later) that it is precisely because religions in the final analysis are supposed to issue ultimate truth claims (in order to maintain their status as responses to the most ultimate questions of life, unless that task is given to some other area of human culture) that Christianity should not abandon its claim to the uniqueness of Jesus Christ as the self-revelation of God and bearer of salvation. This kind of insistence on the uniqueness of Jesus Christ must not necessarily lead to an exclusivism, but rather stands at the heart of inclusivism (including the postconciliar Catholic one). Rather than regarding this as an obstacle to dialogue, it could be presented as a hypothesis to be tested in the dialogue process, open to verification or falsification. And even when it cannot be, of course, conclusively 'verified' (any more than 'falsified') until the eschaton, in light of the history of Jesus Christ, including his death and glorious rising from the dead, it needs to be presented at the dialogue table as a distinctively Christian claim.

Yet another major contention in my interpretation of Dupuis's theory has to do with how he intentionally downplays the role of the church. Here I of course speak as a non-Catholic observer and mean by the *church* the whole Christian church on earth. In the following chapter, as we talk about the proposal by Dupuis's younger colleague D'Costa who in contrast relates the church to his trinitarian scheme (as he sees it biblically warranted), we will have a fuller discussion of the topic. Suffice it to say here that both biblically and in terms of the integrity of trinitarian theology, I do not regard Dupuis's orientation to be very helpful. Dupuis believes that linking salvation and the role of Christ too closely to the church would make the church take the place of Christ. This is an unnecessary and theologically less than convincing fear. I am not so much thinking of the fact that since Christ in the New Testament is depicted as the head of his body, the church, severing the head from the body is unimaginable; more importantly, I refer to the Pauline theology in which the mystery of Christ and the mystery of the church belong together (Eph. 2–3; Col. 1) in God's desire to unite the two (then) opposing entities of humanity, the chosen people and the Gentiles, into one body. Nothing is farther from this thought than to pose the church or Christ as alternatives.

Christ in the New Testament is depicted as the head of the body, the church. Yet the kingdom of God is a wider concept than the church; most, if not all, theologies currently agree on that. But even the kingdom is not unrelated to the concept of the church. The kingdom to come is the kingdom of God that is realized in the person of Jesus Christ in the power of the Spirit. The church is the 'image of the Trinity' and as such the foretaste and sign of the coming of the new creation in which God will be all in all (Rev. 21) (see Volf, 1998). While we should be critical of the way the idea of ecclesiocentrism (*extra ecclesiam nulla salus* especially) has been (mis)used in Christian theology and praxis, theologically, I do not see it right to just downplay the meaning of the church. If the church is made the instrument of salvation only for Christians, then the biblically based (if not explicitly taught) view of the church as the sign of the unity of humankind and the coming of the new creation (Rev. 21) is compromised. Dupuis here appeals to Rahner and others who have talked about the 'provisional nature of the church' on the way to eschatological fulfilment (Dupuis, 1997, pp. 356–7), but I cannot see how one necessarily draws from this the conclusion that the church almost stands in the way of others' entering the kingdom. Dupuis unfortunately devotes only one page to the topic of eschatology and its relation to the reign of God in a book of almost four hundred pages, and so the treatment is very underdeveloped. By my criticism – or an invitation for further work in this respect – I do not mean that we should deny the universality of knowledge of God and deny all the good and notable things outside the sphere of the Christian church. But I fear, biblically and theologically, that to argue for that kind of a subordinate role of the church is misguided.

It should be clear without saying that my rather lengthy critical dialogue with Dupuis is meant to show my great appreciation for his work in that he has really raised the trinitarian theological discourse in relation to other religions to a new level. In the next chapter we will dialogue with the trinitarian theology of yet another Catholic writer, D'Costa, which will also give us the opportunity to refer back to Dupuis and suggest some corrections to his proposal.

Note

1   Ch. 10 will take up a case study between Christianity and Islam as carried on by the Roman Catholic Church.

CHAPTER 4

Gavin D'Costa: A 'Catholic' Trinitarian Theology of Religions

A Trinitarian Critique of Pluralism(s)

While I named Dupuis as the first person to produce a full-scale trinitarian theology of pluralism (Panikkar, of course, has been the first to really take up the issue, but to this day no full-scale trinitarian theology has come from his prolific hand), it has to be said also that Gavin D'Costa is the first to explicitly title a major contribution to Christian theology of religions as being trinitarian. D'Costa's recent *The Meeting of Religions and the Trinity* (2000), while less ambitious than Dupuis's magnum opus, marks a milestone in the development of a distinctively trinitarian approach to other religions. D'Costa's work, while bringing to maturity several themes from his earlier works, is still embryonic and more in the nature of an outline. Yet its contribution to trinitarian theology of religions is significant in many respects, not least because he enters into critical dialogue not only with pluralists but also with fellow-Catholic theologians Rahner, Panikkar and Dupuis, among others. Like his elder Belgian colleague, D'Costa also has an intercultural background: born of Indian parents, he grew up in Kenya and was educated and currently teaches in England.

The scope – if not the size – of the book is broad in that the first part gives a critical assessment not only of the pluralistic theologies of Hick and Knitter, but also of Jewish, (neo-)Hindu and Buddhist theologies of religions. The second part sets out to offer an outline of a specifically Christian trinitarian theology of religions. What is distinctive about D'Costa's proposal is that it is unabashedly and enthusiastically Roman Catholic. It takes its point of departure from Vatican II teachings and engages in an extensive dialogue with papal and other magisterial documents since the council. D'Costa does not build his case on a tradition-specific approach in order to limit it to his own tradition, but sees it as essential to explicate the perspective from which he is speaking; even more importantly, his proposal is meant to be discussed not only by other Christians across the ecumenical spectrum but also by theologians from other faith families (D'Costa, 2000, pp. 12–13, 99–100).

Two major tasks occupy D'Costa in his *The Meeting of Religions and the Trinity*. First, he offers a sharp criticism of pluralisms based on the insight that they are nothing more than representations of modernity's 'hidden gods'. Second, on the basis of conciliar and postconciliar Catholic teaching, he sets out a trinitarian theology of religions, heavily based on a trinitarian pneumatology, to defend a tradition-specific Catholic approach that claims to overcome the errors of pluralism yet avoid the perils of exclusivism. In my understanding, D'Costa's approach represents a type of inclusivism, but he himself eschews the term (as does Dupuis); in my final reflections I will come back to that issue.

D'Costa is no friend of pluralism. The starting point for his relentless criticism of pluralism is that it is a species of Enlightenment modernity.[1] If that applies to Christian pluralism(s), can the same be said of the pluralisms – if there are any – in other religions? D'Costa maintains that even though not all pluralists in other religions are modernists, those who are hold positions that fail. What is the main reason for the failure of pluralisms then?

> Despite their [pluralists'] intentions to encourage openness, tolerance, and equality they fail to attain these goals (on their own definition) because of the tradition-specific nature of their positions. Their particular shaping tradition is the Enlightenment. … The Enlightenment, in granting a type of equality to all religions, ended up denying public truth to any and all of them. (D'Costa, 2000, pp. 1–2)

And the end result is that the pluralists' 'god is modernity's god' (ibid.).

D'Costa laments the fact that even though pluralists present themselves as honest 'brokers to disputing parties', they in fact conceal the fact 'that they represent yet another party which invites the disputants to leave their parties and join the pluralist one', namely, liberal modernity. Therefore, ironically, pluralists end up being 'exclusivists' (D'Costa, 2000, pp. 20, 22). John Hick's view, for example, D'Costa calls 'liberal intolerance' (D'Costa, 2000, p. 24).

But how does D'Costa himself envision Christianity's relation to other religions now that he has discredited pluralistic orientations? D'Costa is no more friendly to exclusivistic attitudes, but rather takes delight in the potential of an encounter with the Other. The main point has to do with how to deal with the Other. 'The other is always interesting in their difference and may be the possible face of God, or the face of violence, greed, and death. Furthermore, the other may teach Christians to know and worship their own trinitarian God more truthfully and richly' (D'Costa, 2000, p. 9).[2] D'Costa believes that trinitarian Catholic theology provides the 'context for a critical, reverent, and open engagement with otherness, without any predictable outcome' (ibid.).

In order for this to happen, D'Costa sets out to redefine radically the three cardinal virtues of pluralism: equality, justice and tolerance. In light of this starting point D'Costa suggests new meanings for the three goals of pluralism that pluralism itself fails to meet. D'Costa argues that pluralism fails exactly because it waters down real differences among religions and regards all of them as the same below the surface. John Hick's pluralism leads to the denial of otherness and difference. Hick mythologizes the differences away so that the religions can be fitted into his system. Consequently, it does not take the dialogue with Other seriously since basically all religions teach the same thing, differing doctrines notwithstanding.

Furthermore, pluralism denies the self-definitions of particular religions and from a distance tells the followers of other religions what is the truth. Thus, pluralism ends up opposing the very virtues it set out to defend (see further D'Costa, 1993, and Hick's response, 1997).

What is D'Costa's corrective? For him, openness becomes 'taking history seriously' and not dismissing it, as pluralism seems to do. Differences do matter and should not be suspended. Tolerance, rather than denying the tradition-specific claims for truth – which in itself, ironically, is one more truth claim among others – becomes the 'qualified establishment of civic religious freedom for all on the basis of Christian revelation and natural law' (D'Costa, 2000, p. 9). Equality becomes the 'equal and inviolable dignity of all persons', which naturally leads to taking the Other seriously, dialoguing with the Other with willingness to learn from the Other and teach the Other (for a tentative analysis, see D'Costa, 2000, p. 9).

But what is the theological basis for D'Costa to replace the pluralist paradigm with a Catholic approach that better fulfils the promise of pluralism, that is, to honour openness, equality and tolerance? We will first exposit the main features of his pneumatological-trinitarian theology and then assess its strengths and weaknesses.

The Spirit, the Trinity and the Church

The main premise of D'Costa's theology of religions can be summarized in this statement: because of the presence in the world of the Spirit of God, 'there too is the ambiguous presence of the triune God, the church, and the kingdom' (D'Costa, 2000, p. 11). The implications of this compact sentence are immense and literally fashion the whole approach of this British theologian. The first part of the premise – an affirmation of the active presence of the Spirit in the world – is agreed on by all Catholics. Not only that, but again based on the teachings of Vatican II, it is also an indisputable fact that not only Christians but also sincere and devout people of other faiths (and possible those of no faith as well) may attain to salvation. These two claims are shared by all who hold to contemporary Catholic faith, and are not subject to debate (D'Costa, 2000, p. 102). The second part of the premise, however, is open to debate, and in fact is being heavily debated among Catholic theologians. That is the question of whether the presence of the Spirit in the world and among religions is related to Christ/Trinity and to the church, and if so, in what way. The last chapter showed us that according to Dupuis, there is an integral connection between the Spirit and Christ/Trinity, but that is not necessarily related to and certainly not tied to the role of the church. Knitter's theology in practice leads to the virtual separation of the Spirit's presence in other religions from Christ. Panikkar relativizes the Spirit–Christ relationship to the point that Christ is only one reference point. Clearly, D'Costa's stance is closest to that of Dupuis, but the difference is still significant: for D'Costa, the Spirit's presence not only implies the presence of the triune God, but also the presence of the church. This is the most distinctive contribution of D'Costa to contemporary trinitarian discourse.

How does D'Costa build his case? He looks for support in both Vatican II documents and postconciliar magisterial teaching, especially in two papal encyclicals quite recently issued on the topic of mission and other religions (D'Costa, 2000, pp. 101–17). When turning to study Vatican II documents, he first asks the question – another one heavily debated in contemporary Catholic theology – of the salvific value of other religions. D'Costa's conclusion – and here he finds agreement with Rahner – is that the question of the salvific value of other religions is *intentionally* left open and should be read as 'no' (or that at least it cannot be read as 'yes', as for example Knitter interprets the silence) (D'Costa, 2000, pp. 101–9, especially p. 105). However, and this is the key point for D'Costa, both Vatican II and postconciliar documents let us understand that the presence of the Spirit among other religions also means the presence of the triune God. Theologically this inference is based on the ancient theological rule according to which the works of the Trinity *ad extra* (outward) are undivided (whereas trinitarian relations can be distinguished from each other; otherwise the Christian God would not be trinitarian!).

In the Council documents, the most explicit mention of the Spirit's role in other religions is found in *Gaudium et Spes* (# 22). It connects the Spirit with Christ and his cross: 'For, since Christ died for all men, and since the ultimate vocation of man is in fact one, and divine, we ought to believe that the Holy Spirit in a manner known only to God offers to every man the possibility of being associated with this paschal mystery.' This passage, D'Costa suggests, needs to be read in light of the *Lumen Gentium* (# 14) view that the church 'is necessary for salvation'. D'Costa's way of making sense of these two seemingly different orientations is as follows:

> The main route for reconciling these tensions lies within the Conciliar teaching that whenever God is present, this is the presence of the triune God; and it is this triune God who is the foundation of the church. Hence, one very important point follows from these Conciliar statements: the Holy Spirit's presence within other religions is both intrinsically trinitarian and ecclesiological. It is trinitarian in referring the Holy Spirit's activity to the paschal mystery of Christ, and ecclesial in referring the paschal event to the constitutive community-creating force it has, under the guidance of the Spirit. (D'Costa, 2000, p. 110)

Accordingly, the presence of the Spirit and thus the triune God in other religions also means some kind of presence of the church, since in the biblical tradition – especially in the Paraclete passages of John 14–16, to be studied in more detail below – the presence of the Spirit is connected to the church.

For D'Costa's argumentation it is crucial to found support in postconciliar magisterial teaching to show that this indeed is the way Council documents are being interpreted, at least by the teaching office of the church. Two papal encyclicals are of prime interest here, the 1994 *Crossing the Threshold of Hope*, a running commentary on *Nostra Aetate* by John Paul II, and the 1991 *Redemptoris Missio* by the same pope. In the more recent teaching letter, the Pope comes closer than any official document has come to affirm a salvific 'root' in all religions even if not the salvific role of other religions. The relevant passage, in reference to *Lumen Gentium*, reads: '... the Council says that the Holy Spirit works effectively even outside the visible structure of the church (cf. *Dogmatic Constitution on the Church* 13), making use of the very *semina Verbi* [seeds of the Word], that constitute a kind of *common soteriological root present in all religions*' (John Paul II, 1994, # 81; italics in the original).

Redemptoris Missio goes into detail in explaining how the presence of the Spirit is related to Christ, his cross and the church. The encyclical connects the Spirit and Christ closely together (# 29; quoted in D'Costa, 2000, pp. 107–8):

> Thus the Spirit, who 'blows where he will' (cf. Jn. 3:8), who was 'already at work in the world before Christ was glorified', and who 'has filled the world ... holds all things together (and) knows what is said' (Wis. 1:7), leads us to broaden our vision in order to ponder his activity in every time and place.

Thus the Pope may affirm that 'every authentic prayer is promoted by the Holy Spirit, who is mysteriously present in every human heart'. Yet the same paragraph warns about not seeing the Spirit's presence as an alternative to Christ, since whatever the Spirit brings about serves as a preparation for the gospel and can only be understood in reference to Christ. Having said this much, the Spirit's presence, related to Christ, is also connected to the Christian church:

> This is the same Spirit who was at work in the Incarnation and in the life, death and Resurrection of Jesus, and who is at work in the Church. ... Moreover, the universal activity of the Spirit is not to be separated from his particular activity within the Body of Christ, which is the Church. (# 29)

> It is true that the inchoate reality of the Kingdom can also be found beyond the confines of the Church among peoples everywhere, to the extent that they live 'Gospel values' and are open to the working of the Spirit who breathes when and where he wills (cf. Jn 3:8). But it must immediately be added that this temporal dimension of the Kingdom remains incomplete unless it is related to the Kingdom of Christ in the Church and straining toward eschatological fullness. (# 20)

Here the Pope sets the record straight and explicitly connects the Spirit with Christ and Christ's church. D'Costa agrees and he is furthermore also happy to note that this presence of the Spirit is not limited to the interior life of individuals but – in light of general Catholic teaching – widens to include cultural, social and religious dimensions: '"The Spirit's presence and activity affect not only individuals but also society and history, peoples, cultures, and religions. Indeed, the Spirit is at the origin of the noble ideals and undertakings which benefit humanity on its journey through history." But this does mean conferring independent legitimacy upon other religions' (# 28; quoted in D'Costa, 2000, p. 113).

Having established, on the basis of contemporary Catholic teaching, his main theological argument, namely, that the presence of the Spirit in the world also implies the presence of the triune God and the church, D'Costa draws implications for his theology of religions.

'The Holy Spirit's Invitation to Relational Engagement'[4]

D'Costa finds a significant clue in the way *Gaudium et Spes* talks about the mutual relationship between the (secular) Western culture and the church. The document encourages the church, 'with the help of the Holy Spirit', to engage in dialogue and discerning work, so that 'revealed truth can always be more deeply penetrated, better understood, and set forth to greater advantage'(*GS* # 44). In other words, the Catholic teaching here affirms the role of the Other to help the church deepen the faith. Yet it does not mean that the teaching can be interpreted as 'sanctifying modernity' any more than that other religions *per se* would be sanctioned as legitimate ways of salvation (D'Costa, 2000, pp. 112–13).

Other religions are not salvific as such, but other religions are important for the Christian church in that they help the church to penetrate more deeply into the divine mystery. This is the first significant conclusion for D'Costa. Earlier on it was mentioned that in contrast to modernity, which tends to water down real differences between religions and thus end up not taking seriously dialogue with the Other, D'Costa, on the contrary, emphasizes the importance of the dialogue. Again, he finds strong support in the magisterial teaching. *Redemptoris Missio* (in the above quoted passage, # 29), having warned about separating the universal activity of the Spirit from the particular activity in the church, strongly encourages dialogue as a way to deepen Christian faith:

> Indeed, it is always the Spirit who is at work, both when he gives life to the Church and impels her to proclaim Christ, and when he implants and develops his gifts in all individuals and peoples, *guiding the Church to discover these gifts, to foster them and receive them through dialogue*. (my italics)

So D'Costa concludes that if 'fulfilment' is understood one-sidedly, as it often is, in terms of other cultures being prepared for the reception of Christ, then something essential is missed. This is nothing less than domesticating the activity of the Spirit in

> that religion, for the Spirit within that culture may call for an even deeper penetration, understanding and application of the truth of God's triune self-revelation entrusted to the church. That is, if the church is not attentive to the possibility of the Spirit within other religions, it will fail to be attentive to the Word of God that is entrusted to it. (D'Costa, 2000, p. 114)

So not only other religions, but also Christianity may be 'fulfilled' by listening to what the Spirit is saying among other religions even if the Other does not bear the gift of God self-consciously. In other words, if the Spirit within the church has the role of helping the church to follow Christ more truthfully 'and coming to indwell the trinity more completely' then this same Spirit when outside the church must also have an analogous role with the other cultures, 'to help make women and men even more Christ-like, individually and in community, however frustrated and thwarted' (D'Costa, 2000, p. 115).

This kind of openness to the Spirit's activity in other religions facilitates a critical and reverential attitude toward other religions. Rightly, D'Costa notes that this kind of acknowledgement of the gifts of God in other religions by virtue of the presence of Spirit (which is not unrelated to Christ and his church) means a real trinitarian basis to Christianity's openness toward other religions. Thus the discernment of the activity of the Holy Spirit within other religions must also bring the church more truthfully into the presence of the triune God, D'Costa argues. All of this is what D'Costa calls the 'Spirit's invitation to relational engagement'. And, once again, it is not separated from the church: 'if the Spirit is at work in the religions, then the gifts of the Spirit need to be discovered, fostered, and received into the church. If the church fails to be receptive, it may be unwittingly practicing cultural and religious idolatry' (D'Costa, 2000, p. 115). The church had better be ready for surprises since there is no knowing a priori what beauty, truth, holiness and other 'gifts' may be waiting for the church (D'Costa, 2000, p. 133).

To back up his case, D'Costa engages in a 'theological exegesis' of the Paraclete passages found in the Gospel of John chapters 14–16, which speak of the Spirit as advocate and guide. The purpose of that exercise is to further highlight the integral connection between the Spirit and church in the framework of a trinitarian high Christology (D'Costa, 2000, pp. 117–18; see further, pp. 119–27). There is neither space nor need to go into details here; suffice it to highlight the main insights. After and by virtue of the crucifixion, resurrection and ascension of Jesus Christ, the Holy Spirit perichoretically indwells the disciples of Jesus, predicated upon the indwelling of the Son and Father, calling the church, the body of Christ, 'to be Christ to the world' in mutual love and sharing, as well as in sharing love with the world, even (as in John's case) over against the hostile 'world' (D'Costa, 2000, pp. 120). The Spirit, facilitating the church's participation in God's trinitarian love, thus brings to focus the trinitarian foundations of the church and thus the integral connection between ecclesiology, pneumatology and the Trinity.

On the basis of this excursus into the Paraclete passages, D'Costa summarizes in a wider theological perspective the response to this corollary question: what does it mean to the church to say that the Spirit is present outside itself – within the world religions? Several implications follow. First, talk about the presence of the Holy Spirit among world religions cannot be abstract and general in nature, but can only be generated in the context of specific Christian engagement with non-Christian religions. The 'claim that the Spirit is active in the world can only be part of the church's discernment (not ownership) of the hidden depths of God's trinitarian action of love'. That claim may not be well received by that particular religion since the claim is an intra-Christian claim. The church in such a context serves both as a sign of judgment and forgiving redemption and a potential receiver of the gift from God through the Other (D'Costa, 2000, p. 128). Thus there can be no question of 'other' or 'new' revelations 'in so much as this might be understood as other "gods," or a cancellation of how God has chosen to reveal God's-self in trinitarian form', since all truth/revelation, 'in whatever form, will serve to make Christ known more fully to Christians—(and to the world?), *without understanding* what this will mean in advance' (D'Costa, 2000, p. 129, italics in the original).

In discerning what the Spirit is doing in other religions, the church may find true Christlike practice in the Other, which, as long as it really is Christlike, can only be brought about by the Spirit. Other religions may produce that kind of practice either in keeping with their own self-understanding or in resistance to elements within that particular tradition. It can also be the case that the church fails to acknowledge it. In a limited sense, then, it is appropriate for D'Costa to use the language of 'saintdom' in reference to other religions, even though it also may be confusing, he adds. The existence of Christlike practice among the followers of other religions makes a crucial theological point:

> It is here that the distinction and relationship of Spirit and Son language takes on one possible meaning in the context of other religions. This never-ending process of nonidentical repetition involves reading all creation in Christ through the guidance of the Holy Spirit, in each and every moment of the church's life. (D'Costa, 2000, p. 130)

For the church, the active presence of the Spirit in the world may be a way of recognizing its own sin and weaknesses. Through the witness of non-Christian lives, the truth of Christlikeness may come to light. The Spirit's presence also has implications for the world and its religions. The world can be held accountable for the elements of truth it might already hold, and 'these elements, when incorporated into Christian articulations and practices, serve to once more give praise to the trine God—even though such incorporation may rightly involve radical discontinuity' (D'Costa, 2000, p. 130).

A case study to test this theory is offered in the form of interreligious prayer. D'Costa wonders if that kind of activity is like marital infidelity or is a genuine mutual dialogue. D'Costa argues that if prayer leads into perichoretic (mutually indwelling) communion with the triune God and his people, there is no reason to limit the perichoretic relations to the boundaries of the church. The same Spirit who helps Christians in their weakness (Rom. 8) is possibly at work in other religions. Prayers from other religious traditions can be moved by and be authentic promptings of the Holy Spirit. Are they directed to the triune God? D'Costa realistically notes that since various traditions are different, they are not commensurate or incommensurate a priori. One can say that while no other tradition explicitly affirms the Trinity, it is not clear a priori that they deny the Trinity. While Christians are bound to pray to the triune God in the name of Jesus, there is no way – nor any need – to try to limit the work of the Holy Spirit who 'offers everyone the possibility of sharing the Paschal Mystery in a manner known to God' (*GS # 22*). This means, D'Costa believes, that the presence of the Holy Spirit must in some manner entail the reality of Christ's presence and therefore the Father's presence within a person's life and devotion. Theologically, it is not possible to claim the presence of the Spirit apart from the perichoretic presence of the Trinity. In the final analysis, D'Costa leaves open the question of the nature and goal of interreligious prayer, but certainly he is leaning towards experimenting with it (2000, pp. 143–66):

> I have been suggesting that plunging into the love of the triune God may well call us to risk finding an even greater love of God through interreligious prayer, and into discovering the darkness and mystery of God afresh. Our marriage to our Lord, may itself suffer infidelity in an absolute resistance to the promptings of suffering love which might entail interreligious prayer. But equally, interreligious prayer may also be an act of irreverent infidelity. The church is called to pray fervently for those who engage in interreligious prayer for the sake of Christ. (D'Costa, 2000, p. 166)

Critical Reflections

To give a critical assessment of D'Costa's proposal without yet venturing into a constructive task is quite challenging, since of all the trinitarian theologies studied in this book his is one of the closest to my own current understanding. Even though as a non-Catholic theologian my doctrinal and spiritual background as well as ecclesial context is different, and therefore I cannot claim this one as my own, there is no denying the fact that my sympathies lie with his general outline and orientation.

The merits of D'Costa's approach are many and significant. Here it suffices to mention them briefly, and the last chapter of the book will pick them up on the way to building a constructive proposal. (The praises given in the context of discussing the Catholic proposals of Rahner and Dupuis, where all three authors agree, are not reiterated here.) D'Costa's criticism of pluralism is very helpful and exposes the blind spots of pluralistic approaches such as their definition of 'openness' and 'tolerance'. Of course, the criticism also raises questions, especially about the heavily debated relationship between modernism and pluralism (and the related question of how modernism and postmodernism are connected, a relevant issue for several reasons, not least since pluralism and postmodernism of course share common values). It might be the fact that the relationship between modernism and pluralism is not as straightforward as D'Costa suggests. But we can also surmise that, for the limited purposes of his book, D'Costa did not say everything about the topic.

In my opinion, D'Costa's trinitarian theology represents the most nuanced response to other religions from the perspective of classical Christian trinitarian faith. The way D'Costa envisions the complementary yet distinct roles of Son and Spirit and their relation to the Father both honours the classical canons and opens up their meaning with regard to other religions, the latter task being one that has not been much pursued in earlier trinitarian theologies. His proposal corrects and expands the dilemma found in Dupuis's, who struggles with how to keep the Spirit's 'independent' ministry within the classical trinitarian rules.

D'Costa's approach is commendable also in that it takes the role of the church as conducive to the relationship of Christianity to other religions. In Christian theology of religions, the first turn was away from the centrality of Jesus Christ in favour of a God-centred approach (theocentrism). That move then led theologians of religions to downplay or ignore the role of the church, the body of Christ. Even in pneumatological theologies of religions, the role of the church is usually bypassed. D'Costa's proposal is bold and innovative: rather than seeing the central role of the church in the programme of the trinitarian God as an obstacle to dialogue, he makes it an asset. Wherever the trinitarian God is present in the world through the Spirit, there is also a link to the church, the new community arising out of the resurrection of Jesus by the Father in the power of the Spirit. Yet this is no exclusivism as 'ecclesiocentrism' can easily be, but rather a call by the Spirit for the church to be mutually involved with communities of other religions to deepen her faith. Dialogue becomes what the term literally means, two parties speaking to each other, learning and growing. Thus interreligious prayer becomes a possibility.

My first query has to do with D'Costa's methodology. I fully agree that – in contrast to pluralists who mistakenly claim a 'neutral' position for their own views (and as D'Costa shows, end up offering yet another option among others, rather than any kind of metatheory) – one's theology is always tradition-specific and thus particular and perspectival. Unless this is acknowledged – and again, that is one major reason why pluralisms fail – a real encounter will not happen. Differences and similarities can only be faced and negotiated when they are acknowledged! To oversimplify the case: why bother dialoguing if all or at least the 'wise men' already know that differences do not really exist, or if they do, they do not count? Certain kinds of pluralisms (but not all, as I hope to show, especially in regard to the type of pluralism advocated by Panikkar, who takes differences seriously), rather than championing dialogue, end up promoting retraining of not only their dialogue partners but in practice the rest of the faithful to see the 'light'. So I am happy that D'Costa not only acknowledges the tradition-specific nature of his trinitarian approach but even makes it one of his assets. So far so good. Nevertheless, in my opinion there are also limits to the extent we should cherish the particularist nature of our theology. It is here that I think D'Costa's otherwise praiseworthy proposal begins to present obstacles. D'Costa's methodology is not only Catholic, but it is a *particular* Catholic approach in that it limits its discourse to Vatican II and selected postconciliar, mainly papal, pronouncements. Here again, he lays his cards openly on the table when in the introduction he explicates the purpose of the constructive section of the book: 'strategically intrachurch dialectics is more important to me in Part II [Trinitarian Theology and the Religions] than the dialectical conversation with other religions and modernity'. Furthermore, he says in the same context that 'any Christian position advanced on these questions must be rooted in, and accountable to, an ecclesial community' (D'Costa, 2000, p. 12).

It is here that I begin to feel uneasy and fear that this methodology is *too* tradition-specific. Let me explain what I mean. First of all, in that D'Costa's approach relies on the official magisterium of the Catholic Church, it has the advantage of dialoguing with the valid Catholic interpretation of faith rather than a myriad of differing voices. At the same time, ironically, that is also a danger: D'Costa's approach has the potential of being interpreted as ecclesio-ideological, in support of the views advanced by the hierarchy. In my reading of D'Costa I do not sense that and certainly he does not belong to the hierarchy himself. Yet when compared to the methodologies of Rahner and Dupuis, D'Costa has really explicitly chosen the narrow path of the current ecclesial teaching office. This is, of course, a stance questioned by many of his Catholic theologian colleagues, and increasingly a number of ecclesiastical colleagues.

What is my point here? Why do I as a non-Catholic theologian concern myself with intrachurch issues like this in assessing D'Costa's theology of religions? The reason is this: if for D'Costa the needed *ecclesial* context for defining a Christian trinitarian theology of religions is a specific Catholic interpretation as advocated by the official teaching office of the church, then I fear it is far too limited to be relevant for an interfaith dialogue. First of all, D'Costa has to convince his fellow Catholics about the validity of his approach, but not only that, he must also convince the rest of the ecumenical spectrum of Christian traditions. Second, even though many non-Catholics who are not content with either pluralism or exclusivism would be happy to go a long way with D'Costa's proposal, for them the materials he alludes to are not authoritative. This also relates to the ecumenical challenge of trying to work for a common witness among Christians to be able to testify to Christian faith before other religions. Thirdly, it is very rare that official documents such as council documents or hierarchical pronouncements, even for those who acknowledge them authoritarian, have the needed theological nuancing to be suitable for a constructive theology such as the one proposed by D'Costa.

Therefore, my suggestion is that in order for the benefits of D'Costa's approach to become a viable option for the church ecumenical and thus more relevant for interfaith dialogue, it should be worked out in critical dialogue with wider Catholic and non-Catholic voices. That would mean that the term 'ecclesial context', rightly emphasized by D'Costa, has to be defined in such a way that it relates in some way or another (also) to the whole Christian church. I do not want to be naïve here: even as a professional ecumenist, I do not envision the future of the Christian church as one single church but rather as a communion of churches, and I do not believe (even if I could pray for it) that an interfaith dialogue in the recent ecumenical climate could be conducted between Christianity (representing one single voice) and another major religion. Rather my concern is a matter of Christian church(es) talking to community/ies representing other faiths. Yet especially in light of the fact that D'Costa partially makes his case in reference to the materials in John 14–16 speaking of the church vis-à-vis the (hostile) world, certainly nothing less than the *whole* Christian church is in view. And everybody agrees that the often-quoted prayer of Jesus for the united witness of his own in John 17 refers in its original context to the undivided flock of Jesus' disciples.

This reference to the Gospel of John and its use by D'Costa takes me to my second query, which also relates to his methodology. It is refreshing to read systematic theology that takes so seriously the biblical witness that it enters into extended exegetical dialogue with the contemporary issues and the text. However, I am surprised again by the limitations of his approach and to some extent with the choice of the biblical materials. I do not think this choice helps D'Costa redeem his promise in the introduction to the book: 'My position is advanced with careful attention to biblical witness' (D'Costa, 2000, p. 12). Careful it is, but very selective. I also suspect that the author overstates the significance of the Paraclete passages in the Gospel of John. Obviously, these passages are not irrelevant for the purposes of a pneumatological theology of religions, but without a 'theological' exegesis (a term that often makes me suspect the danger of eisegesis, or reading something into the text which is not there) one cannot easily make the point D'Costa wants the biblical witness to make. If one really seeks to support one's theological case with the biblical witness, why not select a wider array of biblical materials – especially the Pauline corpus? In this regard Dupuis's approach is helpful in that he covers the whole sweep of biblical materials in the first major part of his book. Passages such as Ephesians 1 with its trinitarian structure (and perhaps also chapters 2 and 3 in their proper contexts) would considerably widen the biblical witness.

My third query is of lesser importance and relates partially to terminology. Like Dupuis, D'Costa eschews the term 'inclusivism', which routinely is reserved for the kind of approach to other religions advocated by Vatican II: all salvation (and truth, at least most of it) comes from Jesus Christ, even though salvation is not limited to those who have conscious faith. In Dupuis's case I have a better understanding of why he is not fond of the term, even though I still count him among inclusivists for want of a better label. For Dupuis, even the contemporary Catholic inclusivism implies restricting the Spirit's sovereignty too much to the confines of Christianity and the Christian church. In D'Costa's case these fears are less felt. Yet to my surprise he is very critical of the term inclusivism. He suggests that inclusivism also collapses into differing types of exclusivism; it is always based on the idea of particularity in a given tradition. Inclusivists, like exclusivists, hold in the final analysis that their tradition contains the truth regarding ontological, epistemological and ethical claims. Furthermore, inclusivism violates the rule according to which each tradition has to be treated as a totality; one cannot affirm only some aspects of another tradition. When one does so, one is still operating from one's own specific tradition and responding to what seems good to it; the aspects the alleged inclusivist affirms or responds to might differ from the self-understanding of the representative of that other religion (D'Costa, 2000, pp. 22–3). This is the way I understand the essence of D'Costa's critique of inclusivism. But frankly, I do not see in this anything substantially different from what he himself affirms! Terminology aside (if a better word can be used, I am more than happy to adopt it), isn't it the case that D'Costa explicitly affirms the tradition-specificity of his approach; takes revelation in Jesus Christ as ontologically true (so that whatever new insights into faith that the Spirit helps Christians to gain from others are still related to the fullness of revelation in Christ); and advocates the kind of approach in which, as part of the discernment process guided by the Spirit, Christians are able to affirm some parts of other religions and their practices, while rejecting others? I am confused here and hope that it is because of my lack of understanding all the nuances of D'Costa's proposal rather than his expressing himself less than clearly!

It is easy to see that, perhaps with the exception of the first query (related to the specificity of the ecclesial context) my criticisms are quite meagre when compared to the merits of D'Costa's approach. There are also several key issues left for further reflection; we have already mentioned that D'Costa's proposal is in the form of an outline, not yet a full programme. One wonders for example how he relates the 'divine mystery' of the biblical faith to the gods of other religions, a topic that Dupuis, among others, has tackled. D'Costa cautiously begins to deal with the issue in the context of interreligious prayer but – wisely, in my opinion, at this stage of theological development – leaves it open as to whether the prayers of followers of other religions (prompted by the Spirit of God) really are addressed to the same God. Here I think D'Costa's cautiousness is very much warranted; earlier on I expressed my reservations about Dupuis's perhaps too hasty desire to identify the gods. Furthermore, one would also raise the question as to the relationship between the church and the kingdom, another issue discussed with Dupuis. While one would guess that with other contemporary theologians, D'Costa would not have a problem in affirming that the kingdom comprises a wider sphere, it would be enlightening to see how he envisions their exact relationship and how that is related to the role of Jesus Christ. A corollary question has to do with salvation: how does D'Costa define salvation brought about by the trinitarian God? These are all questions D'Costa needs to address if he is going to offer a full trinitarian theology of religions.

In the last chapter, I will return to affirming some major elements of D'Costa's trinitarian approach. To conclude our survey of various types of 'inclusivist' trinitarian theologies, two Protestants are to be studied next, Wolfhart Pannenberg and Clark Pinnock.

Notes

1   In his critique of pluralism, D'Costa critically builds on Alasdair MacIntyre and his critical dialogue

partner John Milbank. With his widely debated works such as *After Virtue* (1981) and *Whose Justice? Which Rationality?* (1988), MacIntyre has argued for the pervasiveness of modernity in both contemporary philosophy and theology. In his analysis, 'the Enlightenment project' was doomed to failure because its promise of a rationality independent of any historical and social context was never fulfilled. John Milbank (1990b) critically agrees and laments that the Enlightenment project with its result, modernity, has resulted in the demise of trinitarian theology and Christian practice. Depending on narratives other than the biblical-theological story, modernity has left the world without a God and without teleology (that is, without purpose). 'Deism was the initial home for this unemployed god, but agnosticism, atheism, and secularism were the inevitable trajectories', concludes D'Costa (2000, p. 4) in light of MacIntyre's and Milbank's analyses. Yet D'Costa is not completely happy with the way Milbank especially analyses the influences of modernity on religions, and so he wants to uncover the extent of modernity's influence upon the religions case by case.

2   Here is one instance where D'Costa is critical of his dialogue partners, MacIntyre, who sees the Other as a 'rival', and Milbank, for whom the Other is an object of 'out-narration'.

3   The Pope adds a note in this context warning also about the danger of seeing the Spirit as the one who fills 'a sort of void which is sometimes suggested as existing between Christ and the Logos'. This is a corrective to those who want to separate the Logos too much from Jesus Christ incarnate such as happens in the theologies of Knitter and Panikkar; the tendency is also not totally foreign to Dupuis.

4   Section title in D'Costa (2000, p. 109).

CHAPTER 5

Wolfhart Pannenberg: The Trinitarian Faith as the Resource for the Common Search for the Truth

'Religious Pluralism and Conflicting Truth Claims'

The above title of one of the few essays that Wolfhart Pannenberg (1990), a leading systematic theologian at the international and ecumenical level, has written specifically on theology of religions, brings to focus the main motif of his theology in general and thus his theology of religions, namely, the search for the truth. Even though the subtitle of that essay might indicate otherwise – 'The *Problem* of a Theology of the World Religions' (my italics) – in light of the overall theological programme of this German theologian, one could also say that the competition for the truth gives energy and direction to the rivalry of the gods.

While Pannenberg has established his name among the small number of giants of systematic theologians, if for no other reason than for daring to build a system that attempts to relate faith in the Christian God to all that exists in reality, theology of religions has not been his focus at any point in more than forty years of prolific writing. Many readers might even wonder why the present book devotes a whole chapter to expositing his views. My motive in choosing Pannenberg as one of the representatives of Christian theologians of religions and its relation to the Trinity is that with the publication of his monumental three-volume *Systematic Theology*, a *summa* of his lifetime learning and reflection, it finally became obvious how much potential to speak to this issue his theology carries. Indeed, a whole chapter in volume one is devoted to the topic of history and theology of religions. However, what is somewhat disappointing about the *Systematic Theology* is that after the beginning chapters of the first volume, mainly dealing with methodological issues, Pannenberg does not develop the implications of his theology of religions, not even in his eschatology, which would be one of the loci most pregnant for doing so.[1]

What makes Pannenberg's theology so appealing with regard to the goal of the present book is that for him, unlike pluralists, the doctrine of God occupies the centre of all of his theology. Consequently, Pannenberg takes the term *theology* ('doctrine/study of God') most seriously. For him the object of theology, 'the science of God', is 'the self-communication of a divine reality' (1976, p. 314). Not only that, but a specific kind of doctrine of God is the main structuring principle of his theology, the doctrine of the *trinitarian* God. As will become evident, for Pannenberg salvation history, as unfolded in the biblical canon, conclusively leads us to the idea of God as triune. Yet – unlike Barth, for whom the Trinity is also a structuring principle of theology – Pannenberg does not dismiss the significance of philosophical theology's effort to come to some kind of knowledge apart from Christian revelation. On the contrary, he warns Christian theologians not to write off that ancient enterprise too easily. History of religions matters; religions is the sphere where the ultimate truth question is finally settled.

An appropriate place to begin any exposition of Pannenberg's theology is to highlight the significance of theology – and of religions – to the quest for ultimate truth. He denies all the attempts to ground the truth of Christian claims either in the authority of Scripture alone (after the collapse of the 'Scripture-principle' in Enlightenment criticism), theological or ecclesiastical tradition, personal experience or the piety of the theologian, or God-consciousness (Schleiermacher) (1991, pp. 26–48). The truth of the Christian message – and thus of revelation – can no longer be treated as the presupposition (as in pre-Enlightenment theology) but as its goal (1991, pp. 36, 52). The task of systematic theology is the exposition of Christian doctrine in a way that leads to a coherent presentation in harmony with what we know of God and reality as a whole.[2] In that sense, theological claims have the nature of hypotheses to be tested and if possible confirmed (1991, p. 50). Historical truth by nature is always contestable and open to debate until the eschaton.

An obvious question arises in the mind of Pannenberg's reader at this point. How do we establish the truth of the Christian message or any other message? What is the criterion? Not surprisingly for Pannenberg God is the proper focus and starting point of Christian theology, but in order to achieve 'universal coherence' all the topics need to be related to God's action, to the world as whole (1991, p. 49). But this is not yet the whole answer. How are we humans able to establish that principle? Here eschatology – the end result of the rivalry of gods in the history of religions – comes to play a significant part.

The truth of Christian claims about God – and thus of theological claims – awaits the final confirmation (or lack thereof) till the end of times. 'According to the witness of the Bible the deity of God will be definitively and unquestionably manifested only at the end of all time and history' (1991, p. 54). What about the meantime? Is there any way for us to have at least some kind of certainty before the end? According to Pannenberg, the '[d]ecision regarding their [truth claims] rests with God himself. It will be finally made with the fulfillment of the kingdom of God in God's creation. It is provisionally made in human hearts by the convicting ministry of the Spirit of God' (1991, p. 56).[3] Decisive here is the resurrection of Christ from the dead, a divine confirmation of Christ's claim to be the Son of God and thus the agent to usher in the final victory of God in his kingdom. In the final analysis, what matters in determining the truth of the Christian message – and thus of the existence of and claims to the God of the Bible – is whether 'the idea of God corresponds to an actual reality … [and is] able to illumine human existence, as well as our experience of the world as a whole' (Miller & Grenz, 1998, p. 132). Consequently, if the idea of God must be able to illumine not only human life but also experience of the world, then theology should also. Therefore, Pannenberg does not shy away from arguing for the truth of the Christian message vis-à-vis competing truth claims, even if that is not typical of theology at the end of the second millennium.

The Theological Significance of the History of Religions

Pannenberg has restored religion to the central place in theology.[4] Conducive to his positive appraisal of religions is his foundational anthropological insight according to which faith in God is nothing external imposed on human beings but rather something inherent in humanity. In his view, religion is an essential dimension of human life; it belongs to the nature of humanity to be open to God and search for meaning and truth.[5] Appropriately, he labels his approach a 'fundamental-theological anthropology' (1985, p. 21). This is of course a major factor supporting Pannenberg's claim to the rationality of god-talk. Pannenberg arrives at this fundamental conclusion by way of arguing with Descartes and Schleiermacher that the only way to posit the finite is to assume the infinite as the necessary horizon (1991, pp. 113–18, 136–41). Of course, claiming the 'incurable' religiosity of humankind (1991, p. 157) does not guarantee the truth of theological claims. Rather, that is necessary but not sufficient evidence (1991, p. 93).

Perhaps surprisingly, Pannenberg's point of departure for assessing the value of religions is the phenomenology of religions.[6] But his is a theological interpretation and 'critical appropriation' (1985, p. 18) of religions, that is, theological reflection on the results and approaches of empirical finds in psychology, sociology and history of religions. In other words, the ultimate goal is the investigation of religions, including Christianity as 'to what extent their traditions provide evidence for the self-communication of a divine reality' (1976, p. 315, see also p. 364). Unlike Barth, for Pannenberg religions play a crucial role in revelation since the claim for the truth of god(s) lies at the heart of religions (see further, Grenz, 1989, p. 201). The history of religions represent this endless search for universal truth. Even though Pannenberg believes that God can only be known as God reveals Godself (1991, p. 189), he also acknowledges the fact that the only way to examine divine revelation is through human religion. Christianity is a religion among other religions.[7]

It is the task of the religions to mediate the appearance of the divine in human experience and history. Consequently, religions are both useful and in fact necessary for our knowledge of God. However, Pannenberg is too sharp an observer of religion to ignore the fact that too often the view of religions is falsified because of their tendency to fix on the finite and/or resort to magical means of exerting power (1991, pp. 172–87, especially 182–3). But that tendency does not make void the crucial role religions play in the human search for meaning. Whatever falsifications there are in religions, Christianity for Pannenberg is by nature a syncretistic religion in that it assimilates, incorporates and critically adopts elements from other religious traditions, even those in competition with it. So religions play a vital role in Pannenberg's understanding, but religions also stand under the qualification of provisionality. Not only other religions, but also Christianity, are provisional since the truth that both Christianity and other religions are searching for is not yet fully present.

'The Reality of God and the Gods in the Experience of the Religions'[8]

For Pannenberg, the main thrust of the history of religions is the competition between conflicting truth claims of adherents of various deities. He looks at the phenomenology of religions and concludes that at the heart of the history of religions is the search for a religion that would be able to illumine our experience of the world in the most coherent way. The debate is going on and the final outcome is yet to be determined. While maintaining the provisionality of all religions and their gods, Pannenberg at the same time makes a definite claim for the supremacy of the God of the Bible among other gods. How does he support this claim, which seems not very conducive to dialogue?

Pannenberg's argumentation, rather than focusing on current religions, mainly engages the exchange between Christianity and ancient religions, Judaism included. The first significant step was the emergence of the Jewish view of God (subsequently adopted by Christian theology), which represents a radical advancement over rival ancient religions in that it was able to provide believers with the concept of the unity of the culture. For ancient people, gods were looked upon as the providers of this unity (see Pannenberg, 1976, pp. 311ff.). A transformative change also took place in Israel in that the division into holy and profane was overcome and God's influence was felt to be comprehensive, reaching to all spheres of life. In Israel, as soon as Yahweh was regarded as the one God who was in control of all spheres of life, this foundational tension was overcome and monotheism emerged. It is only against this background that the exclusive claim to worship Yahweh alone can be understood (1991, especially p. 148).

It is, then, on the basis of monotheism that the claim to one God as the ground of the world as a whole as well as human life becomes understandable. Consequently, the dispute concerning religious claims finds its resolution in the sphere of the experience of the world, since the world shows that it is determined by God (Pannenberg, 1976, pp. 300–303). Here again the critical question arises: how is it possible for humans to decide what is the alleged determinative work of God in world experience? For Pannenberg, the determining factor is a specific understanding concerning the relationship between religion and world experience. Pannenberg claims that religious consciousness and beliefs, rather than simply being the results of cultural, socio-political and economic changes (Max Weber[9]), are in fact the driving force behind such changes (Pannenberg, 1976, pp. 311–12, also 206–24).

A final advancement of Jewish faith in God took place, along with the emergence of the apocalyptic vision, when the past-oriented mythical religion began to be transformed into a future-oriented open religion. Unlike typical mythological religions in which historical and religious changes are placed back in the primal age of myth, there arose in Israel the question of the future definitive self-demonstration of the deity of God. This happened in Israel especially in exilic prophecy and was later taken up by apocalyptic writers into expectation of endtime events (Pannenberg, 1991, pp. 169–71). In Pannenberg's opinion, any religion that lives by promise towards the future can 'cope with the vicissitudes of the historical process better than religions related to the past-oriented myth of primordial time' (Braaten, 1988, p. 304).[10] Thus, both Jewish and Christian faith came to view reality as history moving towards a future goal that has not yet appeared. In Christian parlance, the end came to be conceived of in terms of the kingdom of God that would give final evidence of God as the Lord of all people. That would also validate the claim of Christian revelation about the unique place of Christ in the history of religions. Rather than delving into the past, this orientation came to view the future as holding the power to interpret the past. In this 'turn to the future' of Israelite and consequently Christian faith in God, Pannenberg sees another evidence of the superiority of the Christian conception of the deity.

By now it has become clear that Pannenberg regards the biblical concept of God as superior to other gods, even though not unrelated to them and though still awaiting a final, eschatological confirmation. But, more specifically, how is the idea of the *trinitarian* God critical here? Pannenberg's thesis is that the salvation history in the Bible leads Christian theology to conceive of God in plural terms, even if not compromising the unity of God; while the doctrine of the Trinity is a later (philosophical) formulation, the God of the New Testament, who is identical with the Yahweh of the Old Testament, can only be known as trinitarian. Thus we can already say that the only God that Christians may think of and proclaim to others is the Father of Jesus Christ, the triune God.

The Triune God and the Gods of the Religions

The most important way in which Pannenberg revises the traditional discussion of the doctrine of God relates to the order of the topics: while it has been customary to treat the unity of God prior to the Trinity, Pannenberg takes it the other way. The threeness of God is for him the way to talk about the Christian God, even if – as we saw above – talk about the Christian God is not unrelated to philosophical theology. The other distinctive feature in Pannenberg is his grounding his doctrine explicitly in revelation rather than on speculation. By doing so, Pannenberg wants to highlight the fact that the doctrine is based on God's self-revelation and thus it cannot be made an optional appendix but is the crux of the exposition of the Christian God. At the same time, it means that the way to talk about the Trinity is grounded on salvation history: thus, Pannenberg in the main follows Rahner's rule. The way he applies this rule is to look at how the three trinitarian persons come to appearance and relate to each other in the event of revelation as presented in the life and message of Jesus. It is only on the basis of this triune God that Christian statements about the one God and God's essence and attributes can be discussed.[11]

Taking his clue from Barth, who built his trinitarian doctrine on revelation – even if Pannenberg finds fault with Barth in that for him it was not the revelation of salvation history as much as it was a formal statement ('God reveals Godself ...')[12] – Pannenberg begins the discussion of the emergence of the doctrine of the Trinity by looking at how Jesus as Son distinguished himself from the Father and submitted himself to serve the coming of the kingdom (1991, pp. 259ff.). For Pannenberg, the beginning of the trinitarian understanding of God, thus of the Son and Spirit too, lies in Jesus' announcement of the nearness of the rule of God, the God of the Old Testament. Jesus taught us to know God as Father. Jesus' differentiation from and service to the Father establishes Jesus' sonship (1991, pp. 3–5).

The Spirit is introduced by virtue of his involvement in God's presence in the work of Jesus and in the fellowship of the Son with the Father. This is the reason why Christian theology did not adopt a binitarian view but rather trinitarian: 'If the Spirit were not constitutive for the fellowship of the Son with the Father, the Christian doctrine of the deity of the Spirit would be a purely external addition to the confession of the relation of the Son to the deity of the Father' (1991, p. 268).[13]

Having established the overall significance of the doctrine of the Trinity as the proper defining feature of Christian God-talk, how does Pannenberg relate to philosophical theology's tradition of speaking of god(s) apart from particular revelation? Above, we hinted that Pannenberg is not at all willing to dismiss it. So how does the triune God of Christian revelation (and salvation history) relate to the 'god of the philosophers' and to the gods of other religions? According to Pannenberg, Christian theology has too often missed the significance of the fact that in the Bible, the term *god* not only serves as a proper name but also as a general designation. In the Bible, we find both Yahweh (proper name) and *Elohim* (a generic term for God). Proper names, Pannenberg notes, only make sense in connection with terms for species. Therefore, to make God-talk intelligible, Christian theology would be better not to cut off the use of this general term as the background for talking about the particular God, Yahweh, the Father of Jesus Christ. Christian theology needs to affirm the concept of God in philosophical theology. Otherwise it is 'involuntarily regressing to a situation of a plurality of gods in which Christian talk about God has reference to the specific biblical God as one God among others' (1991, p. 69). This also means not shying away from metaphysical talk.

On the basis of this exposition, it is now possible to probe deeper into the implications of Pannenberg's theology for the theology of religions. Stanley J. Grenz, a student of Pannenberg and a well known interpreter of his theology, suggests that two themes in his theology set the stage for interfaith dialogue: the quest for the truth and a trinitarian pneumatology. In addition to these two issues I will also take up several others that speak for the interfaith potential of Pannenberg's theology: the necessity of the doctrine of the Trinity to the Christian conception of God and its implications; Pannenberg's view of the relationship of Christian ecumenism and theology of religions; and finally the role of Christ as the 'inclusive' norm.

'The Theological Basis for Interreligious Dialogue'[14]

Grenz succinctly summarizes the main thrust of Pannenberg's approach to interfaith dialogue on the basis of his trinitarian theology:

> Pannenberg's understanding of the relationship of Christianity to the religions moves from his fundamental conviction that the Christian conception of God is superior to the understandings of ultimate reality found in other religions, whether ancient or contemporary. He is confident that this assertion can be demonstrated by rational inquiry, which in turn becomes the task of systematic theology. At the same time, that very conception of God as the Triune One, when properly understood, provides the foundation for dialogue among the religions. (Grenz, 1989, p. 209)

The significance to the theology of religions of the quest for the truth as the theme of Christian theology comes to focus in two related perspectives. On the one hand, Pannenberg's understanding of truth is tied to God: God is the ground of the revealing of the truth in eschaton. Thus, for Pannenberg, unlike for pluralists such as Hick and Knitter, the Christian conception of God is not something that can be easily negotiated. If the Christian conception of God is treated as only one of the complementary ways of referring to the divine mystery, Christian theology compromises its very foundations.[15]

On the other hand, since for Pannenberg truth is not something timeless (the Greek understanding of truth) but rather an evolving process (as in Hebrew thought), history matters, and especially history of religions. History matters in that resurrection is made a key component in affirming the validity of Jesus Christ's claims of sonship. While Pannenberg shares no sympathies with those conservatives who argue for the historicity of events like the resurrection on the basis of the inerrancy of the biblical tradition, a denial of its historicity would make his system collapse. Thus, any 'metaphorical' theological talk like that of Hick and Knitter as a way to soften the differences is totally foreign to Pannenberg. A corollary implication is that differences between religions are to be honoured and cannot be dismissed. Rather, acknowledging the differences and treating them as hypotheses to be tested is the essence of interfaith dialogue:

> Considering the specific character of the Christian faith as based upon a historical past and related to an eschatological future of salvation, the truth

claims of the Christian proclamation are at its basis, and the differences with other religions finally result from conflicting truth claims. A theology of world religions that wants to be true to the empirical situation in the way the religious traditions confront each other must not evade or play down the conflict of truth claims. If we look to the history of religions in the past, there was always competition and struggle for superiority on the basis of different truth claims. (Pannenberg, 1990, pp. 102–3)

Not only history but also history of religions matters. This leads to the following affirmation: since the truth of the Christian message (in its final, eschatological, sense) is tied to the history of religions, the arena for the competition of gods and their capacity to show which truth can best illumine the world experience, the concept of the triune God of Christian faith is integrally related to other gods. With all his insistence on the superiority of the Christian God – a hypothesis to be tested in the course of and in light of the history of religions – the triune God is not unrelated to world history and the history of other gods. Christian faith needs other religions to come to the conviction of the supremacy of the God of the Bible as revealed in the history of Jesus Christ. Thus for Pannenberg, the claim to the superiority of the Christian triune God is not a dialogue-blocking exclusivism but a public claim based on history and subject to the 'confirmation' of history (of religions). Grenz (1989, pp. 203–4) summarizes well the significance of this perspective. Acknowledging the fact that it is the purpose of the dialogue, in its service of the common quest for the truth, to put forth rival claims to truth and test them in light of their capacity to illumine the world experience, dialogue becomes a necessity:

> This necessity arises from Pannenberg's emphasis on the provisional and contestable status of all religious truth-claims and theological assertions. Theological provisionality means that dialogue never arrives at its terminus. Rather, all dialogue partners must continually remind themselves of the provisionality of their own theological constructs, for, until the arrival of full knowledge of the ultimate reality, all theological statements are subject to revision based on further insight. ... The theological humility that flows from this understanding provides a context for sincere dialogue with all differing religious viewpoints. (Grenz, 1989, p. 204)

A related insight is that dialogue is given a theological basis also by means of Pannenberg's positive evaluation of religious traditions as expressions of a fundamental awareness of divine reality. Religions, even with their flaws, serve a crucial function (ibid.).

In addition to the central role of the truth as the theme, Pannenberg's insistence on the 'necessity' of the doctrine of the Trinity – even in light of the fact that its exact formulations, as with any other theological claims, are subject to development and testing – has enormous implications for his theology of religions. If the talk about Father, Son and Spirit is the only possible way of identifying the God of the

Bible – and thus the God of Jesus Christ and Christian faith – not only is the mythologization of the concept of God (based on salvation history and not on changing religious formulations), as in Hick and others, impossible, but also both Christological and pneumatological strictures are defined by his trinitarianism. Christ's divinity follows from the doctrine of the Trinity. With all the deviations from classical orthodox formulations,[16] Pannenberg's trinitarianism leads him to affirm the divinity of Jesus Christ, thus putting his Christology at odds with those kinds of 'theocentrisms' that prefer God over Jesus Christ. It also leads to a critical attitude towards mythologizations of the doctrine of the incarnation: it is only as the Man, a true human being, that Jesus submitted his life to obedience to the Father; rather than denying his divinity, his true humanity rather confirms it. Humble submission of one's self to the (legitimate) lordship of the Father and thus serving the coming of the kingdom does not mean minimizing deity. This is the essence of Pannenberg's version of the doctrine of *kenosis* ('self-emptying', Phil. 2:7). How Christ acts as 'an inclusive norm' in Pannenberg's theology of religions will be discussed in what follows.

Regarding pneumatology, not only is the divinity of the Spirit affirmed, but the equal role of the Spirit as one member of the Trinity is also fully acknowledged, thus giving the Spirit a central role in the world and among religions. With many other contemporary theologians (such as Moltmann and Rahner), Pannenberg opposes the *filioque* view.[17] Thus Pannenberg is able to 'move beyond traditional Christocentrism and to elevate the Spirit as the trinitarian member most specifically operative in the world' (Grenz, 1989, 204–6; quote p. 204). Rehabilitating the role of the Spirit in the Trinity, Pannenberg's pneumatological approach allows him to see the saving work of God in the context of the divine activity in creation as a whole. A key here – and unfortunately space does not allow elaboration on Pannenberg's pneumatology (see Kärkkäinen, 2002, pp. 117–25) – is the principle of continuity: the same Spirit of God who brings about the new life in Christians and the Christian church is the same Spirit that is the life-principle of everything that exists.

Pannenberg encapsulates this leading principle with the term 'ecstatic' (*ekstasis*, literally 'stand outside' or 'exocentric'): the Spirit elevates creatures above themselves to participate in the life of God. Therefore there is continuity between creation, the new life in faith, and the eschaton, the completion of the creation by the power of the Spirit.[18] And the same Spirit is present in the religious expressions of the human person, which have given rise to the various religious traditions of human history (Grenz, 1989, pp. 204–5). Furthermore, on the basis of his understanding of trinitarian relations, according to which the task of the Spirit is to glorify the Son and through the Son give honour to the Father's claim of unique lordship, Pannenberg is able to maintain that everywhere in relations where the divine mystery is at work, the Son is too. Now it may be that there are distortions and mispresentations present in religions, but still the Son, as the mediator of all creaturely existence, is 'behind' this quest for meaning and truth. And the same

Spirit of God, who lifts up creatures, especially human beings, above themselves to share in the divine life, is at work in correlation with the Son.

Thus pneumatology represents universality, while Christology in a sense becomes the point of tension between the historical particularity and the eschatological universality, though not in an exclusive way, but rather in a way that opens up Christianity for dialogue with others. 'The rule of God which Jesus proclaimed and pioneered in his own life, death, and resurrection can be seen in light of the apostolic message as the power at work in all the religions of humanity' (Braaten, 1988, p. 305).

Therefore, the possibility of salvation is not confined to the church. This takes us to Pannenberg's understanding of the role of Jesus Christ as the 'inclusive norm'. While Pannenberg certainly does not limit salvation to the members of the Christian church, in the final analysis he leaves the fate of nonbelievers open. But he sets forth the Christological criterion: Jesus is 'the universal criterion of judgment or salvation, but not the indispensable historical means of salvation'.[19] What matters is how closely people's lives conform to the standards set forth by Jesus and the kingdom (Pannenberg, 1990, p. 98). Yet it has to be noted that – again, in contrast to pluralists such as Hick for whom the 'transformation' of lives, whatever the sources, is the essence of salvation – 'salvation' in the Bible goes far beyond this worldly concept of opening up to others in selfless love; the New Testament in Pannenberg's reading links salvation primarily to the eschatological judgment of God and to participation in the communion of the kingdom (1990, p. 101). Thus, to make the 'salvations' of different religions denote the same reality does not work for Pannenberg for reasons deriving from his trinitarian theology. In the New Testament, Jesus' claims to the transcendent reality of God in his ministry (as in exorcisms) put Jesus in a different category from other divine figures (see further, 1990, p. 102).

Clearly, Pannenberg's understanding of truth as the theme of theology (of religions) and its linking to the triune God – combined with his understanding of election, according to which election does not mean sealing the eternal fate of certain individuals but rather bringing about the divine goal through the involvement of the people of the world – 'serves to move the focus of interreligious dialogue away from the question of who ultimately belongs to the people of God and toward the task of looking for the activity of the divine reality in the world and engaging all peoples in the mandate to foster the divine program' (Grenz, 1989, p. 206).

There is one more crucial theme in Pannenberg's theology that has bearing on the shape of his theology of religions, something that his interpreters seemingly have missed, namely, the relationship between Christian ecumenism and theology of religions and their relation to the kingdom of God, the cause of which Jesus serves as the obedient Son. In Pannenberg's ecclesiology, the church is an anticipation and a sign of the unity of all people under one God (1998, p. xv; see further, Kärkkäinen, 2002, pp. 115–17). The church is the anticipation of the kingdom of God; therefore its essence is constituted by the kingdom, of which it is the sign. The church 'serves both as a sign, pointing to a future society of peace and justice that no political system can bring into existence and as a reminder of the transience of all social orders in contrast to the finality of God's rule' (Grenz, 1990, p. 153). For Pannenberg, it is crucial that the kingdom of God is directed beyond itself to the unity of humankind under one God. The essential goal of the church is a sign and tool of the coming kingdom of God; the church has its end not in itself but in the future of a humanity that is reconciled to God and united by common praise of God in his kingdom (Pannenberg, 1998, p. 45). The challenge of ecumenism – one church under one triune God – is thus directly tied to the unity of humankind: 'If Christians succeed in solving the problems of their own pluralism, they may be able to produce a model combining pluralism and the widest moral unity which will also be valid for political life' (1977, p. 138). The unity and peace between Christians and between them and their God is a proleptic sign of renewed humanity.

Having highlighted some critical themes in Pannenberg's theology that in my understanding shape his approach to interfaith dialogue, how would the dialogue process look in light of those affirmations? Pannenberg comes to the dialogue table with adherents of other religions with the set of commitments outlined above. He takes the differences seriously. The purpose of the dialogue is not to soften the differences between religions and consequently to blur the importance of the search for a unified truth. Pannenberg's programme naturally sets the tone for the encounter, that is, a common search for a truth. Rather than trying to extrapolate an alleged 'core' of religions in an attempt to create a new kind of 'universal' religion, the positive religions in their own distinctiveness have to be honoured as legitimate ways of reaching for a unified truth. That religion which has the potential of offering an explanation of the experience of the world in a most satisfactory way most probably will prevail or at least offer itself as the most viable religion.

Since it is only at the eschaton that the truth of any religious claim can be finally established, the dialogue process becomes a real *process*. Not only the truth claims but also the religions themselves are provisional in nature. At best, they approach the truth. Therefore, any kind of haughty claim for the superiority of any religion can hardly stand the criticism of an honest dialogue. On the contrary, even the final result of the dialogue cannot be guaranteed beforehand. Provisional truth by definition is open for corrections and adjustments. And since not only Christianity but perhaps all other living faiths are also syncretistic in nature, interreligious dialogue is as much a learning experience as it is an opportunity to share about one's convictions and let others test one's own hypotheses.

At the end of the dialogue process one has to ask if the god(s) of other religions are the same as the God of the Bible. Pannenberg argues that while the face of Christ can be seen in some persons of other religions, as well as God's providence, one cannot be sure if the God that a Hindu or Sikh prays to is the God of Jesus Christ. Ultimately, this is a question to be decided by God, not us (Pannenberg, 1990, p. 103). Even when there is a high quality of religious life and the fruit of the transformation of lives, for Pannenberg, the question is whether that corresponds to the Christian hope, in that Christianity 'hopes for an eschatological transformation of our bodies by participation in the glory of God' (ibid.). Christians should hope that God will look graciously upon others, but one difference remains: 'The Christian has the promise of God in Christ. The other religious traditions do not provide that particular promise' (Pannenberg, 1990, p. 104).

Critical Reflections

As with D'Costa's proposal, many of my sympathies go with Pannenberg's bold suggestion for honest 'co-learning' among religions. Yet it is not without problems, and those have to be taken up to advance the discussion. The first one has to do with his theological method and the primacy given to the common search for truth. Living as we do in postmodern times, Pannenberg of course represents a minority voice, harshly criticized especially by Anglo-American postmodernists. That Pannenberg, even in his magnum opus, does not engage the current discussion concerning the concept of truth after the advent of postmodernism (or even before it), represents an anomaly very difficult to understand for a theologian who in his earlier career had established himself with methodological writings. While Pannenberg derides the dogmatism of much of older Christian theology, he borders on another dogmatism himself by claiming that taking the coherence theory of truth (according to which, with regard to theology, faith in God has to cohere with everything that exists) is the self-evident criterion of truth. For many it is not, and I am not even thinking only of contemporary theologians but also of the long history of Christian theology. Corollary issues are many and challenging: are proponents of various religions able to agree on what is 'historical' and what is not? What I mean here is Pannenberg's insistence on the historicity of resurrection as the key to establishing the truth of the Christian message (proleptically at the present, awaiting the final eschatological resurrection of all). And even if they were able to agree, would all religions be willing to take 'historicity' as *the* criterion? I doubt it, since not all the people of the world follow the discourse of Western modernism. Too bad. Pannenberg gives the impression that the coherence theory of truth, as based on a critical exposition of Western theological discourse, is directly applicable interculturally. He never bothers to even cite let alone dialogue with voices from other religio-cultural contexts.

Let me be open about my own standpoint: I am no friend of that type of postmodernism that mistakenly imagines being able to leave behind the truth question in favour of 'perspectivalism' (that each 'truth claim' only represents one perspective and cannot even begin to assume universality), and I am not suggesting Pannenberg should. But what I am concerned about is that in order for Pannenberg's proposal to make sense to contemporary philosophical and theological discourse, he should subject his theological method to critical dialogue with those who disagree about the method.

I applaud the desire to make theology of religions discourse 'rational' in the sense of rehabilitating the truth question as central, and thus helping to make God-talk rational. In secular discourse, God-talk is relegated to the interiority of personal life without any claim to public validity. Thus, efforts by Pannenberg (and for example, the late Lesslie Newbigin) are to be welcomed. But one has to ask if Pannenberg is making theology (of religions) discourse one-sidedly rational. It is true that in his *Systematic Theology* he has introduced the concept of doxology. He admits that with all its logical and rational power, in the final analysis 'talk about God becomes doxology in which the speakers rise above the limits of their own finitude to the thought of the infinite God'. In this process, 'the conceptual contours do not have to lose their sharpness. Doxology can also have the form of systematic reflection' (1991, p. 55). However, he does not expand on how the introduction of doxology relates to the basic orientation of theology in the service of public, coherent truth. I agree in principle with Pannenberg that the truth question ought not to be dismissed and that if it is, as in most pluralistic theologies, implications are felt in the concept of God (as is evident with, say, Hick and Knitter). Yet focusing one-sidedly – and we may want to say, almost exclusively – on the pursuit of truth as the theme of theology and interfaith dialogue could become an obstacle for a true dialogue. Furthermore, as the long history of Christian theology shows, there is a celebrated tradition of the mystical, apophatic[20] approach to faith in and worship of God; while the mystical must not be set in antithesis to the effort to pursue truth, the mystical approach contains many other elements, too. Living faiths – all of them, even Buddhism with its philosophical atheism – do contain a lot of mystical elements.

That brings me to my next concern: how viable is Pannenberg's proposal of interfaith dialogue as a common quest for the truth? For a scientific community that may work in terms of gathering scholars from various religions to advance the quest for their understanding of God. A *religious* dialogue may not work from that sole premise: commitment to a certain faith and its conception of God contains elements that go beyond intellectual conviction of the truth of that particular faith. Thus, with all the admiration for Pannenberg's proposal for a model of interfaith dialogue, my guess is that it would be depicted as having a Christian bias rather than being a universal, 'neutral' method.

Another methodological issue needs much clarification: what is the way concretely to assess which religion is best equipped to illumine the world experience? I doubt if there is any 'neutral', 'objective' – even any commonly agreed upon – way of doing so. How we assess the religions' capacity to do this is, of course, related to our understanding of what is crucial in religions and about the world. This is true especially in light of the fact that differences – and with Pannenberg and others I do affirm radical differences between religions – do touch the very basics of worldview and approach to reality. How to define 'truth' is of course dependent on the underlying philosophical and religious framework. Therefore, while in principle Pannenberg's proposal regarding religions' capacity to illumine world experience sounds adequate, I fear that it remains too abstract and can hardly be either validated or invalidated in practice.

In line with the most recent focus of theology of religions, Pannenberg does not make the question of salvation the sole – nor even the primary – focus of discussions. Yet what he says about the eschatological nature of salvation, in contrast to the 'this-worldly' transformation of personal and collective lives (as pluralists maintain), is valid in my assessment. What does trouble me is that with all his analytical and rational powers, Pannenberg surprisingly leaves the question of the extent of salvation open. While I agree with Pannenberg that in the final analysis it is only God who knows it, Pannenberg's trinitarian theology would have resources for addressing that question more deeply. For example, his approach to the crucifixion in terms of the concept of 'inclusive substitution' in contrast to 'exclusive substitution' may have some bearing on the topic.[21] His insistence on revelation as history could also shed some light on the issue of salvation: even with the 'brokenness' of revelation in the current world, it is open to anyone to see, he maintains. These, and other resources (such as the above-mentioned idea of corporate election), would give seedthought for probing more deeply into the issue of salvation and corollary topics. Maybe the fact that Pannenberg has so little directly engaged interfaith dialogue explains why he has never majored on that issue.

Finally, I come to the crux of my assessment of Pannenberg's proposal. In the main outline, I take it as a helpful corrective to much of the desire of pluralisms to leave behind the classical faith of the Christian church with its appeal to the history of salvation of the triune God of the Bible. Yet I think that in light of challenges coming both from the current Western discourse on modernism/postmodernism (and related issues, especially those concerned with 'truth') and from an honest acknowledgment of radical differences between religions (so that, for example, Buddhists and Hindus cannot be expected to embrace a particular agenda as the 'universal' one), Pannenberg's proposal should be seen more modestly as *a Christian*, and thus particular, commitment. Pannenberg, no more than Hick (with his implied idea that the followers of all religions are 'wrong' in assuming the absolute truth of their own faith) or theologians from other religions, cannot take a seat above other dialogue members and assume that his own agenda is more universal. Let me be precise here. With Pannenberg, I agree that the Christian message, even in its particularity, claims a universal truth based on the triune God who is believed to be the God of all, the only true God, and thus pluralisms that leave behind an appeal to universality also leave behind the conception of the triune God of the Christian tradition. That is not my concern here. What is my concern has to do with methodology and approach: Pannenberg's proposal is a particular approach to interfaith dialogue and nothing more. Most probably other dialogue partners will not accept it as *the* agenda. Nevertheless, its commitment to the triune God of the Bible as the guarantor and basis of truth is a bold attempt to rehabilitate the triune God as the focus of interreligious affairs.

Notes

1 In addition to the essay mentioned above, see the classic essay by Pannenberg titled 'Toward a theology of the history of religions' (1971).

2 For his definition of theology along these lines, see Pannenberg (1991, pp. 59–60).

3 Pannenberg's reference to the conviction of the Spirit here must not be taken out of context. It is not pietism's insistence on the subjective certainty in the believer's heart of the certainty of God and the truth of the Christian message but is based on historical events, primarily on the resurrection of Jesus Christ.

4 A comprehensive treatment of the topic is found in Pannenberg (1991, pp. 119–36). In his *Theology and the Philosophy of Science*, Pannenberg had already announced his programme: 'Theology as a science of God is therefore possible only as a science of religion, and not as the science of religion in general but of the historic religions' (1976, p. 31).

5 For a short statement, see Pannenberg (1991, pp. 54–7 especially). For a full-scale treatment, see his *Anthropology in Theological Perspective* (1985), which in fact is an attempt to fight against the opponents of religion on their own field, namely, psychology, anthropology, sociology and history.

6 'Today, the phenomenological method is obviously the dominant one among the science of religions' (1971, p. 72).

7 By this, however, Pannenberg does not join the mainstream of contemporary research into religions in which the turn to anthropology has eliminated God from religions. For a critical dialogue with several phenomenologists of religion, see Pannenberg (1991, pp. 136–51). Pannenberg bemoans the inner contradiction that contemporary research into religions has created in denying the existence of God, since this hypothesis brings the study of religion into opposition with the intentions of religion itself. 'In religion God is the agent in the relation to humanity, but the study of religion looks only at humanity's relation to God and tells us nothing about God's action" (1991, pp. 143–4). Even the famous phenomenologist G. van der Leeuw noticed this, but obviously regarded this contradiction as unavoidable.

8 Section title for Panenberg (1991, vol. 1:119–87); the basic ideas are already present in Pannenberg (1972, pp. 65–118).

9 Even Max Weber himself noted that, with regard to Protestant ethics, this ethos has been a catalyst of social changes.

10 Note the comment by Pannenberg: 'Whoever lives on the basis of the archetypal and strives to achieve for the present only its optimal participation in the archetypal reality, lives unhistorically. To this extent, archaic peoples close themselves off from the historic future' (1971, p. 109).

11 See especially Pannenberg (1991, p. 200), where he summarizes his method of approaching the Trinity. In another context, Pannenberg critically surveys the whole of Christian theology from the Fathers to Barth and concludes the following: 'Any derivation of the plurality of trinitarian persons from the essence of the one God, whether it be viewed as spirit [as Hegel] or love [as Social Trinity], leads into the problems of either modalism on the one hand or subordinationism on the other. Neither, then, can be true to the intentions of the trinitarian dogma' (1991, p. 298).

12 For the criticism of Barth, see e.g. Pennenberg (1991, p. 296).

13 The key to Pannenberg's trinitarian doctrine, then, is to study carefully 'The Reciprocal Self-distinction of Father, Son, and Spirit as the Concrete Form of Trinitarian Relations' (1991, p. 308). Applying Hegel's concept of 'self-differentiation', which means that by giving oneself to one's counterpart one gains one's identity from the other, Pannenberg maintains that the Father is 'dependent' on the Son for his identity, and the Son and Spirit on the Father and each other.

14 This subheading is taken from Grenz (1989, p. 203). My exposition under this title, however, includes several key points not present in Grenz.

15 By using the term *foundation*, I am not necessarily suggesting that Pannenberg is a foundationalist philosophically (foundationalism means that in the final analysis, an irrefutable ground/foundation is assumed on which the rest of the theological/philosophical system lies). Recently, it has been

suggested that Pannenberg is rather 'postfoundationalist', a term not easy to define (see Shults, 1999). Personally, I do not see how Pannenberg's system would work without some kind of foundationalism; yet in the confines of the present chapter it is not possible to support my opinion.

16   Pannenberg is not happy with the language of 'two natures' (human and divine); his doctrine of atonement avoids most traditional theories, and the crucifixion does not play a crucial role in his theology.

17   The Latin *filioque*, 'and from the Son', means that the Holy Spirit proceeds both from the Father and the Son.

18   For a programmatic statement, see Pannenberg (1970, 1997).

19   See Pannenberg (1984, p. 136). Earlier in his career Pannenberg proposed the idea that the disputed passage of 1 Peter 3:19–20 about the descent into hell of Christ after the crucifixion opens up hope for those who have not heard the gospel (1972, p. 95).

20   'Apophatic theology' (in contrast to 'kataphatic') means an orientation in which theologians and worshippers of God are content to identify what God is not, but not what God is like. Of course, this approach raises the question whether one is able to identify negative elements if no understanding is available of what the 'object' is supposed to be. That question cannot be pursued here and does not directly affect our line of questioning.

21   For Pannenberg Jesus acted as our substitute in his crucifixion and resurrection. Jesus did not die so that we can avoid death, as the exclusive view maintains; instead, in tasting death for us he has radically altered it. No longer do we need to be terrified by death. Because we participate through faith in the new life brought by Christ, we look forward to participating in God's life beyond death.

CHAPTER 6

Clark Pinnock: A Pneumato-trinitarian Theology of Religions

An Evangelical Spokesperson

The theological locus of Clark Pinnock, a Canadian professor of theology emeritus, is found, broadly speaking, in the so-called Evangelicalism[1] of the English-speaking world. While he has been criticized by the right wing of the movement for being too open to other religions, his views can be regarded as representative of a more progressive, ecumenically conscious segment of the rapidly growing Christian family of churches, which is not united by a common denominational label but rather a set of theological convictions.[2] In recent decades, the Evangelical movement, which is transdenominational and global, representing not only all sorts of Protestants from Lutherans to Presbyterians to Baptists to Pentecostals to Anglicans,[3] has distanced itself from the more reactionary Fundamentalism, even though most Fundamentalists regard themselves as 'true' evangelicals. My reference to 'evangelical theology' here follows the main usage in the English-speaking world, namely, various (mainly Protestant) Christian traditions who are open to the dialogue with all other Christians and want to cherish the classical Christianity as explicated in the creeds and mainstream confessions, yet also remain open to the latest developments in theology and other academic fields.

Traditionally, evangelicals have been both very missionary-minded and suspect of (or even hostile to) the notion of interfaith dialogue. In 1970, a defining document was drafted in Germany under the leadership of the prominent missionary Peter Beyerhaus. The 'Frankfurt Declaration', as it came to be known, soon established itself as the evangelical statement on other religions on both sides of the Atlantic Ocean. Beyerhaus drafted the document as a counterposition to the perceived liberalism of the theologies of religions of the World Council of Churches. The declaration stated that only the Bible is the proper frame of reference and criterion for Christianity's relation to other religions. Salvation can be found only through the cross of Christ and is available only through 'participation in faith'. On the basis of these convictions, the proponents of the Frankfurt Declaration 'reject the false teaching that the nonchristian religions and worldviews are also ways of salvation similar to belief in Christ'. This means that there is 'an essential difference in nature' between Christianity and other religions and that dialogue with other religions may not be seen as a substitute for proclamation.

Four years later, another significant document called the 'Lausanne Covenant' was issued. In the main, it advocated the views of Frankfurt, but sought to do so in a more conciliar way. The Lausanne meeting, with almost 2,500 participants from 150 countries, also wanted to combat the liberalism of the World Council of Churches and its diminishing missions agenda. The main concerns were syncretism, universalism and de-emphasis on evangelism.[5] Under the rubric of 'The Uniqueness and Universality of Christ', paragraph # 3 affirmed the unique status of Jesus Christ among religious figures. What made Lausanne's approach to other religions and Christian mission more conciliar was its strong support for social concern (# 5) along with proclamation and its acknowledgment of the value of dialogue as part of Christian mission.

Pinnock, representing the 'left wing' of Evangelicalism, has tirelessly challenged his fellow evangelicals to open up to the concept of dialogue with others. By doing so, he is both echoing other evangelical voices and countering opposition.[6] Pinnock's open-minded evangelical theology of religions is based on truly trinitarian foundations: (1) Open theism, which has challenged the traditional view of God as immutable and uninvolved with the happenings of the world; (2) Christology, which regards Christ as the norm but not as exclusive of other ways of connecting with God; and (3) full-blown pneumatology, which depicts the work of the Spirit in cosmic terms. In hindsight, one could say that Pinnock as a leading evangelical theologian started his move towards inclusivism with Christological convictions; simultaneously, his work with Open theism encouraged this move; and it came to its recent state finally through a fresh focus on pneumatology. Pinnock has not yet produced a full-scale work on the Trinity even though his theology has a definite trinitarian shape. In his *Flame of Love: A Theology of the Holy Spirit* (1996), he sets forth his main trinitarian ideas in relation to the Spirit.

'Open Theism' and a Hermeneutic of Hopefulness

This Canadian theologian has joined the growing number of contemporary theologians who associate themselves with the social doctrine of the Trinity. In this understanding, the Trinity is a 'transcendent society or community of three personal entities. Father, Son and Spirit are members of a divine community, unified by common divinity and singleness of purpose. The Trinity portrays God as a community of love and mutuality' (Pinnock, 1996, p. 29). In the loving communion, the Spirit is the love that bonds the Father and Son, mediating the relationship (1996, p. 37). Plurality is thus real plurality and relationality belongs to the essence of God. This kind of relational understanding accounts for the narrative of salvation. The Father sends the Son, and his suffering and resurrection release the Spirit. 'The story reveals God as a fellowship of Persons who are open to the joy and pain of the world' (1996, p. 41). The relational depiction of God as loving communion naturally leans toward Pinnock's understanding of God as 'open' to world happenings.

In his most recent book, titled *Most Moved Mover* (2001), Pinnock brings to maturity the programme of Open theism already presented initially in a collection of essays coproduced with some of his evangelical colleagues, *The Openness of God* (Pinnock et al., 1994). The starting point for Open theism is a criticism of the classical view of God. Open theists are not happy with the way God's sovereignty, majesty and glory have been depicted by tradition. In their interpretation, which echoes some concerns of Process theology, classical theism regards God as the final explanation of everything that occurs. God has sovereignly created the universe to fulfil his eternal purposes and receive glory to his name. His will being irresistible, everything that happens in the world is a result of his will and working. The proponents of Open theism often caricature what they call the 'perfect being theology' of classical theism deriving from Anselm and others.[7] This 'unchanging God' of classical theism does not appeal to them. Theirs is 'the God who faces a partially open future'.[8]

In contrast to classical theism, they claim, the new view supports an understanding of a loving God: 'love is the most important quality we attribute to God, and love is more than care and commitment; it involves being sensitive and responsive as well' (Pinnock, 1994, p. 15). God as loving, caring parent is a more suitable image than say God as King or Lord. God acts in relation to human beings and is affected by and is moved by human action. Pinnock laments that conventional theism did not leave enough room for relationality and communion in God's essence. He quotes the Catholic Walter Kasper's chiding remark according to which classical theism's God is 'a solitary narcissistic being, who suffers from his own completeness' (Pinnock, 2001, p. 6).

It is easy to see that this kind of Open theism tends to acknowledge the possibility of the knowledge of God outside the limited boundaries of the Christian religion, yet owing to it. In his main study on theology of religions, titled *A Wideness in God's Mercy* (1992), Pinnock wrote to this effect:

> From the earliest chapters of the Bible we learn a fundamental (if neglected) truth, that salvation history is coextensive with world history and its goal is the healing of all the nations. This is a testimony which stands as a corrective to so much Western theology, which has not been universal in its orientation but rather has narrowed God's saving purposes to a tiny thread of history and limited participation in salvation to the adherents of church and synagogue. These witnesses tell us that God has in his heart to bless the race and does not want only to rescue a few brands plucked from the burning. (1992, p. 23)

Pinnock champions a view of God of 'unbounded generosity'. This God is committed to the salvation of all humankind. 'The God we love and trust is not One to be satisfied until there is a healing of the nations and an innumerable host of redeemed people around his throne (Rev 7:9; 21:24–6; 22:2–6).' This is what Pinnock calls a hermeneutic of hopefulness (1992, pp. 18–20). This is already to be seen in the Old Testament, which he notes in relation to 'pagan saints', those who came from outside the elected community, yet were included (1992, 25ff.).

Not only theology proper (the doctrine of God) but also Christology and pneumatology contribute to a dialogue-enhancing orientation in Pinnock's trinitarian theology. Appropriately, the main work on theology of religions cited above has the subtitle *The Finality of Jesus Christ among World Religions*.

The Finality of Christ and the Optimism of Salvation

The main task of Pinnock's theology of religions is to try to avoid these two perils: one is to say dogmatically that all will be saved (universalism), and the other is to say that only a few will be (in Pinnock's terminology, 'restrictivism'). The two poles of the Christian message, the universal will of God to save all and the finality of salvation only in Christ, are to be handled in a way that does not do away with the uniqueness of Christ, but on the other hand does not make salvation unavailable to most people. Pinnock has become weary of the insistence of right-wing Evangelicalism according to which the only possibility for encountering God and receiving salvation is to exercise explicit faith in Jesus Christ in this earthly life (1992, p. 12). As an alternative to an evangelical theology of religions he presents the dynamic governed by two foundational parameters. On the one hand, there is the biblical and theological basis for an optimism of salvation grounded in the love of God for all humanity. This opposes the 'fewness doctrine' according to which only a small number of people will be saved. The second foundational concern is Christological. Pinnock's theology represents high Christology in that it takes the uniqueness of Jesus Christ for granted, but does not understand it in a way that closes the door of salvation to the majority of people. While resisting attempts to conceive of incarnation as mythical (Hick and others) or truncate the orthodox doctrine of the Trinity, Pinnock 'will insist just as emphatically that a high Christology does not entail either a pessimism of salvation or an exclusivist attitude toward people of other faiths' (1992, pp. 13–14).

While critical of 'an ideology of pluralism which celebrates choice in and of itself and claims that choice is good no matter what is chosen' (1992, pp. 9–10), Pinnock sets forth the uniqueness of Jesus in a way that attempts to widen the scope of God's mercy significantly:

> A fundamental point in this theology of religions is the conviction that God's redemptive work in Jesus Christ was intended to benefit the whole world. ... The dimensions are deep and wide. God's grace is not niggardly or partial. ... For according to the Gospel of Christ, the outcome of salvation will be large and generous. (1992, p. 17)

But once again, Pinnock notes that a high Christology does not necessarily mean exclusivism. The theological basis of an open attitude to all peoples is the doctrine of the triune God and of his prevenient grace. In Christ, 'God's secret plan for the creation is disclosed'. Therefore, the incarnation 'does not weaken but seals and strengthens our confidence in the universal salvific will of God'. The Logos, which was made flesh in Jesus of Nazareth, is present in the entire world and in the whole of human history. 'Though Jesus Christ is Lord, we confess at the same time that the Logos is not confined to the segment of human history or one piece of world geography' (1992, p. 77). According to Pinnock, this optimistic hermeneutic was lost early in Christian theology with the introduction of the Augustinian notion of the doctrine of election that focused on individuals and often led to apathy before the sovereign choice of God. The doctrine of election needs to be recast into a communal focus and the possibility of salvation rather than irrevocable damnation of individuals (1992, p. 35).

But alongside the optimism of salvation Pinnock also holds to the uniqueness of the person of Jesus Christ. This claim, indeed, causes embarrassment to many, both Christians and others. Therefore, Pinnock goes into a quite detailed biblical and dogmatic inquiry into the basis for a high Christology to argue for the finality of Jesus Christ among religions and religious figures. He is critical of the reinterpretations of Christology that are common among pluralists and argues that they distort the historical faith of the church. With several critics of pluralism (D'Costa among others), Pinnock believes that theological pluralism is a metareligious conviction, an attitude that is not at all open-minded or tolerant to nonrelativist ways of thinking. It does not allow the presentation of truth claims of religions (1992, ch. 2).

Pinnock's focus during the last years has been on pneumatology. A revised pneumatology has helped him formulate a truly trinitarian doctrine of religions.

The Ministry of the Spirit in the World and Among Religions

Pinnock argues that access to grace is less of a problem for a *pneumatologically* based theology of religions as it for an exclusively Christologically anchored one. Whereas the incarnation of the Son was confined to a specific place in time and history, its universal effects through the ministry of the Spirit can be transmitted to the farthest ends of the earth (1992, p. 188). If Father points to ultimate reality and 'Son supplies the clue to the divine mystery, Spirit epitomizes the nearness of the power and presence of God' (1996, p. 9). The same Spirit who is the bond of love among trinitarian members reaches out to creatures, catches them up and brings them home to the love of God. Thus the Spirit makes the redemption in Christ universally accessible, he maintains (1996, pp. 21–2). Here is the theological basis for Pinnock's criticism of what he call 'restrictivism'. Against restricting access to God's grace only to those who are conscious of belonging to God's people, he argues that it is not only God's nature as Father and the universality of the atonement of Christ, but also the ever-present Spirit, 'who can foster transforming friendship with God anywhere and everywhere' (1992, pp. 186–7). The gateway for Pinnock to an appreciation of a more unlimited ministry of the Spirit is the 'cosmic range to the operations of the Spirit' (1996, p. 49). Emphasis on the Spirit's work in salvation should not be read as a denial of his work in creation on which it is based, as too often has been the case (1992, p. 51). Pinnock argues that by acknowledging the work of the Spirit in creation we are actually allowing a more universal perspective of the Spirit's ministry in which the work of preparing for hearing the gospel is not set in antithesis to the fulfilment of the gospel in Christ. 'What one encounters in Jesus is the fulfillment of previous invitations of the Spirit' (1992, p. 63). In the final analysis, the ministries of the Son and Spirit cannot, of course, be put in any kind of opposition; rather, they are to be seen as 'both-and'. 'Christ, the only mediator, sustains particularity, while the Spirit, the presence of God everywhere, safeguards universality' (1992, p. 192).

It is on the basis of this dynamic trinitarian pneumatology that Pinnock approaches the question of the role of religions. That the Spirit is working not only in the world but also among other religions means that the triune God is present. He says:

> If the Spirit gives life to creation and offers grace to every creature, one would expect him to be present and make himself felt (at least occasionally) in the religious dimension of cultural life. Why would the Spirit be working everywhere else but not here? God is reaching out to all nations and does not leave himself without witness (Acts 14:17). Would this witness not crop up sometimes in the religious realm? (1996, pp. 200–201)

A truly revolutionary insight for an evangelical theologian is that religions, rather than being either futile human attempts to reach God (conservatives) or outright obstacles to a saving knowledge of God (the young Barth), can be Spirit-used means of pointing to and making contact with God (1996, p. 203). Not only that, but everyday human experiences can likewise be used by the Spirit, since human beings 'as spirit' are created to be open to God (1996, p. 73).[9]

With all his appreciation towards religions as God-chosen means of helping people in their search for God, Pinnock is not blind to the errors and weaknesses in world religions; religion can be 'dark, deceptive, and cruel. It harbors ugliness, pride, error, hypocrisy, darkness, cruelty, demons, hardheartedness, blindness, fanaticism, and deception. The idea that world religions ordinarily function as paths to salvation is dangerous nonsense and wishful thinking' (1992, p. 90). On the other hand, '[a]ccording to the Bible, there also exists among the nations religious faith which lies at the other end of the spectrum. It recognizes faith, neither Jewish nor Christian, which is nonetheless noble, uplifting, and sound.' Listing a number of 'pagan saints' (such as Abel, Melchizedek and Lot), Pinnock goes on to say that they 'were believing men and women who enjoyed a right relationship with God and lived saintly lives, under the terms of the wider covenant God made with Noah' (1992, p. 92). So there is a dark side to religion, but also a happy side. As with Pannenberg, in Pinnock's opinion religions play a crucial role as a venue for the search of God. It seems that the criterion for the value of religions in the Bible is whether the person fears God. Another criterion seems to be the pursuit of righteous behaviour (1992, p. 96).

Pinnock engages the questions of truth and revelation from a pneumatological perspective; in other words, he asks how the Spirit reveals God's identity and brings revelation to fruition.[10] God's Spirit is never confined to parochial interests but is always intended for the nations. The Spirit is 'guiding, luring, wooing, influencing, drawing all humanity, not just the church' (1996, p. 216).

Unlike most of his evangelical colleagues, Pinnock expresses hope concerning other religions. Since religions are not static but constantly changing over time, he believes that it is possible for the Spirit of God to impact them. Being more positive, however, does not require one to conclude that every religion is a vehicle of salvation or an ordinary way to salvation (Pinnock, 1992, pp.106–7 and ch. 3). Therefore, the Christian church in her mission to the nations should take seriously the meaning of religions, he exhorts. 'Religions as cumulative traditions have to be viewed in this context like everything else. The sweeping action of the kingdom of God, through the mission of the church, will inevitably overtake them' (1992, p. 118).

Critical Reflections

There is no doubt that Pinnock's trinitarian theology of religions, even if not yet presented in any systematic form in one place, builds significant bridges between those forms of Evangelicalism that view interfaith dialogue as neither fruitful nor desirable and those which espouse pluralisms of various sorts. Pinnock's theology clearly represents the left wing of Evangelicalism and situates itself in a moderate form of inclusivism fully anchored in orthodox Christianity. Thus Pinnock's locus can be found somewhere in the vicinity of Pannenberg in the Protestant camp and D'Costa in the Roman Catholic camp. To my knowledge, he is the first evangelical theologian who has laboured hard and long in building a responsible theology of religions gleaning from (if not always explicitly mentioning) classical trinitarian resources.

The merits of Pinnock's approach are many and deserve commendation, especially in light of the theological climate in which he operates. While almost self-evident, the way Pinnock takes up the tension between universalistic and restrictivistic elements while holding on to classical orthodox canons is a most helpful starting point for any theology of religions. In my mind, he is not able to solve the problematic and I highlight some areas of ambiguity below, but what he is up to is noble and advances the discussion beyond the confines of his own camp. Departing from pluralisms that deny difference, Pinnock boldly tackles the issue of the particularity of the Christian faith – and thus the affirmation of true differences – in a way that does not lead to a typical evangelical impasse.[11]

Pinnock's theological pilgrimage strikes notes familiar to anyone who has observed developments in Christian theology of religions during recent years. He began struggling with the impasse of Christologies that did not acknowledge the universality of God's grace. Rather than buying into the cheap form of theocentrism which sooner or later leads to the denial of trinitarian doctrine and makes Jesus less than divine, he moved on to consider pneumatological resources. Again, his implicit trinitarian orientation safeguarded Pinnock from embracing pneumatologies in which the integral relationship between the Spirit and Christ or Spirit and Yahweh/God is torn apart. Pinnock linked the Spirit both to Christ and to God. So the path he chose is commendable in my assessment as another trinitarian theologian. That I have to offer some criticism is not meant to be critical of Pinnock's direction, but rather to point out the way his trinitarian theology is still in need of clarification and explication.

There are several concerns and questions in my mind that, if addressed by Pinnock, would make his theology of religions more viable. I would like to identify here two major ones since I see both of them as crucial not only for theology of religions in general but also for an *evangelical* theology of religions, the context of Pinnock's work. The first has to do with the relationship between Christ and the Spirit. I applaud Pinnock for devoting one whole chapter in his *Flame of Love* to considering Spirit-Christology (1996, ch. 3). In a very helpful way, he points to the necessity of making the relationship between the Spirit and Christ more integral than the typical Logos-Christology has done, even though the latter is not to be dismissed. Nearly everybody agrees with Pinnock that the Spirit represents universality and Christ particularity, and our discussion has raised that issue several times. I do not have any queries with that. But the theological/trinitarian question arises here: what exactly is their relationship? And a corollary question (crucial to Pinnock's pneumatological theology) asks: how is the Spirit's presence in the world related to the presence of the triune God? It is not enough to affirm that Christ's incarnation was limited to a geographical location while the Spirit is operative all over the cosmos. That is a truism. Classical trinitarian theology believes (and certainly Pinnock does not disagree) that there is universality to the person of Christ as Logos as well (however the precise relationship between the incarnate Jesus and the eternal Son is being depicted). Pinnock agrees that the particularity of Jesus Christ does not necessarily imply restricting God's mercy to only a few, but beyond that affirmation he does not offer a theological rationale, so it is expressed more in terms of a wish.

Quite surprisingly, when talking about nontrinitarians, Pinnock agrees with them that to call God spirit means that in the encounter with the Spirit we encounter God (1996, p. 25); but it is precisely the same claim that trinitarian theology makes: when we encounter the Spirit, we encounter God. Pluralists who are not trinitarian may distinguish the Spirit's presence from the presence of the Son and Father in a way that makes the Spirit an 'itinerant minister', but for anyone wishing to stay within the contours of trinitarian doctrine, that kind of difference cannot be posited. I am sure Pinnock could learn from D'Costa, among the Catholics the closest in mindset to him. D'Costa argues theologically why it is that we have to acknowledge the presence of the triune God when we discern the work of the Spirit in the world.

This brings me to my second query, again not unrelated to what D'Costa brings up. It has to do with the role of the church as the community of God in Christianity's relation to other religions. D'Costa, as we saw, on the basis of biblical exegesis (which in my estimation in itself was not totally satisfactory) maintains that the presence of the Spirit, and thus triune God, presupposes and is integrally related to the presence of the community of disciples. I have no doubt that Pinnock as an evangelical theologian would be happy to affirm this view, but oddly enough he does not discuss it, even though it is a crucial issue to his evangelical constituency. With his high Christology, dismissing the church, the body of Christ, does not seem an appealing option and there is nothing in his theology of religions that compels him to ignore the place of the church. The ambiguity concerning the relation of the church to the presence of the triune God in the world is perhaps due to a lack of sophistication in outlining the trinitarian dynamic as to how the Spirit's presence is related to the presence of the triune God.

Since Pinnock's theology of religions is still in the making, it is appropriate to suggest some further tasks and challenges. While his programme of Open theism is still in an embryonic form and some aspects of it require much more clarification, the implications of that sort of challenge to classical theism could be brought to bear on theology of religions in a much more significant way than Pinnock has done thus far. Combined with his idea of God as relational – and thus affirming plurality and diversity within the one godhead – the implications for Christianity's relation to other religions are worth exploring in future investigations. I am convinced that this kind of doctrine of God could help us move beyond 'theocentrism', which denies a unique mediatorial role of the Son, a tendency not evident in Pinnock's theology. Furthermore, his quite innovative doctrine of Scripture (again, especially in light of the theological family he comes from) may have noteworthy implications for how revelation is to be thought of outside of Christian special revelation. If revelation can be found out there and the task of the Spirit is to make the reader capable of discerning it, would that open up some knots in the traditional problem of how people outside of the covenant may appropriate revelation?

Notes

1   On Evangelicalism, see Tidball (1994).
2   The term *evangelical* in its current usage possesses at its best several different meanings and at its worst is being used as an almost sectarian defensive weapon. In its original meaning, the term *evangelical* denoted Protestant theology as opposed to Catholic theology; thus for example the 'Evangelical-Lutheran Church' or 'evangelical theological faculty'. Another meaning was added in the twentieth-century English-speaking world, mainly in the United States of America but also in Great Britain. Now it denotes those Protestants who adhere to the more orthodox version of

Christianity as opposed to the liberal left wing. Thus there arose an 'evangelical doctrine of Scripture', which held the Word of God as divine in its origin and trustworthy in all regards.

3   Recently, there is also a movement within the Roman Catholic Church identifying itself as 'evangelical'.

4   The full text of the 'Frankfurt Declaration', from which the present citations come, can be found in *Christianity Today* **14** (1970), pp. 3–6.

5   The text can be found, e.g. in 'Lausanne Congress, 1974' (Anderson & Stransky, 1975, pp. 239–48).

6   For evangelicals who share Pinnock's more open attitude, see, e.g. N. Anderson (1984), Grenz (1994), Sanders (1995) and Yong (2000). For representative literature of evangelicals who are reserved about or opposed to the idea of salvation outside the church (with the exception, for example, of unbaptized babies), see, e.g. Glasser (1981), Geivett & Phillips (1995) and Clendenin (1995).

7   See, e.g. Rice (1985, pp. 14–15).

8   Title for ch. 2 in Boyd (2000).

9   Here one can see the influence of Karl Rahner on Pinnock's thinking, although he doesn't explicate it in this context. Wolfhart Pannenberg's theological anthropology also operates with this idea.

10 The basic argumentation is found in Pinnock (1984), especially the chapter titled 'Word and Spirit'.

11 A younger evangelical colleague of Pinnock, the Pentecostalist Amos Yong, has significantly added to the rapidly growing literature of pneumatological theology of religions, but his focus has been less on a trinitarian vision and more on the role of the Spirit among religions. See further Yong (2000).

Part III
The Christian Trinitarian Faith as an Embrace of Pluralism

CHAPTER 7

John Hick: The Doctrine of the Trinity as Problematic

Religions Revolving Around the 'Ultimate Reality'

Having assessed proposals by five theologians, both Catholic and Protestant, who by the standard terminology can be classified as inclusivists, it is time to consider three pluralistic theologians. Mention has already been made of the fact that these three theologians, Hick, Panikkar and Heim, represent vastly different approaches and that their presence together in one camp really stretches the boundaries of pluralism. On the other hand, this makes more valid the claim that when speaking of pluralisms we should in fact use the plural, *pluralisms*, rather than *pluralism*. My exposition and assessment will make evident their similarities and differences.

As early as 1970, the English theologian John Hick, currently the most prolific and hotly debated defender of radical religious pluralism, published with some of his colleagues a critical manifesto titled, 'The reconstruction of Christian belief for today and tomorrow'. Hick concluded that doctrines such as divine revelation, creation *ex nihilo*, the virgin birth and the resurrection, no longer speak meaningfully to contemporary men and women; thus, they had either to be left behind or reinterpreted in a new way. Even though that pronouncement did not yet deal specifically with other religions, Hick's idea of the need to radically reassess the whole concept of Christian doctrine has become one of the backbones of his pluralism. Hick is a prolific writer and debater, and his theology is constantly in the making, complicating the interpreter's task. In this chapter, I take the liberty of limiting my exposition greatly to consider only those aspects of his thought that bear directly on the doctrine of the Trinity. Hick's views are well known in the field of theology of religions, and there is no need to give a full exposition here.

His own emerging pluralistic view, according to which there is more than one way of salvation, was inspired by considering factors that challenge exclusivism: the diversity of religions (Christians are the minority in many areas of the world), the tie between ethnicity and religion, the lack of missionary success, the quality of religious life in non-Christian religions and the phenomenological similarity of religions; visiting worship places of other religions reveals so many similarities. He came to the conclusion that religion represents a human interpretation of reality, not absolute fact statements, and consequently all religions are in contact with and describe the same reality.

Hick compares his pluralistic theology of religions to Copernicus's astronomical model. The centre of all religions, around which they revolve in the way of planets, rather than being Jesus Christ as in the traditional view, is God, the Ultimate Truth:

> And the needed Copernican revolution in theology involves an equally radical transformation in our conception of the universe of faiths and the place of our own religion within it. It involves a shift from the dogma that Christianity is at the center to the realization that it is God who is at the center, and that all the religions of mankind, including our own, serve and revolve around him. (1983, p. 82)

In Hick's view, the essence of pluralism means that there is 'both the one unlimited transcendent divine Reality and also a plurality of varying human concepts, images, and experiences of and responses to that Reality' (1983, p. 83). Thus, all religions, whether Christian or Hindu (1980, p. 83; 1973, p. 131) or Buddhist (1988, p. 48; 1993, p. 134) are challenged to move from a 'Ptolemaic' view in which a particular religion stands at the centre and other religions are being judged by the criteria of that centre, to a genuinely pluralistic view of God (1995, p. 44). To accomplish this task, Hick contends that the views of the adherents of religions cannot be taken at face value, but rather each religion has to be confronted by the challenge of de-emphasizing its own absolute and exclusive claims (1989, pp. 2–3; 1993, p. 135). Various conceptions of God/god(s)/divine, such as Yahweh, Allah, Krishna, Param Atma or Holy Trinity, are but aspects of the Divine (1973, pp. 140–41) or like maps or colours of the rainbow (1988, p. 80).

While earlier on in his career, Hick was content to speak of *God*, later, in order to do justice to his understanding of the nature of religious language, Hick has shifted from speaking about God to speaking of the '(Ultimate) Reality'. This term is more flexible than the personal term *God*. For Hick, the great religions of the world are different – and one may say complementary – ways of approaching this Reality that exists beyond the human capacity of knowing. The Sanskrit term *sat* and the Islamic term *al-Haqq* are expressions of that, as is also *Yahweh* and the Christian *God* (1989, pp. 10–11). Here Hick builds on the Kantian distinction between *phaenoumena* (the way we see things) and *noumena* (the thing in itself, which is unknown to us), and he maintains that there is a part of the divine/Reality that is totally unknown to us and a part about which we know at least something. The Hindu concept of *nirguna Brahma*, in contrast to *saguna Brahma*, refers to something that cannot be fathomed at all by human means of knowledge. Similarly, the 'eternal Tao' of Taoism about which we know nothing is distinguished from the 'expressed Tao'. Irrespective of these differing names and approaches to the Reality, in Hick's view there is only one Reality, the ultimate divine. This he postulates mainly on the basis of astonishingly similar concepts of the divine in various religions (1995, p. 69). Consequently, he posits a unified soteriological structure in all religions (1993, p. 136; 1988, p. 69). This he calls a move from self-centredness to reality-centredness.

The Metaphorical Nature of Theological Language

The background for this pluralistic conception of God is Hick's understanding of the nature and functions of religious language. He does not totally deny the cognitive function of religious language, as many other contemporary pluralists do, but rather uses two kinds of approaches to deal with the existence of competing truth claims. Hick divides the differences between seemingly contradictory claims of various religions into three categories. The first level of differences relates to historical conceptions, such as the Christian belief in the death of Jesus on the cross vis-à-vis the view of the Koran according to which he only seemed to die. The only way to solve a conflict of this level is by an appeal to historical evidence, which, of course, is lacking (e.g. 1989, pp. 363–5). The second level is that of suprahistorical claims, or as Hick also calls them, 'quasihistorical' claims, such as the doctrine of reincarnation. Obviously, there is no way to reconcile the differences between those religions that do support the idea (Buddhism, Hinduism) and those that do not (Islam, Judaism, and Christianity). Consequently, the only sensible way to deal with this level of conflicts – his first approach – is to adopt an attitude of mutual respect and acceptance (1988, pp. 89–95; 1989, pp. 365–72). The third level of conflicts concerns the conceptions about the Ultimate Reality. Ideas of personal god(s), such as *Yahweh, Shiva, Vishnu, Allah*, and impersonal conceptions, such as *Brahma, Tao, nirvana, Sunyata* or *Dharmakaya*, cannot be easily reconciled with each other. So what should be done according to Hick is to treat these seemingly contradictory descriptions of the divine as complementary to each other (1988, pp. 90–95; 1989, p. 374).

Another way to try to ease the conflict between contradictory truth claims is to appeal to the mythical nature of religious language. The 'myth' is based on 'metaphor', which means that we speak 'suggestive of another' (1993, p. 99). In this understanding, metaphors that are not meant to be taken at face value still convey meaning, but do so in terms of eliciting emotions and associations familiar to a group that shares the common context of meanings. In an important sense, myth is an expanded metaphor. Even though it is not literally true, it 'tends to evoke an appropriate dispositional attitude' (1993, p. 105; 1989, pp. 99–104). Its purpose is to change our attitude and thus influence our thinking in a real way. The story about Buddha's flight to Sri Lanka, the creation story of the Old Testament, or the legend of the dance of Siva all function like that (1989, pp. 103, 347–72). Rather than inquire into the truth of the myth, one should rather ask how it functions in that life situation and context for which it was created. Then Yahweh and Krishna are not set in antithesis since they operate in their own distinctive spheres (1989, 267–8).

On the basis of his understanding of language, Hick divides the basic elements of religions into two categories: essentials and more superficial elements. In other words, even though different religions seem to have dramatic differences at the surface level, deep down there is a common foundation. For Hick, the differences on the surface level, even when they are to some extent cognitive in nature, do not create insurmountable conflicts, and here the use of the two strategies described above are of help.

Christ and Incarnation

Christology, a theme crucial to any trinitarian doctrine, is a case in point here. Traditional talk about incarnation has to be demythologized and set in harmony with other major religions, Hick contends. What incarnation is all about is making real the presence of the Divine to all men and women. It is not about a god becoming a human being; that kind of idea is totally repulsive to contemporary people (see, e.g. Hick, 1988, p. 14). Moreover, Jesus' divinity has to be understood metaphorically (1980, p. 74; 1983, p. 9). A mythological interpretation of Christology has the potential of serving a pluralistic theology of religions, Hick argues. In that view, Christ is depicted as the embodiment of divine love, complementary to what Buddhism reveals about the divine in the intense experience of release from suffering, or to Hinduism's source of life and purpose. Logos for Hick transcends any particular religion and is present in all of them (1980, p. 75). Consequently, talk about incarnation is not indicative, but rather expressive (1980, p. 78). Hick also makes reference to the way two lovers express themselves to each other. Even though expressions such as 'I love you more than anybody else' seem to be absolutist in nature, they are not exclusive; other lovers may freely use them as well, and still they are true in their own context and for the purpose they were meant.

What are the grounds for positing such an interpretation of Christology? Hick mentions three main reasons beyond the need to be relevant for contemporary people to whom traditional language does not convey much. In his *The Metaphor of God Incarnate: Christ and Christology in a Pluralistic Age* (1993), he says first that Jesus himself did not claim to be God nor God the Son incarnate (1993, p. ix). Rather, the Jesus of history would probably have considered such claims blasphemous. In response to those who maintain that even though Jesus did not explicitly claim to be divine, there was much in his person and ministry that implies divinity, Hick responds in various ways; one response is that the use of *Abba* did not connote a unique closeness, as scholarship has maintained, but rather is a common way of addressing 'father' (1993, p. 32). His conclusion is that 'it is hazardous to rest a faith in the deity of Jesus on the historical judgment that he implicitly claimed this' (1993, p. 33). Second, Hick argues that the doctrine of Christ's divinity has had dire historical consequences such as hatred of Jews, colonialism and oppression of women (1993, p. 86). Third, Hick takes as the most important reason for his revised Christology the claim that orthodox Christology has never been spelled out in a way that is philosophically coherent and religiously acceptable. I will come back to these three issues below. First I will look at the shape of his doctrine of the Trinity on the basis of his understanding of language and his revision of some key Christian doctrines.

A Modalistic Version of the Trinity

How then does Hick conceive of trinitarian doctrine?[1] Hick rightly notes that in the doctrinal system in which Christian thought was imbedded from the beginning, the doctrine of incarnation, atonement and Trinity cohere together (1987, p. 30; 1990, p. 90). Thus, denying the factual nature of incarnation (and reinterpreting atonement as a sort of expression of divine love and benevolence) removes classical trinitarian doctrine as a viable option.

Hick's view is best described as modalistic or unitarian, thus denying real 'personal' distinctions in the godhead/divine reality. Based on what he calls either 'degree' or 'inspiration' Christology – meaning that Jesus, as an 'incarnation' of God's love, inspires us to love our neighbours and that Jesus' 'uniqueness' differs in degree from the uniqueness of some other religious figures – Hick himself defines his stance in the following way (1987, p. 32; see also 1989, pp. 170–72, 271–2):

> An inspiration Christology coheres better with some ways of understanding trinitarian language than with others. It does not require or support the notion of three divine persons in the modern sense in which a person is a distinct center of consciousness, will, and emotion—so that one could speak of the Father, the Son, and the Holy Spirit as loving one another within the eternal family of the trinity, and of the Son coming down to earth to make atonement on behalf of human beings to his Father. An inspiration Christology is, however, fully compatible with the conception of the trinity as affirming three distinguishable ways in which the one God is experienced as acting in relation to, and is accordingly known by, us—namely, as creator, redeemer, and inspirer. On this interpretation, the three persons are not three different centers of consciousness but three major aspects of the one divine nature.

In line with his metaphorical understanding of religious talk, Hick can understand the doctrine of the Trinity 'not as ontologically three but as three ways in which the one God is humanly thought and experienced' (1993, p. 149).

In Hick's view, this kind of modalistic version of the doctrine of the Trinity has parallels with other religions such as Islam's threefold name of God as omnipotent creator and ruler of the universe, God as gracious and forgiving and God as intimately present to us (1990, p. 98).

Critical Reflections

That I focus here on critical comments on Hick is not an indication of a lack of respect for his work. The reason for offering only critical observations is rather due to my limited purpose in this study: whatever positive features there are in his pluralism, Hick's view of the Trinity and related issues such as Christology do not commend his approach to me at all and I do not regard it as helpful. When it comes to other aspects of his theology of religions, I do not engage the discussion here unless it relates to the Trinity.

I do not take issue with Hick's contention that Christian doctrines are to be regarded as human attempts to grasp the religious meaning of the Christ event rather than divinely formulated and guaranteed propositions (Hick, 1990, p. 89). Nor do I find it difficult to say that the doctrine of the Trinity is not yet developed in the Bible (ibid., pp. 96–7). All theologians agree that while there is a trinitarian orientation in the way salvation history happens in the New Testament, no trinitarian doctrine yet exists. It is a later intellectual effort to make sense of biblical orientations. But what I do not accept is Hick's contention that the Trinity (and orthodox Christology) is a development foreign to the New Testament and as such in need of radical revision in the form of inspiration Christology and nontrinitarian modalism.

Let us begin with revisiting the three main reasons why Hick sees it necessary to revise Christology as expounded above. How one thinks of Christology shapes considerably one's trinitarian doctrine,[2] and thus Christology provides an appropriate place to start the critical dialogue with Hick. Regarding Jesus' reluctance to regard himself as divine, mainstream current New Testament scholarship, albeit divided on the issue, does not uniformly support Hick's view. Hick's view is much closer to the older, now discredited, Quest for the Historical Jesus approach. All agree that Jesus did not go out proclaiming himself to be divine, and a majority of biblical scholars are very reserved about how much the Jesus of history really even implied his own divinity; yet a number of leading scholars do support the idea that Jesus claimed to be divine.[3] This idea is no more 'hazardous' than Hick's view. With appeal to historical matters, especially resurrection traditions (as Pannenberg and others have done), the evidence gets much stronger. Second, Hick's reluctance to follow traditional Christology on the basis of its abuse is no compelling reason for anybody; any theology or ideology can be misused and that can never take the place of the criterion of truth. However, it reflects a general orientation among pluralists, namely, a functional understanding of doctrine (see Griffiths, 1990).

The functional view of doctrine bypasses the truth question, a strategy that I see as a serious problem. According to Hick, statements of the doctrines that express an 'inspiration' Christology are not to be taken as 'true', but should be accepted because they 'work' better in relation to other religions. Hick's view makes it very difficult for him to pay proper attention to the substantive content of religious doctrines. Yet he assumes that his view of the metaphorical nature of religious language is to be taken as true! Later I will argue that to deny the claim to (universal) truth for religion is to deny religion or to give that function to something else in culture that takes instead religion's role of responding to ultimate questions. Every society seems to need what sociologists of knowledge (like Peter Berger) call 'plausibility structures', the body of assumptions and practices that, in any society, determines which beliefs are plausible and which are not. And some concept of God/Ultimate Reality seems to be a part of any plausibility structure. With

Pannenberg I believe that ultimately it is the conception of God that backs up the truth claims of any religion, and for Christianity that is the triune God. I will come back to this issue at the end of the book.

Hick's third and most significant objection in his opinion to adhering to traditional orthodox Christology is that the doctrine has never been formulated in an intelligible and religiously adequate view. For him, it leads to contradiction and paradox. Of course, there is no denying the mysterious or paradoxical nature of the doctrines of Christology and the Trinity. But one needs to be careful here. Paradox does not necessarily mean contradiction. Contradiction denotes an opposition between *p* and not-*p*. Following the rules of logic (which, of course, with the advent of postmodernism have been challenged but not in my mind discredited), a contradiction cannot be true ever. Paradox, or 'mystery', may be true. 'Religious mysteries are paradoxical religious claims that typically stretch the mind and are difficult or even impossible (given human cognitive weaknesses) to comprehend, but which (it is claimed) there is good reason to believe' (Davis, 1999, p. 258). So an appeal to the classical doctrines of Christ and the Trinity *prima facie* cannot be regarded as intellectually or religiously absurd, as Hick's most severe criticism implies. On the other hand, Hick's own theology of religions is not free from paradoxes that are just as challenging, if not more so. For example, Hick maintains that even though nothing can be known of the Ultimate Reality, still we 'can know' that all conceptions of the divine ultimately point to this something unknown. Sometimes Hick speaks of the inability of humans to experience the Reality and other times he mentions that the Reality is 'variously experienced'.[4] I agree with the Finnish theologian Martti Amnell whose dissertation ends up criticizing, among other things, a very vague – and paradoxical – view of the divine in Hick's theology:

> Hick attempts to say two things which are opposite to each other: God can be experienced – God cannot be experienced. There can be knowledge of God – There is no knowledge available concerning God. In one case the ultimate Reality seems to convey information about itself in a way that suggests continuity with the way people experience the divine. In the other, there is such a wide gap between the ultimate Reality and experienced Reality that it leads towards agnosticism, since the foundation of all religious experiences is totally outside the realm of experience. (Amnell, 1999, pp. 136–7; my translation from Finnish)

Furthermore, I agree with Armin Kreiner's (1996, pp. 129–30) observation that if something is experienced as *x* even though it is not *x*, it is usually regarded as illusory. In other words, if there is not a real experience of the Reality, even though religions claim to experience it, that cannot be regarded as a real religious experience in any legitimate way. We do not need to take up any more examples to make our point: Hick's appeal to the paradoxical nature of the Christian doctrines of Christ and the Trinity is not compelling, and one wonders if ideological reasons

(Hick's desire to promote understanding between religions at any cost) play the crucial role here.

One could also point to the vagueness of Hick's view of incarnation. Of course, he does not regard the incarnation as the Son of God literally coming to occupy human life, but understands it rather in a metaphorical way: 'Jesus embodied, or incarnated, the idea of human life lived in faithful response to God, so that God was able to act through him, and he accordingly embodied a love which is a human reflection of the divine love' (1993, p. ix). This is a confusing way of using language, which does not promote understanding any more among Christians than between religions. The Christian doctrine of the incarnation simply cannot be reduced to an idea of an embodiment of love; nor can Hindu or other versions of incarnations (in the mainstream, at least) be defined like that. Why then keep on using the traditional religious language of incarnation? Honestly, I do not see any reason for it. It confuses and further reinforces the impression that Hick takes his stand outside existing religions and seeks to teach the followers of religions the 'true' meaning of classical doctrines (see also Davis, 1999, pp. 265–8).

Hick's truncated Christology alone makes his theology nontrinitarian, which he himself confesses: 'To question the idea of Jesus as literally God incarnate is also, by implication, to question the idea of God as literally three persons in one. For the doctrine of the Trinity is derived from the doctrine of the incarnation' (Hick 1993, p. 152; see also Davis 1999, p. 268). The basis for Hick's nontrinitarian theology seems to be his desire to go beyond personalist and nonpersonalist conceptions, ending up, in my opinion, advocating a generic conception of God not to be identified with any particular religion. This is unacceptable since it puts Hick in a place outside of existing religions, as someone above everyone else telling the followers of other religions that they are in fact in error and need to be enlightened by this new religion (Hick's own view is, of course, only one among others). But not only that, it is also unacceptable because it compromises the basis of the Christian religion. I agree with Stephen Williams' incisive criticism:

> [T]he logic of his [Hick's] general argument carries him away from belief in divine personhood. For he insists that we cannot know the Real *an sich* [in itself] and that conceptions of the Real as impersonal are not less valid than conceptions of the Real as personal, as far as we can judge. The Real has given no effective revelation of his reality as personal. For if there had been such an effective revelation, it would not be optional, but mandatory, so to regard the Real. If there is no such revelation, the Real is either unwilling or unable to reveal. If the Real is unwilling, then we may have a personal being, but one utterly unlike the personal deity of Christian belief. If the Real is unable, then we do not have a personal being at all in the sense conceived in Christian thought. On neither account is the Christian option open. Hick, therefore, is not really allowing that it is valid to think of God as personal provided that we concede that other ways are valid. He denies that we may validly think of God as personal in any way resembling the tradition. (Williams, 1997, p. 38)

Therefore, as Williams again rightly notes, the doctrine of the Trinity elucidates the claims both to a particular revelation and to a universal presence that Christians have wanted to make on behalf of a personal God (Williams, 1997, pp. 37–8). Hick's nontrinitarian view does not allow that as possible.

With regard to Hick's comment that he is not happy to employ the language of 'person' in reference to God and thus finds a modalistic view more compelling, his reasoning is flawed. He says that it is inappropriate to understand the concept of person as separate individuals or even separate centres of consciousness (Hick, 1987, p. 32). But it has to be noted that Christian theology should not think of personhood in that sense in the first place; that is a much later Western conception. With the ascendancy of communion theology, as explicated in the introductory chapter of this book, Christian theology has been able to revive the patristic and biblical idea of 'person' as in communion, not as an individual. This kind of communion understanding, in fact, would rather support Hick's theology of religions (even apart from his reluctance to appeal to classical trinitarian language); unfortunately, he seems to be unaware of the developments in trinitarian theology during the past two decades or so.

Regarding Hick's desire to connect Christian talk about the trinitarian God (however that is defined) with other religions' conceptions of the divine – as in his example, cited above, of Islamic thought – I am not convinced at all. It is one thing to find triadic patterns in religions' conceptions of the divine and another thing to maintain that a particular religion's view of God – as is the claim with regard to the Christian God – is triune. The best these parallels can do is serve as illustrations not unlike Augustine's psychological analogies. Christian trinitarian theology makes the bold claim that God exists as a triune communion and that the only way to the knowledge of God is through the portals of the Trinity: it is only through the Son that we may know the Father in the Spirit. Furthermore, Christian theology claims that this view is not based on phenomenology of religions or abstract speculation, but is the structure of salvation history as revealed in the Bible.

In sum, whatever assets Hick's revisionist theology may have, for the purposes of the present book his proposal gives little if any help. Hick, if I understand him correctly, not only regards the Trinity as a useless later theological development, but also a real obstacle in interfaith dialogue. One cannot go with Hick's proposal if one wants to stay within the contours of the classical Christian view of God as triune.

Two other pluralists discussed next take radically different routes to the significance of the Trinity in Christian theology of religions when compared to the virtual dismissal of the doctrine by Hick. For Panikkar, the Trinity is a key to interfaith dialogue in the sense that a trinitarian structure can be found in all major religions. While Panikkar's formulation of the Trinity in interreligious dialogue does not live up to the expectations of his initial proposal, it is refreshing among pluralists in that it takes tradition very seriously. Yet another pluralist, S. Mark Heim – in a way, perhaps the most pluralist of all since he ends up positing the possibility of different destinies for the followers of various religions, each of them legitimate in their own contexts – differs radically from Hick in that he takes the doctrine of the Trinity as the main interpretative framework for his theology of religious ends, and he differs from Panikkar in that for Heim the *Christian* doctrine of God, rather than an *interreligious* interpretation of the Trinity, is the key.

Notes

1   A helpful discussion can be found in Davis (1999).
2   Evans (2001, p. 29) notes: 'Apart from the divine identity of Jesus as the Son there could not be a Trinity – at least not in the traditional Christian sense. The concept of Trinity expresses the idea that the three Persons that make it up are fully divine: God the Father, God the Son, and God the Holy Spirit.'
3   See further, Moule (1977, p. 4), O' Collins (1983, pp. 184–5), Dunn (1980, p. 60); see also Davis (1999, pp. 252–5).
4   See Hick (1989, p. 249), which makes these two contradictory statements on the same page.

CHAPTER 8

Raimundo Panikkar: The Cosmotheandric Trinitarian Mystery

The Cosmotheandric Structure of Reality and the Trinity

The often quoted autobiographical comment by Raimundo Panikkar according to which he 'left' Europe as a Christian, 'found' himself as a Hindu and 'returned' as a Buddhist, without ever having ceased to be a Christian (1978, p. 2), is a striking illustration of the unique pilgrimage of this Catholic thinker who was born in Spain to a Spanish Roman Catholic mother and a Hindu father. Panikkar believes himself to have been placed at the confluence of the four rivers: Hindu, Christian, Buddhist and secular (1964, p. 30). After living in Europe and Asia – and having completed three doctorates and acquired a mastery of a number of languages – he did his major life work in California, regularly commuting between continents. One of the most creative intercultural and interreligious theologians of our time, Panikkar does not lend himself to easy exposition, let alone interpretation.[1] Again, I take the liberty of being very selective and focused regarding themes taken up for scrutiny in this most prolific writer's corpus; only that which highlights and contributes to the role of the doctrine of the Trinity in relation to other religions is of interest here. In Panikkar's case we are fortunate in having a theologian to whom Trinity serves as an interpretative key to reality and religions. He is the 'exception that proves the rule, a pluralist who *does* invoke the Trinity and who believes it to be at the heart of all human religions' (Vanhoozer, 1997, p. 58, italics in the original).

Even though Panikkar's theological vision – and in his case it is far more appropriate to talk about 'vision' than 'doctrine' – is multidimensional, the various strands come together in his notion of 'cosmotheandrism'. The literal meaning of the term 'theandrism' is not difficult to establish (coming from two Greek terms meaning 'God' and 'human person' respectively).[2] Yet, the neologism 'cosmotheandrism' has a kind of technical sense in Panikkar's thought; as an elusive thinker, however, he is not too concerned about always using the term in exactly the same way. Panikkar himself defines it in this way: 'The cosmotheandric principle could be stated by saying that the divine, the human and the earthly—however we may prefer to call them—are the three irreducible dimensions which constitute the real, i.e., any reality inasmuch as it is real' (Panikkar, 1979, p. 74). He can also state it in this way: 'There is a kind of perichoresis, "dwelling within one another," of these three dimensions of Reality, the Divine, the Human and the Cosmic—the I, the you and the it' (Panikkar, 1979, p. 214). Or, 'There is no God without Man and the World. There is no Man without God and the World. There is no World without

God and Man' (quoted in Ahlstrand, 1993, p. 134). In other words, in Panikkar's vision the cosmotheandric principle expresses the fundamental structure of reality in terms of intimate interaction of God, humankind and the world or cosmos. There is no hierarchy, no dualism; one of the three does not dominate or take precedence.

Before expositing Panikkar's doctrine of the Trinity, a tentative understanding of his theocentric Christology is in order. In his Christology, we can discern a change taking place, from an initial inclusivistic Catholic understanding of a close relationship between Jesus and the Christ to a pluralistic theocentrism in which the Christic principle is wider than the history and saving significance of Jesus.

The Universal Christ and the Particular Jesus

In his earlier major work *The Unknown Christ of Hinduism* (1964; revised 1981 with some significant changes as noted below), Panikkar argued that in the historical Jesus the fullness of revelation had occurred, even though not in an exclusive way. Even at this point his Christology was open to acknowledging the presence of God among religions. For him, God always works in this world through Christ, and where God is present, there is also Christ and the Spirit. This triune God works in all religions and forms the common foundation for all religions. Thus Christ, the Logos, is present in the holy writings of Hinduism. Christ is also present mystically where people reach for union with God. God himself is the Mystery, Absolute, even though he is not so acknowledged. Panikkar sees correspondences and similarities between Christ and Hindu figures, such as *Isvara*.

But in his significantly revised version of *The Unknown Christ of Hinduism* in 1981, he moved definitely towards a pluralistic version of Christology. In that book, he rejects all notions of Christianity's superiority over or fulfilment of other religions. The reason for this rejection is simply that the world and our subjective experience of the world have radically changed since the Christian doctrine concerning Christ was first formulated. And along with the change of our experience of the world, our understanding should also be modified.

Panikkar's revised understanding is based on the distinction between the universal Christ and the particular Jesus. This is the key for him to an 'authentically universal' Christology. 'Christ is … a living symbol for the totality of reality: human, divine, cosmic' (1981, p. 27). As such, Christ represents an intimate and complete unity between the divine and the human. Panikkar calls this a 'non-dualist vision': God and the human being are not two realities, but rather one. God and the human being presuppose each other for the building up of reality, the unfolding of history. The meaning of the confession 'Christ is God the Son, the Logos' is that Christ is both symbol and substance of this nondualistic unity between God and humanity.

But what, then, is the relationship between this universal Christ and the historical Jesus? With Catholic theology Panikkar affirms that the Logos or Christ has been incarnated in Jesus of Nazareth. But he departs from orthodoxy by denying that this incarnation has taken place solely and finally in Jesus. Arguing for the opposite of what he argued in the first edition of *The Unknown Christ of Hinduism*, in which he posited a unity between Christ and Jesus, he now rejects it. According to his revised Christology, no historical form can be the full, final expression of the universal Christ. The universal symbol for salvation in Christ can never be reduced to a merely historical personhood, he argues. Panikkar claims that 'Christ will never be totally known on earth, because that would amount to seeing the Father whom nobody can see' (quoted in Knitter, 1985, p. 156). Total identification between the universal Christ and the historical Jesus would lead in Panikkar's understanding to a sort of idolatrous form of historicism. The saving power of Jesus, indeed, is to be found in the fact that he embodies a reality that is beyond every historical form, the universal Christ. On the other hand, as a Catholic theologian, Panikkar is not willing to lose all historical contours. He issues a warning against diluting the Christian belief that Christ has appeared in the form of the historical Jesus. The connection is to be maintained, if not the complete identity, but in a way that does not hinder dialogue with people of other faiths as it has tended to do in the past. For Panikkar, this means that one can at the same time make a genuine confession of Christ, the 'Supername' (Phil. 2:9), and yet in one way or another acknowledge that all religions recognize and acknowledge Christ.

The Doctrine of the Trinity and Religions

As mentioned, Panikkar takes very seriously the function of the doctrine of the Trinity for interfaith dialogue, thus differing radically from Hick and most other pluralists. He firmly believes that the idea of the Trinity is not a specifically Christian idea, but that it can be found in all religions though taking various forms. Trinity is 'the junction where the authentic spiritual dimensions of all religions meet' (1973, p. 42). In light of this, what would Panikkar's version of the Christian doctrine of the Trinity look like? Unlike many pluralists, while Panikkar is always in search of parallels and ways to overcome anomalies between religions, he is not in search of a new, 'universal' religion in the spirit of Hick. He honours the existing differences, and even though he believes that eventually there will be a convergence of all religions, he does not seek to deny their differences. Thus he offers his own understanding of a distinctive Christian theology of religions and then connects it with other religions, since all religions are founded on a trinitarian structure.

In his small yet important book *The Trinity and the Religious Experience of Man* (1973) Panikkar develops his trinitarian theology on the basis of his theandric vision. He regards the term *trinitarian* as synonymous with (cosmo)theandric (1973, p. 71). And the main reason Panikkar chooses to resort to trinitarian language in his wide and inclusive religious vision is that the notion 'trinitarian' – as of course also cosmotheandric – genuinely reflects the structure of reality. The doctrine of the

Trinity is not a forced concept. Panikkar speaks of 'the intuition of the threefold structure of reality, of the triadic oneness existing on all levels of consciousness and of reality, of the Trinity'. In other words, 'the Trinity is the acme of a truth that permeates all realms of being and consciousness' (1973, p. xi).

Seen in this way, the Trinity is a way to structure the world, to recognize its trinitarian nature and its spiritual traditions, an exercise taken by Christian theologians of old, especially St Augustine. Before explicating any further how this applies to the Father, Son and Spirit, it is equally important to pay attention to Panikkar's use of the Hindu notion of *advaita*. The term *advaita* means 'nonduality' (literally: not two), a cherished Asian way of thinking. This notion, of course, belongs together with theandric nondualism. According to Panikkar:

> there are not two realities: God and man (or the world), as outright atheists and outright theists are dialectically driven to maintain. Reality is theandric; it is our way of looking that causes reality to appear to us sometimes under one aspect and sometimes under another because our vision shares in both. (1973, p. 75)

Thus Cousins calls Panikkar's trinitarian view 'Advaitic Trinitarianism'.[3] Applied to the ancient problem of unity and diversity in the trinitarian God, the advaitic principle implies that Father and Son are not two, but they are not one either; it is the Spirit who unites and distinguishes them (Panikkar, 1973, p. 62).

For Panikkar, the Father is best described as 'Nothing'. What can be said about the Father is 'nothing'; this is the apophatic way, the way to approach the Absolute without name (1973, p. 46). What is the basis for this unique notion in Christian theology? Panikkar sees this in the Johannine saying that no one comes to the Father except through the Son. It is not possible to approach the Father directly, because there 'is' no Father *per se*, only a Father in relation to the Son. There is no such thing as the 'Father' in himself, the 'being of the Father' is 'the Son'. In the incarnation, *kenosis*, the Father gives himself totally to the Son. Thus the Son is 'God' (1973, pp. 45–7). Panikkar believes this is the needed bridge between Christianity and Buddhism as well as advaitic Hinduism. What *kenosis* (self-emptying) is for Christianity, *nirvana* and *sunyata* are for these two other religions.[4] 'God is total Silence. This is affirmed by all the world religions. One is led towards the Absolute and in the end one finds nothing, because there *is* nothing, not even Being' (1973, p. 52).

'It is the Son of God who is, and so is God', Panikkar affirms (1973, p. 51). In that sense, the Son is the only 'person' of the Trinity. For this statement to make sense, Panikkar notes that the term 'person', when used of the internal life of the Trinity, is an equivocal term that has a different meaning in each case. Since the 'Father' is a different kind of 'person' compared to the 'Son', and the 'Spirit' differs in nature from both, it is not advisable to use the term 'person' for these different meanings. In that qualified sense, it is also understandable when Panikkar says that there is in fact 'no God' in Christian theology in the generic sense of the term. There is only 'the God of Jesus Christ'; thus the God of theism is always the 'Son', the only one with whom human beings can establish a relationship (1973, pp. 51–2).

What about the Spirit? The Spirit is 'immanence'. Yet it is challenging to make the meaning of the Spirit as immanence more concrete (a fact acknowledged routinely in all theologies for that matter): 'immanence is incapable of revealing itself, for that would be a contradiction of terms; an immanence which needs to manifest itself, is no longer immanent'. Panikkar uses images and paints pictures to say something more about the Spirit: the Father is the source of the river, the Son is the river that flows from the source, and the Spirit is the ocean in which the river ends (1973, p. 63). The Spirit is the mediator, as in classical theology. We do not pray to the Spirit, we pray to the Father through the Son; thus it is the Spirit who prays, and the prayer is a trinitarian conversation (1973, p. 59). In his desire to build bridges, Panikkar searches for analogies from Hinduism and Buddhism. The Spirit can be described as Hinduism's 'Divine *Sakti* penetrating everything and manifesting God, disclosing him in his immanence and being present in all his manifestations' (Panikkar, 1981, p. 57). Panikkar is convinced that Hinduism and Christianity are not antagonistic in the final vision. Christ 'is not only at the end but also at the beginning. Christ is not only the ontological goal of Hinduism but also its true inspirer, and his grace is the leading, though hidden, force pushing it towards its full disclosure' (1964, pp. ix–x). 'It is Christianity and Hinduism as well that belong to Christ, though in two different levels' (1964, pp. 20–21). He also believes that Buddhism has developed a spirituality of the Spirit.[5]

Trinity, Christianity and the Spiritualities of the World

Panikkar posits three different yet complementary spiritualities among world religions (1973, ch. 1). The first he calls 'iconolatry' or the path in which the karma, the icon or image serves as the focus for religious practice. The characteristic elements are moral aspiration in an effort to transform the world. The desire to give religious practice a concrete form in the world is both its strength and temptation; it easily leans towards idolatry. The second spirituality is 'personalism', a way of devotion. The emphasis is on worship, and it desires love, mercy and joy. A focus on the human (anthropomorphism) is thus its temptation. The third one is 'mysticism': it desires unitive knowledge with the divine forgetfulness of self. Its temptation is indifference to the world.

Now it is only in the trinitarian concept of reality that we can see a synthesis of these three spiritualities and their reconciliation. How this happens is unfortunately less than clear in the writings of Panikkar. As a creative writer, he is not always keen on maintaining consistency and so, even in his small book *Trinity and the Religious Experience of Man*, he proposes two sets of spiritualities in a triadic form (the above-mentioned triad and one that includes 'nihilism' related to the apophaticism of the Father; 'monism' related to the radical immanence of the Spirit; and 'theism' related to the spirituality of the Son) (1973, ch. 3). So the question of how exactly the Trinity relates to the diversity of religions is left open. A significant clue, though, is given in Panikkar's comment that 'in the Trinity a place is found for whatever in religion is not simply the particular deposit of a given age or culture' (1973, p. 43). In other words, while the particularities of religions are affirmed, the trinitarian structure points to universality and the coming convergence of all religions. But again the precise content of this claim is not sufficiently explicated. Panikkar can say that it is in the 'trinitarian possibilities of the world religions, in the striving of each in its own fashion towards the synthesis of these spiritual attitudes, that the meeting of religions—the kairos of our time—finds its deepest inspiration and most certain hope' (1973, p. 55), but how this relates to the three spiritualities of 'iconolatry', 'personalism' and 'mysticism' remains vague. The closest Panikkar comes to relating the trinitarian members to these three spiritualities is in his much later work *The Cosmotheandric Experience* (1993): the Father, 'unknown' in himself, is related to the silent, empty God behind God; the Son to a spirituality of a personal deity who manifests God; and the Spirit to a spirituality of mystical union, forgetful of all distinction.

What is clear, however, is that the Trinity is not the unique or sole property of Christianity: 'It simply is an unwarranted overstatement to affirm that the trinitarian concept of the Ultimate, and with it the whole of reality, is an exclusive Christian insight of revelation' (Panikkar 1973, p. viii). Indeed, the Trinity is hardly understood by Christianity and therefore a real appreciation of its meaning and significance requires constant interaction with other religions. Christianity can learn from others, but it also has a significant role to play in leading 'to the plenitude and hence to the conversion of all religions' (1973, p. 4). In the final analysis, the end of this process (and the goal of Christianity) is 'humanity's common good'. Christianity 'simply incarnates the primordial and original traditions of humankind' (1987a, p. 102). If I understand Panikkar correctly, he maintains that Trinity is a doctrine unique to Christianity, but not exclusively, since the whole structure of reality reflects Trinity.

'Ecumenical Ecumenism': The Vision of the Future of Religions

Panikkar invites us to consider what he calls the 'Christic principle' based on his theandric vision and theocentric Christology. This is not a universal religion nor a particular event, but 'the center of reality as seen by the Christian tradition' (1987a, p. 92). He refers to three stages in the historical consciousness of Christianity in relation to other religions, metaphorically, three rivers: the Jordan, the Tiber and the Ganges. The Jordan represents Judeo-Christian faith with a traditional exclusivism; the Tiber, the imperial expansion of Christianity into an inclusivist faith; and the Ganges, the emerging pluralism of religious faiths. These he calls 'Christianity', 'Christendom' and 'Christianness', respectively:

Only the last is appropriate for the present *kairos* of a pluralist world. Christianness stands for 'experience of the life of Christ within ourselves', an experience 'that I and the Father are One'; it is freed from monotheistic assumptions of a totally intelligible Being, holds lightly to ecclesiastical creeds and traditions, recognizes myth as 'the horizon that makes thinking possible' and that 'no single notion can comprehend the reality of Christ', regards security as of no importance, and lives by 'confidence' in the future, not by concern over truth-claims. (Ramachandra, 1996, p. 82)

Thus Panikkar believes that the religions are approaching each other, and he expects a convergence, not necessarily at the doctrinal level, but at an existential level, in the 'cave of the heart', as he puts it. Doctrinal conceptions create differences and conflicts, whereas the meeting of hearts fosters unity. This is the call, in Panikkar's words, of 'ecumenical ecumenism'. This interreligious ecumenism works out of a common origin and goal, a 'transcendental principle' or mystery, a basis for shared experience active within all religions. Panikkar calls this shared mystery 'the fundamental religious fact' that does not lie in the realm of doctrine, nor even of individual self-consciousness, but is present everywhere and in every religion. The whole purpose of ecumenical ecumenism is to deepen one's grasp and living of this mystery. For this to happen, all religions, Christianity included, have to give up any claim of uniqueness, let alone absolute normativity.

Instead of pluralism, Panikkar prefers here the term 'parallelism': all religions run parallel to meet only in the Ultimate, at the end of time (see further, Panikkar, 1978). According to his vision, 'the Christian, in recognizing, believing and loving Christ as the central symbol of Life and Ultimate Truth, is being drawn towards the selfsame Mystery that attracts all other human beings who are seeking to overcome their own present condition' (1981, p. 23). In that vision, the Mystery may be called by various names, but yet is one and the same. It is neither 'one' nor 'many' since in the Ultimate Reality the dualism–nondualism distinction does not hold. As we saw above, Panikkar has strong leanings towards the Buddhist emphasis on ultimate silence.

In the very beginning of his career Panikkar became convinced that there 'is a living presence of Christ in Hinduism'. And not only that, but also Christ 'is not only at the end but also at the beginning. Christ is not only the ontological goal of Hinduism but also its true inspirer, and his grace is the leading, though hidden, force pushing it towards its full disclosure' (1964, pp. ix–x). 'It is Christianity and Hinduism as well that belong to Christ, though in two different levels' (1964, pp. 20–21). Therefore, Christ does not belong only to Christianity; he belongs only to God. Thus, theocentrism.

In Panikkar's theocentric vision there is a special relationship between Hinduism and Christianity. Hinduism has a place in the Christian economy of salvation. On the one hand, Hinduism 'is the starting-point of a religion that culminates in Christianity', 'Christianity in potency'. On the other hand, there is a need for 'conversion', 'a pascha', a mystery of death and life for Hinduism. In other words, it is not a matter of total continuity or of fulfilment in terms of the fulfilment theory of religions. The final result is not another religion but rather a 'better form of Hinduism'. Christ has been at work in anticipation in Hinduism, and now the task of Christian revelation is the 'unveiling of reality'. 'The Christian attitude is not ultimately one of bringing Christ *in*, but of bringing him *forth*, of discovering Christ' (Panikkar 1964, pp. 58–61; see also Dupuis, 1997, p. 150).

The Interfaith Potential of Panikkar's Theandric Vision

Everett H. Cousins, a respected interpreter of Panikkar's thought, succinctly summarizes the significance of his trinitarian vision for interfaith issues. Cousins mentions that no doubt Panikkar is a classic theologian in putting the Trinity at the centre of theology. Yet he does this in a way that makes his trinitarian vision innovative. First, he sees the Trinity in relation to other religions, which most earlier Christian theologians did not have contact with or knowledge about. Second, he has related the Trinity to the advaitic heritage of Asia; Cousins dubs Panikkar's approach 'Advaitic Trinitarianism'. Third, Panikkar sees that the Christian doctrine of the Trinity reveals a structure of reality that is more comprehensively universal than was perceived in the classical tradition of Augustine and others that sees in creation and human beings vestiges of the Trinity (Cousins, 1996, pp. 119–20).

In Panikkar's view, Christian understanding of the Trinity is in need of deepening from other religions; on the other hand, Christianity contributes to a fuller understanding of that vision among other religions. Exclusivism is avoided by maintaining that Christianity, no more than other religions, can never absolutize its current historical understanding. Pluralism, in terms of watering down differences, is also avoided by insisting that differences among religions are real and that they matter, even in light of the expectation of the coming convergence (cf. Heim, 2001, p. 150).

Let me first register the positive contributions offered by Panikkar to our topic as I see them and then offer critical comments. There is no denying the fact that Panikkar has significantly advanced the discussion of the relation of the doctrine of the Trinity to interfaith dialogue. Against the prevailing pluralistic idea of the 'rough parity' of all religions, Panikkar affirms the principle of diversity:

> We have to work towards a healthy pluralism which would allow for the conviviality and coexistence of cultures and civilizations that no single culture, religion or tradition has the right to claim to represent the universal range of human experience, nor the power to reduce the diversity of humanity to one single form, broad as this may be. (Panikkar, 1996, p. 206)

As A.S. Raj puts it, in 'the pluralistic approach of Panikkar, differences between cultures and religions are neither absolutized nor ignored but they are transformed into creative polarities' (Raj, 1998, p. 39). This is based on Panikkar's view of a genuine diversity in the Trinity: 'The mystery of the Trinity is the ultimate foundation for pluralism' (Panikkar 1987a, p. 110). And: 'In the Trinity a true encounter of religions takes place, which results, not in a vague fusion or mutual dilution, but in an authentic enhancement of all the religious and even cultural elements that are contained in each' (Panikkar, 1973, p. 42). Plurality *ad intra* (among the trinitarian members) is reflected in the plurality of reality (Panikkar, 1987a, pp. 109–10; see further Knitter, 1996a, pp. 180–81).

At the same time, Panikkar maintains that religions need each other and are mutually dependent (see further, Ahlstrand, 1993, p. 184). Thus, Panikkar distinguishes himself from Hick and others who not only dismiss real differences between religions as something having to do with surface features only, but also claim for themselves a 'neutral' standpoint to judge all existing religions. Panikkar's cosmotheandric vision sees the need to affirm diversity and posit mutuality on the basis of trinitarian relations. Even when Panikkar uses metaphors such as the rainbow to illustrate plurality, the point is not that some see the entire rainbow while others are content with just one colour (cf. the famous elephant story used often by pluralists). The point rather is that there are different colours and that it is impossible to see anything at all except through one particular colour (see further, Ahlstrand, 1993, p. 194; Cobb, 1996, pp. 46–7; Veliath, 1988, pp. 173–5). All attempts toward universalization, so prevalent in Western culture as he sees it, are an anathema to Panikkar (see further Lanzetta, 1996, p. 97).

One term Panikkar uses to speak of the diversity and complementarity is *perichoresis*, an ancient way of referring to the intermutuality among the trinitarian persons or between the two natures of Christ. For Panikkar, the idea of *perichoresis* implies the mutual conditioning and transformation of religions in their diversity on the way to convergence. I agree with K. Ahlstrand (1993, p. 184) that this is not what the term *perichoresis* means in Christian trinitarian or Christological discourse and so Panikkar uses the term idiosyncratically. Terminology aside, the idea itself is something worth entertaining since it takes seriously the historical form and developments of religions in God's economy, an idea not far from Pannenberg (even though Pannenberg does not affirm pluralism in the way Panikkar does). Another implication of the idea of *perichoresis* is that plurality as such is not a problem for Panikkar, but rather an asset. The goal of pluralistic theologies is not to water down or dismiss plurality but enhance it. Therefore dialogue matters; through interaction religions condition and enrich each other. Each religion comes out of the encounter with a deeper sense of its own identity, yet with the awareness of needing each other.

Another asset of Panikkar's trinitarian theology is that he genuinely wrestles with the ancient problem of one-and-many. Here the Asian advaitic thinking, an affirmation of nondualism, is of help. Panikkar is hardly able to solve the problem that has plagued philosophy from of old, but he sheds some light on the topic. Both trinitarian doctrine and advaita desire to go beyond both monism and dualism. The Father and the Son are not two, but they are not one either: it is the Spirit who unites and distinguishes them (Panikkar, 1973, p. 62). Panikkar notes that if 'being' can be ascribed to each of the trinitarian members, it leads to tritheism; if 'being' is ascribed only to God as a single Being, then modalism is inevitable (Panikkar & Barr, 1989, p. 141).

Even though I find serious problems in Panikkar's exposition of the doctrine of the Trinity, as will become evident in what follows, I see his approach as helpful not only in that he avoids tritheism and modalism, but also in that he has a desire to approach the problem of one-and-many from an intercultural perspective. Often what happens is that Western and Asian ways of thinking are just set in opposition (and differences there are indeed!); Panikkar is not content with affirming an impasse, but makes a significant, even though less than satisfactory effort to overcome it.

Significantly enough, Panikkar also joins the contemporary trinitarian discourse by preferring the principle of relationality instead of the 'substance' approach typical of older theology: 'God's radical relativity *ad extra* is a mirror image of the same radicality *ad intra*: that is to say, the whole universe, as image or 'vestige' of the Trinity, is endowed with the character of radical relativity. ... Things are but reciprocal constitutive relationships' (Panikkar & Barr, 1989, p. 142). This principle also serves as a catalyst for interreligious dialogue: 'To Panikkar, the cosmos reflects the interrelatedness at the heart of the Trinity and thus draws all of creation into a oneness of distinctions, which, like the relationship of the three Persons in the one God, cannot be said to be either "one" or "two"' (Lanzetta, 1996, p. 96). All religions are in movement towards the Mystery, whether that mystery is termed *nirvana* or Christ. 'Humans yearn toward that which they are not yet, toward the ground of their being' (Lanzetta, 1996, p. 96).

All in all, Panikkar places the world's religious traditions interior to the Godhead and depicts them as pluralistic self-revelations of divinity. 'The Trinitarian life is one of pluralism in oneness, or distinction in unity, that is constantly replenishing itself' (Lanzetta, 1996, p. 95). A bold vision indeed, and a most creative way of relating Trinity to the world and world religions. Panikkar's vision, however, is not without problems and challenges, and to those we turn next.

Problems and Challenges

My first query has to do with how Panikkar approaches Christology. I noted above that a change has taken place in his thinking towards a more typical pluralistic model in which Jesus of Nazareth is perceived as one – if, in Panikkar's case, a determinative – expression of the principle of Christ. While there is not necessarily a compelling reason to make a total identification between Jesus and Christ, neither is it possible to make the kind of separation that Panikkar's 1981 edition of the *Unknown Christ of Hinduism* posits. The approach of the first edition (1964) is healthier theologically in that it leans towards a dialogue but still holds on to the uniqueness of Jesus to Christ, while not totally exhausting it. The main problem with his later approach is that, according to Christian theology, one does not have access to Christ, at least in the biblical-historical sense, apart from the person of Jesus of Nazareth. By making a reference to the Christ-principle without the 'From Below' method (i.e. working to the deity of Jesus of Nazareth on the basis of the historical materials related to the Jesus event as narrated in the Gospels) is nothing other than trying to rehabilitate the 'From Above' method in Christology, in other words, defining the meaning of Christ apart from historical contours and then reading the narrative of the Gospels in light of this preconceived 'theology'. Methodologically, this is as unwarranted as the traditional 'From Above' approach in which the 'Christhood' of Jesus of Nazareth is presupposed rather than argued for.

While it is of course possible to expand the Christic principle beyond the figure of Jesus of Nazareth as Panikkar does, one pays a high price: historical and theological criteria are left behind and one operates in a milieu in which personal opinions count as much as historical investigation. The reason I am so hard on Panikkar regarding this issue is that in contrast to Hick and most other pluralists, Panikkar claims to hold on to the traditional trinitarian doctrine. Since Panikkar is not a systematic thinker in terms of traditional theology, he seems to be unaware of the difficulties brought about with this kind of theocentric approach. Holding on to the trinitarian doctrine (even in the unique way of his) seems to be very problematic if the Christic principle is divorced from history and salvation history. Especially in light of the fact that in Panikkar's trinitarian doctrine the Son is the whole focus of deity, his pluralistically constructed Christology – and it really is *Christ*ology rather than *Jesus*ology – creates internal contradiction. Occasionally he himself seems to acknowledge the danger of separation by speaking of the importance of not letting Jesus and Christ be too much divorced from each other, but for the purposes of not making the Jesus of history a stumbling block to dialogue, he has the need to emphasize the universality of the Christ principle at the expense of the particularity of the historical figure of Jesus. In my reading of Panikkar's corpus, he leaves the question open and is willing to live with ambiguity. While the danger of 'historicism' may be real in some quarters, for Panikkar the danger is the opposite. His Christ has a strong tendency to separate from historical contours. Sometimes he seems to support this with reference to the 'mystical' or 'Mystery', or to the idea of advaitism or nonduality, but the concrete meaning intended by this kind of appeal is vague.

This brings me to critical observations concerning his trinitarian doctrine. Apart from his truncated Christology, as I see it, his trinitarian doctrine also suffers from some serious problems and open questions. In the first place, one may ask the question Panikkar poses to himself: 'Why do I persist in still speaking of the Trinity when, on the one hand, the idea that I give of it goes beyond the traditional idea by Christianity' (1973, p. 43). Notwithstanding the centrality of the idea of an advaitic cosmotheandrisim/trinitarianism in his thinking, Panikkar's interpretation goes well beyond any boundaries set forth by classical Christianity. He himself acknowledges it, but believes that his own ideas do not imply departure from but rather development of Christian trinitarian doctrine; he argues for the continuity (see 1973, p. 43). Such continuity is less than self-evident, I fear.[6] The reasons are many, not only the above-mentioned Christological ones.

Panikkar's interpretation of the Johannine sayings that no one comes to the Father except through the Son (Jn 14:6; Panikkar, 1973, p. 47) cannot be supported by any stretch of exegetical or theological imagination. What Christian theology has understood from this saying is not that the Father does not exist, as Panikkar maintains – making the 'Father' a god with a generic name but without any kind of 'personality' – but rather that the only way to know the Father is through the Son sent by his Father. I understand Panikkar's motive here – to relate the Father of Christianity to the godhead in the Buddhist concept of *nirvana* and *sunyata* (1973, p. 47) – but I fear he is mispresenting both Buddhist and Christian sources here. Whatever similarities there might be with the basically a-theistic, nonpersonalist Buddhist notion of *nirvana*, in my opinion no amount of stretching of the meaning of the concepts could make it compatible with the personalist, theistic notion of the Father in Christian faith. This is to confuse the way we talk about God (in apophatic terms) with how God exists (if in Buddhism there is any kind of concept of the divinity). Rather than trying to connect Buddhism and Christianity with the help of this most suspect twisting of terms, Panikkar should rather be faithful to his foundational idea of radical differences between religions and their concepts of the divine. So I think Panikkar has committed the most typical sin of pluralism (of which he is often critical), namely, dismissing the real differences among religions and their conceptions by assuming a similarity behind the terminology. A strong case could be made for the claim that the conceptions of the divine in Buddhism and Christianity are incompatible; that should be taken as an issue to deal with in the interfaith dialogue rather than positing a superficial similarity. I am not saying that bridges could not be built between the trinitarian conception of the deity in Christianity and Buddhism; what I am saying is that Panikkar's version does not appeal to me, neither from the Christian nor from the Buddhist perspective.

I also fear that Panikkar's claim to apophaticism is forced: what Eastern Christianity (and some strands of Western Christianity) have meant with apophaticism is not the virtual 'nonexistence' of the Father but rather the principle of negativity regarding statements about divinity; this apophatic principle applies as much to the Son and the Spirit as to the Father.

Likewise, Panikkar's interpretation of the Son can be criticized for being forced. In Christian trinitarian theology the Son is not the focus. Thus, ironically, Panikkar's version of trinitarianism is to be judged as too 'Christocentric': in the biblical canon, especially in the Gospel of John, it is made clear that even the Son's equality to the Father never implies taking the place of the Father. On the contrary, as Pannenberg and others have shown, the point of the New Testament incipient references to the subsequently formulated trinitarian understanding of God is to emphasize the voluntary submission of the Son to the lordship of the Father.

Panikkar refers to the meaning of the term *person* in analytical philosophy as a way to negotiate the seeming paradox that if the Father is not 'person' but 'nothing', how can talk about the Trinity make sense in the first place (1973, pp. 51–2)? *Person* means to be in relation, but how is this possible if there are not three persons? Panikkar says the term *person* has different meanings; the Father is a different kind of 'person' from the Son. If so, it is not very practical to use the term *person* at all for the three of them. It is of course possible to continue using traditional theological terms such as Father, Trinity, person or apophaticism and cast them into a new meaning, but the rationale for that is less than evident. Does that not confuse theology of religions discourse? Unless there are compelling *theological* reasons to change the meaning of terms, theology, in my opinion, should rather try to operate with the commonly agreed terminology.

Apart from the Christological and trinitarian problems combined with serious terminological difficulties, I also have to raise the question of the status of truth claims in Panikkar's vision. Several issues are involved here. His reference to the principle of advaita is not the problem in itself. But its use is problematic. It seems to me that often when Panikkar encounters a real theological/logical problem, he resorts to either the advaitic or mystical principle. And in doing so he opens the door to that kind of relativistic understanding – or dismissal – of truth that in the final analysis also works against his own idea of holding on to the doctrine of the Trinity while acknowledging real differences between religions. G.J. Larson, in a recent appraisal of Panikkar's pluralism, puts this basic problem in perspective by saying that Panikkar's 'notion of pluralism becomes unintelligible in a two-valued (truth–falsehood) logic, inasmuch as the principle of the excluded middle is violated' and therefore, 'the notion of pluralism so formulated is as self-defeating as any formulation of relativism and as tripped up by the problem of self-referentiality as any formulation of universalism or absolutism' (Larson, 1996, p. 72). Panikkar acknowledges this dilemma by saying, 'We cannot, by definition, logically overcome a pluralistic situation without breaking the very principle of noncontradiction and denying our own set of codes: intellectual, moral, esthetic and so forth' (Panikkar, 1987b, p. 125). Any kind of universal theory, in Panikkar's opinion, denies pluralism; he opts for the latter (1987b, p. 132). But, of course, Panikkar's own notion of pluralism cannot be a universal theory and therefore truth itself is pluralistic (see Larson, 1996, p. 77). Panikkar, however, no more than any other relativistically oriented thinker, does not live up to his philosophical claims to relativism. His position, as much as that of other pluralists, makes certain propositional claims and thus requires a propositional network and operates with truth–falsehood logic (apart from those detours when an irreconcilable dilemma appears and he resorts to advaitic or mystical principles) (see further Larson, 1996, p. 81). His trinitarian doctrine would never make any sense apart from a propositional network, even when it refers to the Father as 'nothing'. Or his appeal to the Christic-principle: how could it ever make sense apart from some propositional, 'universal' appeal (see further, Lanzetta 1996, p. 102–3)?

This, once again, brings us back to the devaluing of 'history' in Panikkar's thought, another aspect of his tendency towards relativism. While it may be true to some extent that the West lives under the 'myth of history' (see further, Ahlstrand, 1993, p. 162), just dismissing the question of historicity – as a way of affirming the 'Indian mind' as Panikkar claims – is a dubious method. If scrutiny of historical facts ends up being counterproductive, all contours of rational reasoning are left behind (see also Ahlstrand 1993, pp. 161–4).

I think Panikkar confuses rather than clarifies the truth issue by his statement that 'to understand is to be convinced', as the title of one of his essays puts it (1975, p. 134). What Panikkar means by this is that rather than positing common, taken-for-granted criteria of meaning and validity, on the 'religious' plane, understanding what a statement means is the same as acknowledging its truth. Or to put it the other way round, a false proposition cannot be understood at all. In fact he says, 'To understand something as false is a contradiction in itself.' Therefore, one cannot really understand the views of another if one does not share them. But how do we then assess the truthfulness (in any traditional sense of the term) of religious statements?[7]

Implications for interfaith dialogue are obvious. Panikkar's attempt to avoid impasse by proposing that in dialogue neither the claim that universality is inherent in Christianity nor the negation of this claim are viable options does not commend itself to me. What options are left then? Panikkar's suggestion is that religions will meet only in their transformation into Spirit. Religions 'meet skies—that is, in heaven' (Panikkar, 1987a, p. 92). But is this a helpful way to further dialogue? I doubt it and am confused by Panikkar's apparent lack of desire to tackle the issue. No more helpful is Panikkar's famous resort to a 'cosmic confidence' that allows 'for a polar and tensile coexistence between ultimate human attitudes, cosmologies, and religions' (1987b, p. 148). No amount of references to the 'animating' Spirit as creating a shared 'agon' or 'pathos' despite the lack of 'one rational view' sounds very convincing here (1987b, 147). I agree with Knitter (1996a, pp. 183–4) that Panikkar ends up affirming too much diversity in terms of 'bourgeois mystical understanding of religious pluralism and dialogue' (as Knitter puts it) that may eventually lead participants in dialogue to simply delight in diversity without ever really judging the differences. Therefore, again agreeing with Knitter (1996a, p. 184) – who, himself, is of course a self-pronounced pluralist – it has to be said that for Panikkar to avoid the peril of relativism, he must make clearer how he can come to discern what is true and false or good and evil.

A final question that I want to present to Panikkar concerns his understanding of the nature of salvation and the religious ends in religions. Panikkar postulates a coming convergence of religions: does that mean envisioning one single end for all? Or, as S. Mark Heim, our last dialogue partner suggests, different goals for different religions? A related question, one that Panikkar has not really dealt with much in his writings, is the question of the relation of the Trinity to existing religions of the world. E.H. Cousins (1996, pp. 128–9), based on personal conversations with Panikkar in the 1960s, outlines the relationship in this way: Buddhism is the religion of the silence of the Father; Judaism, Christianity and Islam, religions of the revelation of the Son; and Hinduism, the unity of the Spirit. Does this vision, then, entail a common goal for all? If so, how is the unity of the triune God to be maintained? According to classical trinitarian canons, *ad extra* trinitarian persons always work together: positing different ends for the religion of the Father from that of the Son or Spirit would compromise the very basics of trinitarianism, an issue I will also raise regarding Heim's proposal, to which we turn next.

Notes

1   A fine, up-to-date discussion by a number of leading scholars from various persuasions concerning Panikkar's thought is *The Intercultural Challenge of Raimon Panikkar*, edited by Joseph Prabhu (1996).
2   The term has roots especially in Eastern Christian theology (Dionysius the Areopagite and Maximus the Confessor). It was related to the two 'energies' in the person of Jesus Christ in his saving work; deity and humanity are joined together in his person.
3   The term coined by Cousins (1996); for the term *advaitic*, see especially p. 120.
4   Cf. the title of another book by Panikkar, *The Silence of God: An Answer of the Buddha* (Panikkar & Barr, 1989).
5   This is not yet explicated in his earlier trinitarian work but comes to focus in *The Silence of God* (Panikkar & Barr, 1989) and later works.
6   See also the serious reservations expressed by Ahlstrand (1993, especially pp. 152–6).
7   For an incisive assessment of Panikkar's view of truth, see Krieger (1996, pp. 201–3).

CHAPTER 9

S. Mark Heim: A Trinitarian Theology of Religious Ends

Making Pluralisms more Pluralistic

Theologically, the most innovative and most recent approach to the question of the Trinity and religions is offered by S. Mark Heim, who comes originally from an evangelical background and has moved subsequently to an understanding of theology of religions that is very difficult to classify. Many would say that Heim probably represents the more pluralistic pluralism in entertaining the idea of the validity of multiple religious ends in God's economy. Others may say that Heim is still a quite orthodox Christian theologian who only expands the limit of a more or less inclusivistic understanding of other religions, in which Christian trinitarian grammar serves as the guiding criterion and in which Christian salvation in terms of communion with God is the highest norm.

What is clear about Heim's programme, the main thesis of which was presented in his 1995 *Salvations* and further nuanced, and slightly altered, in a subsequent work titled *The Depth of the Riches: A Trinitarian Theology of Religious Ends* (2001), is that he is critical of all kinds of pluralisms that end up denying real differences among religions. In Heim's opinion, the pluralisms of Hick, Wilfred Cantwell Smith and Knitter fail since they deny the possibility of differing religious ends for religions and instead assume an underlying common foundation of a 'world religion'.[1] This kind of attitude makes void the particulars of existing religions (1995, p. 3). Echoing (but not giving reference to) the critique of D'Costa, Heim concludes that pluralisms of that sort end up being self-contradictory and do not, in fact, radically differ from inclusivism (1995, pp. 101–3).

The title of Heim's book needs to be taken seriously: there is a possibility of more than one type of 'salvation' (1995, p. 6). 'One set of religious ends may be valid for a given goal, and thus final for that end, while different ways are valid for other ends' (1995, p. 3). Thus he sets forth his distinctive approach to theology of religions: 'I argue for a true religious pluralism, in which the distinctness of various religious ends is acknowledged' (1995, p. 7).[2] Thus, *moksha* or *nirvana*, explained in Buddhist scriptures, can be achieved in an authentic way only through Buddhist practice; the same applies to salvation as communion with God as promised by the Christian scriptures (2001, p. 31). While Christian theologians have spent a great deal of time considering whether there are varying ways to salvation, Heim suggests we should rather consider that there are different, yet real and valid, ends that are not Christian (2001, p. 3). Heim contends that both liberal and conservative theological approaches share a largely undefended assumption that there can be only one religious end, one actual fulfilment: for liberals, it is the universalist type of common end for all; for conservatives the divide between eternal bliss and perdition (with some exceptions such as unbaptized babies) (2001, pp. 17–18). Heim suggests that these are not the only option. In his programme, then, truth and differences are recognized in various religions, even if Heim as a Christian theologian does not shy away from setting forth communion with God as the essence of salvation (1995, p. 124).

In his earlier work (1995), Heim dubs his approach 'orientational pluralism', even though in his later book (2001) he hardly mentions the term (and does not give any explanation for the lack of it). It comes from Nicholas Rescher's *The Strife of Systems* (1985). Rescher – attempting to go beyond the impasse familiar in philosophy of having to say either *yes* or *no* to questions that seem to demand only one response or the other – suggests the possibility of a multifaceted reality (see Rescher, 1985, p. 117), which means that one and only one position is rationally appropriate from a given perspective, but that we must recognize that there is a diversity of perspectives (Heim, 1995, p. 134). This perspectival view affirms then an irreducible plurality.

What, then, is the difference between Heim's orientational pluralism and conventional pluralisms? The orientationalist responds that it is perfectly possible to argue for the equal validity of varying faiths, as one doctrine among others, but not – as conventional pluralists claim to do – that one can step out of a perspectival position onto some mountain top and issue metatheological judgments such as the 'rough parity' of all religions notwithstanding all the apparent differences. The orientational pluralist, again in contrast to the conventional pluralist, freely acknowledges that his or her position is 'doctrinal', not 'neutral' (1995, pp. 142–3). Orientational pluralism 'affirms that more than one [religion] may be truthful in their account of themselves, and that these truths are distinct' (1995, p. 147).

Naturally, then, Heim sets himself on a path that does not follow the typical theology of religions discourse focusing solely on the postmortem fate of individual persons. Moreover, rather than putting forth, say, heaven or *nirvana* as exclusive options, he is ready to say that they are only contradictory if one or the other is supposed to be the fate of all human beings. On the contrary, if *nirvana* is the preferred end of Buddhists and heaven of Christians, no self-contradiction necessarily follows (1995, pp. 148–9; see also 2001, pp. 4–5, 20–21).

These are, roughly speaking, the main theses of Heim's first work. Towards the end of the book, he already begins to make connections to the doctrine of the Trinity as the driving force, expressing his sympathies especially with some leading ideas of Panikkar's cosmotheandric trinitarianism. Yet it is only in his recent book that Heim – holding on to the possibility of the diversity of religious ends as the guiding principle – develops a trinitarian theology and its implied diversity in the triune God. This also helps him to clarify his understanding of the relationship between the

Christian view of salvation and its relation to other religious ends as well as the role other religions play in relation to Christianity and in God's economy.

The Diversity in the Trinity and Diversity of Religious Ends

It might be helpful to go ahead and try to set forth as accurately as possible the main arguments in Heim's trinitarian theology of religions and then unpack it in light of the doctrine of the Trinity. Moreover it is significant to note that he is not purporting to present a full-scale theology of religions but rather more modestly a trinitarian theology of religious ends (2001, p. 3; see also p. 12). The following accurately expresses his main approach:

> We can ... see the connection between the Trinity and varied religious aims. The actual ends that various religious traditions offer as alternative human fulfillments diverge because they realize different relations with God. It is God's reality as Trinity that generates the multiplicity of dimensions that allow for that variety of relations. God's threefoldness means that salvation necessarily is a characteristic communion in diversity. It also permits human responses to God to limit themselves within the terms of one dimension. Trinity requires that salvation be communion. It makes possible, but not necessary, the realization of religious ends other than salvation. (2001, p. 180)

Another quotation develops this foundational thesis:

> Salvation is precisely communion with God across the breadth of these complex dimensions of God's nature, a communion whose fullness requires participation in relation with other persons and with creation. Humanity realizes its deepest encounter with the plenitude and diversity of the divine nature through this web of communion, this shared relation with God. ... The 'one way' to salvation, and the 'many ways' to religious ends are alike rooted in the Trinity. (2001, p. 209)

There is, on the one hand, an affirmation of the reality and validity of varying religious ends as the proper fulfilment of particular religions and, on the other, 'a "hierarchy" between full communion with the triune God [salvation] and lesser, restricted participation'. But all the types of relation with God 'are grounded in God, in the coexisting relations in God's own nature' (2001, p. 179).

The unity and diversity in the triune God is based on the understanding of God as communion.[3] 'In articulating Trinity as the character of ultimate being, Christians affirm an ontology in which the differences of the persons are basic and integral. There is no being without both difference and communion' (2001, p. 175). Thus we can say that theologically, the validity and reality of more than one religious end is based on the idea of diversity in the triune God: there is oneness in God, yet there is irreducible diversity. God's personal reality is complex: God is 'made up' of personal communion-in-difference. 'Therefore any full communion with God will have to participate in that same complexity' (2001, p. 62). Trinity provides a particular ground for affirming the truth and reality of what is different. 'Trinitarian conviction rules out the view that among all the possible claimed manifestations of God, one narrow strand alone is authentic'; therefore, Heim claims that a simple exclusivism and a simple pluralism are untenable (2001, p. 127). In that sense, the Trinity, as Heim says, is Christianity's 'pluralistic theology'. Its basis was set by the disciples' conviction that their encounter with Jesus could be correlated with the encounter with Israel's one God (2001, pp. 132–3).

The salvation envisioned by Christian faith and the religious ends of other religions (to be expounded below) mean varying degrees of being in communion with God and/or related to God (2001, ch. 2). Therefore, salvation, whatever 'degree' is attained, means being in relation. Relationality, based on God as being-in-relation (communion) encompasses three interrelated dimensions: to God, to fellow humans and to creation. Salvation, the religious end Christians know and seek, is 'a relational state and not a simple one'. This same principle also applies to other religions: 'It is this composite character that opens the possibility of different but real religious ends, ones whose limitation leads to distinct definition, whose isolation leads to a special purity' (2001, p. 9).

Incarnation as the Fullest Expression of Communion

What, then, is the role of Jesus Christ in Heim's trinitarian theology? Unlike conventional pluralists who tend to relativize the uniqueness of Christ, Heim rather points to the necessity of Jesus' incarnation as the condition of seeing God as communion. Thus the incarnation of Jesus Christ, rather than being an obstacle in relation to other religions, makes the Christian understanding of God as communion understandable and reasonable: 'In the incarnation God forms an irrevocable relation with a human being at the deepest possible level. The personal character of the relation of God and humanity, of creator and creature, is realized and confirmed'. Furthermore, the communion with God in which Jesus participated in the incarnation as a human being is now a continuing possibility for us through a universalized relation with Christ (2001, pp. 56–7).

To understand the full force of this last argument we need to recognize the specific type of trinitarianism Heim supports: in contrast to Panikkar with whom he dialogues quite extensively,[4] Heim does not propose a generic and symbolic scheme of abstract threeness (such as the 'trinities' of *Brahma-Shiva-Vishnu* of Hinduism as parallels to the Christian trinitarian doctrine). Rather, Heim takes the biblical salvation history, culminating in the incarnation of the Word as crucial revelation and act of God, as the key to distinguishing the triune God. Christians' belief in the incarnation affirms that in Jesus the internal relations that constitute God's divinity (the trinitarian relations) and the external relations between God and humans (the creator–creature relations) participate in each other (2001, pp. 130–31). But does this make Heim's theology exclusively Christ-focused? He responds: 'If people object that one incarnation is too few, they may miss the point that the Christian doctrine of God does not limit the going out of God into creation to just one instance. God's living presence in the world has a complex variety' (2001, p. 133). Heim summarizes his understanding of the role of Christ like this:

> The Trinity teaches us that Jesus Christ cannot be an exhaustive or exclusive source for knowledge of God nor the exhaustive and exclusive act of God to save us. Yet the Trinity is unavoidably Christocentric in at least two senses. It is Christocentric in the empirical sense that the doctrine, the representation of God's triune nature, arose historically from faith in Jesus Christ. And it is so in the systematic sense that the personal character of God requires particularity as its deepest mode of revelation. (2001, p. 134)

The Taxonomy of Religious Ends

In Panikkar's cosmotheandric vision, each member of the Trinity was related to a particular type of religion. Heim takes a different route. For him, the whole Trinity is related to all religions, but diversity within the Trinity generates the existence of varying religious ends as presented by varying faiths.[5] In principle there are four broad types of human destinies: salvation as communion, religious ends of other religions, human destinies that are not religious ends at all (instances of human beings clinging to created reality in place of God) and negation of creation itself leading to annihilation (2001, pp. 272–3).[6]

The first two human destinies, namely, salvation and religious ends, interest us here. Even though Heim sometimes uses the term 'hierarchy' (2001, p. 179), it is perhaps more appropriate in terms of his overall theology to use a term like 'taxonomy'. The basic idea is expressed like this: 'Alternative religious ends represent an intensified realization of one dimension of God's offered relation with us' (2001, p. 179). Based on this theological rationale, there is a threefold typology, a kind of ascending ladder, if you will, each level further divided into two alternatives, making six altogether (2001, pp. 184–97, 210–13).

The first dimension is an 'impersonal identity', a connection that does not require personhood, with two variations each rooted in aspects of the triune life. The first variation, a more apophatic one, is grounded in the emptiness by which each of the divine persons makes space for the others. This is God's active contraction, withdrawal from creation, the 'emptiness' of God in the Buddhist parlance. Such insight and a rigorous practice based on it leads to a kenotic process as described in Buddhism in terms of *nirvana*. This state is of course quite distinct from the Christian view of salvation as communion with God, but in Heim's opinion is one legitimate end for those who desire and yearn for it. The second variation of the impersonal identity is economically expressed through God's sustaining presence in creation, in, with and under the natural order; this is God's immanence in creation, most aptly embraced by pantheistic faith in which the small 'I' of the particular creature resolves into a perfect identity with the one existing 'I' of the absolute being.

The second dimension is a type of relation with God, which Heim calls 'iconographic' (borrowing from Panikkar). Within the Trinity, each trinitarian person encounters the others as a unique character. Regarding the human–divine encounter, two variations can be found here as well. The first kind focuses on encounter with the divine life under an authoritative but not explicitly personal 'icon': a law, order or structure, like that of the Buddhist *karma* or the *Tao* of Taoism. The other variation focuses on God as a personal being and on personal encounter with the divine. Law and morality are in view here, but more in the context of command, promise, trust and faith. This is still an 'I–thou' relation, but a more impersonal one, and the religious end is faithfulness and obedience. For Heim, Islam is the most noted example of this kind of vision of the religious end.

The last dimension of the triune life is based on real communion, *perichoresis*, a mutual indwelling of human and divine. There is a real communion, yet each one's unique particularity is left intact (as in the Eastern Orthodox doctrine of deification). The first variation is that of putting these different 'frequencies' of relation side by side, emphasizing parallelism and nonconverging absolutes. Traditional polytheism and some postmodern theological perspectives reflect this approach. The second variation proceeds through an 'explicit trinitarianism, a particular vision of the inner complexity in the life of the one personal God' (2001, p. 212). This is the vision of Christian salvation.

Even though Heim does in fact use the term *hierarchy*, he claims not to be saying that one religious end is above or below another, but simply acknowledging their differences. Of course, it would be natural to take the impersonal as basic, the personal as a further addition and the trinitarian as the culmination, but that is not the whole picture. It is possible, for example, to focus on the personal and yet gain a deeper appreciation of the impersonal dimension in the divine. In addition, the fact that Christianity envisions the communion identity does not mean that its vision necessarily includes all that there is on the 'lower' level (2001, p. 213).

What about biblical support of Heim's view? He is too good a theologian – and one who explicitly wants to build on mainline Christian traditions, biblical and historical, even though he admits going beyond it – to dismiss the biblical warrant. In chapter three of *The Depths of the Riches* (2001), Heim investigates the teaching of the Bible regarding religious ends. Having noted the ambiguity and relative silence of the New Testament concerning the fate of the unevangelized, he also acknowledges that the traditional stance according to which there are two opposite ends, heaven and hell, seems to be the mainline biblical view. To balance this, he refers to arguments presented during church history that seem to give some hope to those who have never heard the gospel, such as the treatment of 'pagan saints', Jews before the coming of Christ, and so on.

In addition to biblical and historical considerations, Heim turns to Dante's *Divine Comedy* to make his case for the existence of more than two religious ends (heaven and hell) during church history. One of the main points of Dante's vision, based partially on medieval and ancient Christian traditions and speculations, is that the presence of God can be found even among those in hell. Heim draws on this idea from Dante to support his foundational thesis according to which salvation is relational in essence and so are other religious ends, too, in this case even the end of those who fare very poorly in their afterlife experience. Heim concludes: 'We have seen that the *Comedy* in fact presents us with a variety of ultimate ends. There is great diversity within hell, purgatory, and paradise' (2001, p. 117). This is, of course, an argument in support of Heim's overall programme. Yet, in fairness to Dante, Heim also acknowledges that 'the scriptural twofold division between salvation and loss as the overarching structure' is maintained (2001, p. 118).

Heim's theology of religious ends, as mentioned, is open to the possibility of loss. This is because of the reality of the human freedom given by the Creator. This possibility, moreover, stems from God's 'withdrawal' from humans in creation to provide the space for self-existence and self-determination (2001, p. 182).

The Eschatological Plenitude

One final question awaits a response before we look at the practical implications for interfaith dialogue and subsequently begin a critical dialogue, namely, how does this vision of Heim's relate to the most obvious objection coming from the perspective of eschatology: doesn't this theology of religious ends compromise God's victory at the end? In other words, doesn't a variety of final destinies compromise the very unity of humanity under one God and thus frustrate the original goal of creation, as if God had 'failed'? Setting aside the option of universalism, which Heim agrees in principle would be the most logical response – but one that has not met with much approval in Christian theology – Heim disagrees that a variety of ends compromises the traditional Christian eschatological vision. He champions this view by referring to leading principles of his theology of religions that have bearing on this topic (2001, pp. 246–8):

1   God's universal saving will: God wants all to be saved.
2   The decisive and constitutive place of Jesus Christ as saviour: all who are saved are saved in communion with Christ.
3   The universal accessibility of salvation: if God's saving will is universal, and the decisive saving act in Christ is particular, then there must be means by which these two are connected.
4   The freedom of the creature is based on the withdrawal of God from his creatures.
5   The possibility of loss is a real option.

6 The idea of 'plenitude' is the guiding principle in addressing the above objection
and it deserves to be looked at in more detail (1995, pp. 163–71; 2001, ch. 7).

The idea of 'plenitude' – which simply means that God's infinite nature
mandated the proliferation of the greatest variety of *types* (but of course not,
number) of beings – has a rich history of debate both in philosophy and theology
(and especially in philosophical theology). Heim's understanding of the 'theological
principle of plenitude' is as follows. Plenitude is a qualitative description of the
divine life as triune; a personal communion-in-difference can be judged to be better
than a pure divine substance. Furthermore, this divine fullness is expressed in all
God's creation, with humans created with freedom and thus capable of choosing
whether they desire communion or not. And, as Heim has argued, in harmony with
the expansiveness of God's creation in diversity, God's purpose for creation allows
that variety to work itself out in different ways. This God-chosen principle of
plenitude, so clearly represented by the endless variety of creation, is maintained by
God through the multifarious communion with God and in being in relation,
personal or impersonal, to those attaining other religious ends. According to Heim,
the 'alternatives to salvation are in fact constituents of salvation, standing alongside
each other. These ends are not evil or empty. They could not be real unless they were
relations to God' (2001, p. 255).[7] So Heim presents a vision in which there is a
plenitude of communion within salvation, but also a plenitude of religious ends
alongside it.

Mission and Dialogue

Heim argues that his hypothesis of multiple religious ends, unlike other options
available, is conducive to interfaith dialogue and relations between various religions
at least in these three respects: first, it affirms the significance of careful study of
faith traditions in their particularity; second, it recognizes the truth and validity of
varying religious paths; and third, it affirms the validity of witness on the part of any
one faith tradition to its 'one and only' quality, 'indeed to its superiority in relation
to others' (2001, p. 29; see also 1995, p. 7).

A great deal of energy has been devoted to the question whether
mission/evangelization or dialogue should be the primary mode of the Christian
church's relation to other religions. A related question, of course, asks about the role
of Christ in relation to other religions. Heim wants to overcome this dual dilemma.
Both mission and dialogue are needed as essential aspects of Christian presence in
the world. Regarding mission and evangelization, he states,

> The Christian imperative to preach the gospel 'to the ends of the earth' is an
> authentic gospel of Christian revelation. This book affirms the legitimacy of
> Christian confession of Christ as the one decisive savior of the world. But it

> does so by means that will no doubt seem unusual and perhaps paradoxical to many Christians: affirming that other religious traditions truthfully hold out religious ends which their adherents might realize as alternatives to communion with God in Christ. These are not salvation, the end Christians long for. But they are real. (2001, p. 7)

Mission and proclamation of one's faith is thus not only permissible but essential to holding onto one's faith as 'the' way, yet not denying the value of other religions to their particular followers. On the other hand, since Heim appeals to the capacity of trinitarian approaches to comprehend or integrate other religious truth within their vision of reality, there should be a 'competition' among the faiths as to seeing which can most adequately take account of the distinctive testimony of others.

> To put it another way, the question is whether one faith's sense of the ultimate is such as to allow it to recognize that real (if limited or less than full) relation to that ultimate exists in another tradition, *in terms largely consistent with the distinctive testimony from that tradition itself.* The faith that proves able to do this for the widest possible range of compelling elements from other traditions will not only be enriched itself, but will offer strong warrants for its own truth. (2001, p. 128; italics in the original)

The last sentence in the quotation brings to light the significance of listening to and learning from other religions, not only to be able to grasp in a more authentic way their own self-understandings, but also to be deepened in one's own faith. Belief in the unity of various dimensions of divine life, as expounded above, means that Christians are obliged to recognize validity in the unique claims of many religions, obliged even to recognize a ground for their distinctive criticisms of Christianity. On the other hand, Christians also testify to others about their distinctive vision of the possibility of true communion (2001, p. 214).

Christians should also keep in mind that there can be two-way traffic here, with some followers or groups of other religions moving towards the communion vision and some Christians moving away from communion to the other dimensions (2001, p. 215).

The following summary attempts to put these various challenges to mission and dialogue in a dynamic perspective:

> Some Christian theologians have maintained that the various world religions ordinarily serve as the means for their adherents' salvation (i.e. attainment of the Christian end). Christianity would be (for those adherents) simply an extraordinary means of doing the same thing. Would it not make more sense to regard these traditions as ordinary and primary means of attaining their own unique ends, in contrast with the Christian aim? This recognition does not deny that these religions could secondarily, at the same time, serve those so inclined as the path to 'anonymous' (and necessarily, finally explicit) Christian faith. Where this process takes place, it involves not only a conversion to Christ as

God's Word but a conversion to communion in Christ as the nature of the end desired. The two go together. (2001, p. 216)

Towards a Renewed Christian Theology of Religions

After this exposition of the main themes of Heim's trinitarian theology, it is time to pause for assessment. To conclude this chapter, I will first highlight the contributions of Heim's proposal to Christian theology of religions and interfaith dialogue and second, express my concerns and point to quite serious challenges that need much further probing.

The merits of Heim's trinitarian theology of religious ends are many and significant. His is a fresh voice and an honest attempt to make the central Christian doctrine speak to other religions in a way that would honour the distinctness of each tradition, yet give room for the claim of uniqueness to both Christian and other faiths. It is a challenge many would consider too big, yet an ideal most theologians of religions envision.

With D'Costa, Heim presents one of the most incisive and successful critiques of the pluralisms that dominate the theology of religions discourse. Heim shows convincingly that the pluralism of Hick and like-minded colleagues not only fails to achieve its goal, namely, to take seriously the diversity of religions, but also ends up being self-contradictory in superimposing an external system on the self-understanding of religions, thus denying the Other's right to be different. Even though the routes – and consequently the stances – taken by D'Costa and Heim differ considerably, both desire to make the unity-in-difference in the triune God the basis for affirming both the legitimacy of differences and the right to regard one's own faith (for Christians, faith in Jesus Christ) as unique, yet not in an exclusive way. And that Heim expresses his harsh criticism of pluralisms while himself wanting to represent a kind of pluralism is even more significant. His desire is to present a more viable pluralism.

Heim's programme comes closest to Panikkar's in that the doctrine of the Trinity is not only made *a* Christian resource in relating to other traditions but *the* special asset. Yet there is a significant difference, one noted by Heim himself: whereas Panikkar's trinitarianism is based on a generic idea of the trinitarian structure of reality (and thus of religions), Heim builds on the biblical salvation history and subsequent Christian tradition (see 2001, pp. 130–31). By doing so, Heim is much closer to D'Costa than Panikkar, the latter of whom more freely gleans from different faith traditions.

Heim's approach can be labelled 'theological' in the full meaning of the term, in that he takes seriously both biblical and historical Christian traditions. Again echoing the style of D'Costa (and Dupuis), Heim devotes a considerable amount of space to a meticulous dealing with the issue of salvation and religious ends in Christian traditions. The way he links biblical and historical trinitarian traditions to the contemporary renaissance of the doctrine of the Trinity and especially communion theology is a highly commendable enterprise. Whereas for Hickian pluralism there is a tendency to either ignore or downplay the significance of Christian tradition,[8] Heim unabashedly builds on distinctive Christian views.

I am not highlighting this aspect of Heim's work only to give credit to his desire to be 'theological', but also because it illustrates his methodological orientation: if the distinctness of each faith tradition is to be honoured, then the Christian tradition should also. And to give voice to the distinctness of that tradition requires a careful sorting out of biblical, historical and contemporary viewpoints. It is ironic that often in theology of religions the distinctive contributions of other religions (say, in Panikkar, the advaitic principle of Hinduism) are given due attention, but there is a reluctance to bring to the dialogue table the distinctive features of one's own tradition. Heim's treatment of the doctrine of incarnation is a showcase example here: in stark contrast to those pluralists for whom the idea of incarnation is either problematic or has to be widened to the point of losing all Christian criteria, Heim takes it as a supreme example of his communion theology. Heim is one of the few, if not the only major pluralist theologian, for whom both the incarnation and resurrection of Christ are necessary elements of a Christian theology of religions.

In a remarkable way, Heim also tries to keep together a new openness to other religions and the necessity of continuing Christian proclamation and mission, the latter call of which is being ignored – or resisted – in typical contemporary pluralistic theologies. If this can be maintained it also has significant effects on interfaith dialogue: the purpose of the dialogue, the results of which are not announced before the 'game' as it were, is not only a needed mutual learning experience (to help both parties come to a deeper understanding of their counterpart's tradition as well as of their own), but may lead to real changes. Followers of other religions may be led to move towards the Christian vision of salvation and Christians may also shift their location.

The rest of this chapter enters into a quite extensive critical dialogue with Heim's main arguments. That this section is longer than that of other dialogue partners (and quite heavy-handed) does not imply any lack of respect nor overly negative reaction; rather, the opposite is the case. Heim's proposal is of such quality theologically and philosophically that it deserves a most focused and detailed scrutiny. Even with all its flaws, as I see them based on my careful reading of his works, it signals a decisive step forward in the ecumenical and interreligious discussion of the role of the Trinity in relation to other religions. I divide my critical notes into two major parts: first, I target my criticism on the failure of his trinitarian logic, which is based on reasoning that is unfounded and that ends up compromising God's unity; second, I criticize Heim's overemphasis on diversity as something not in tune with the intentions of religions and something that imposes a Christian conception of God upon other religions even though it purports to be pluralistic.

A Trinitarian Logic that Fails

In the assessment of Heim's theology of religious ends one needs to remind oneself that the author himself, as noted in the beginning of the chapter, has taken on a modest yet challenging task: to set forth a trinitarian theology of *religious ends*, rather than a full-fledged theology of religions. Yet at the same time we have to acknowledge that in order to present a *trinitarian theology of religious ends*, one cannot avoid dealing with several leading issues of theology of religions. Therefore, even if the critique presented below touches issues that Heim has hardly included in his proposal explicitly, they are of such a nature that need to be tackled as part of this kind of programme.

A terminological note is in order first concerning the term *salvation* (or as Heim prefers, in the plural, *salvations*). The book title *Salvations* implies that there is more than one mode of salvation. But that indeed is confusing since Heim explicitly makes a distinction between 'salvation' and 'religious ends'. He uses the term '"salvation" to refer to the human fulfillment that Christians believe is offered to us by God through Christ. This is the characteristic use of the word in Christian theology' (2001, p. 8). The title of the later book, which refers to 'religious ends', is thus more appropriate in Heim's terminology: 'salvation' denotes the Christian religious end; otherwise, the term 'religious end' refers to ends other than Christian salvation.

In his case for pluralism on the basis of the manyness in the triune God, Heim builds on the argumentation of both D'Costa and Panikkar (Heim, 1995, pp. 166–71) and claims to find support for his own view according to which there is, in fact, no divisive line between inclusivism (D'Costa) and pluralism (Panikkar), but this apparent impasse can be overcome with the help of the Trinity. In what follows, I argue (in agreement with D'Costa) that it is not possible to be a pluralist based on the Christian understanding of the Trinity. Here I will focus on how accurately Heim interprets the views of his dialogue partners. I do this not because I want to play teacher to another teacher, but to bring to light the underlying self-contradiction in Heim's theology of religions.

Heim's reference to Panikkar is far from the target: that kind of generic trinitarianism, which takes its point of departure in the biblical salvation history and Christian tradition, but feels free to move beyond it (at least in my assessment) in its desire to find a common trinitarian structure of religions, may well support Heim's pluralistic orientation. That, however, goes against Heim's own explicit purpose: he does *not* want to build on a generic concept but on a specifically Christian concept of the Trinity as it has been revealed in the biblical salvation history and formulated by the conciliar Christian tradition (2001, pp. 130–31). Heim does not endorse Panikkar's approach. Rather, Heim wants to go with D'Costa, whose approach comes from a self-professed Christian (and particularly Catholic) trinitarian theologian. D'Costa's trinitarianism makes him an ardent opponent of pluralism; it is true that D'Costa's critique targets that kind of pluralism that denies differences and ends up being intolerant. But the trinitarian grammar of D'Costa, keeping the works of the Trinity *ad extra* together and relating them to the church, the community of God on earth, makes his theology hostile to the idea of varying religious ends. In sum, I have to conclude that neither Heim's appeal to Panikkar nor to D'Costa supports his own approach.

But that is not the main point here. Panikkar and D'Costa aside, how does Heim's theology fare in light of biblical and theologico-historical considerations? This is a task incumbent for any reviewer of Heim, since Heim purports to build on biblical and historical traditions, albeit stretching the interpretations.[9] With regard to biblical considerations, the faithfulness to the Bible of any trinitarian theology can only be evaluated in light of later theological developments, since the Bible does not yet have a doctrine of the Trinity. So we have to ask, does Heim's interpretation of the Trinity coincide with the (early postbiblical) Christian reading of biblical salvation history that resulted in the doctrine of the Trinity? The main impetus for the rise of the doctrine of the Trinity in early Christian theology, as Heim correctly notes himself (2001, p.131), was to secure the closest possible union between Yahweh of the Old Testament and Jesus Christ. This was necessitated by the uncompromising monotheism of Judaism, on which incipient Christian faith built and insisted that the Father of Jesus Christ is the Yahweh of the Jewish faith. The Trinity was also needed to hold simultaneously to two premises, perceived as contradictory to other monotheisms, namely, the transcendence of God and the historical particularity of the incarnated Son as the very revelation of God. So the original purpose of the doctrine of the Trinity was not so much to affirm diversity in God as it was, in light of the incarnation and giving of the Spirit, to affirm belief in one God. In that sense, the way Heim works towards his theology of the Trinity is exactly the opposite.

But that in itself must not necessarily be seen as a deviation from the orthodox way. There is a process of doctrinal development and a need to respond to new challenges. What we have to ask now is the next question: is the way Heim expands the classical trinitarian doctrine still in keeping with the basic intention and theological parameters of the doctrine in light of the biblical revelation? It is here, I fear, that we have to raise serious doubts both in terms of the lack of integrity of Heim's interpretation, logical gaps in his reasoning, and the corollary problems it brings about, especially the frustration of the biblical vision of gathering all people under one God at the end.

In his desire to read into the Trinity the idea of pluralism (which then is translated into diverse religious ends, a chain of reasoning that is not self-evident), Heim has the tendency to overstate his case. His observation of the disciples' connecting their encounter with Jesus with the God of the Jewish faith (2001, p. 133) as an indication of the plurality of ways God relates to human beings is of course a fact; but I do not easily see how that in itself supports his idea of the kind of pluralism in the Trinity that leads to positing varying religious ends. The identification of Jesus with Yahweh rather speaks to the unity in the Trinity, not of the diversity. And even if it did, it is a long, long way from this observation to the idea of the plurality of ends!

So this takes me to what I consider one of the foundational flaws in Heim's reasoning: while it is no problem to affirm diversity in the triune God – apart from diversity, it would not make any sense to speak of three different 'persons' in the godhead – it is a completely different thing to say that because of the diversity in God there follows a diversity in religious ends. That is simply an unfounded line of reasoning. Logically, it may or may not be a valid conclusion, but in light of the biblical and historical Christian tradition, it is not plausible at all. One reason for the implausibility – but not the only and perhaps not even the strongest one – is the fact noted above that this works against the whole purpose of the emergence of the trinitarian doctrine. It is true that the biblical teaching about religious ends (but not of the nature of salvation, which clearly points to communion with God) has room for interpretation as attested by the rise during church history of challenging views (universalism) or supplementing ideas (purgatory among others) to qualify the seemingly clear twofold division between salvation and lostness. Therefore, in my reading of Heim's proposal, it hardly has the needed biblical attestation. On the contrary, it seems to be seriously at variance with the biblical vision of the gathering of all people in the New Jerusalem under one God (Rev. 21–2). In fact, Heim is not trying too hard to establish his case biblically; rather, he focuses his scrutiny of the biblical materials on supporting the idea that the traditional teaching is not as clear as often thought – which I do not think is a much contested claim. The following quotation from a fellow pluralist, the leading American Catholic Paul Knitter, brings to light the problem I am trying to highlight here:

> Christians have always taken for granted, and still do, that because there is one God, there is one final destination. Heim's efforts to draw out the possibility of many salvations from the Christian doctrine of the Trinity go only half-circle. Yes, Christian belief in three divine persons does mean that diversity is alive and well and a permanent part of the very nature of God; and this could well mean, as Heim concludes, that it is alive and well and enduring among the religions. But that's only the first half of the circle of Christian belief in God as triune; the other half swings back to oneness: the three divine persons, Christians also affirm, have something in common that enables them to relate to each other, enhance each other, achieve ever greater unity among themselves. Heim does not seem to apply this part of the Trinitarian cycle to the world religions: as diverse as they are, as incommensurable as their differences may seen, they also, like the persons of the Trinity, have something in common that enables them to transcend their differences without doing away with them. (Knitter, 2002, p. 231)

The same principle applies to the evaluation of Heim's proposal in light of the history of theology. With all its disputes about individual eschatology, there is hardly much in Christian tradition that supports Heim's idea. As with the biblical considerations, what he is attempting to do is to convince the reader that the twofold divide is not as absolute as is often held. That is the point, I believe, in his extensive commentary on Dante's vision. But again, that is hardly a highly disputed question.

In the late medieval period, with the rise of speculative eschatology, all kinds of fancy theories about the afterlife were presented. Christian theology, however, has been quite cautious about the use and validity of those visions. And certainly, whatever inspiring ideas works like Dante's *Comedy* present to the curious reader, at their best they can only be regarded as the products of a creative artistic mind, echoing – but not authoritatively interpreting – Christian speculations. Let us for a moment admit that there may be levels in heaven and hell and that, as Dante lets the reader understand, the presence of God is not absent from any level. How easily can one logically and theologically draw from this observation the idea that therefore whatever religious ends other religions envision – in their own self-understanding totally unrelated to the biblical revelation – they need to be taken as valid in Christian theology? And not only that, but in fact, they are anchored in the plurality or diversity in the triune God? There are so many huge leaps in this argumentation that it demands much more nuanced reasoning to make it convincing.

Too Much Difference is Too Much!

What about the nature of the 'salvation' Heim envisions? I am compelled to raise the question posed by Knitter: 'Can many salvations save our world?' (Knitter, 2002, p. 229 subheading). Knitter rightly acknowledges the desire of Heim to affirm diversity among religions (a feature less evident in earlier proposals of Knitter), but he wonders how, if there is a total lack of symmetry (in this case, regarding the final ends), can the religions talk to each other and understand each other:

> With his notion of *salvations*—salvation in plural—Heim told us that religions differ not only in the means they use but in the ends they pursue. But if two people have different goals, if the momentum and motivation and hopes of their lives are moving in different directions, how will they ever be able to understand each other, help each other in reaching their goal, or perhaps confront each other about the value of what they are seeking? ... When the religious communities of the world are on journeys that have divergent final destinations, then all they can do is wave at each other as they pass; to join each other on their journeys just doesn't seem possible. (Knitter, 2002, pp. 229–30; italics in the original)

For a dialogue to work, there has to be some commonality that will help establish lines of communication between such real, valid differences. Otherwise, as Knitter ironically remarks, the common ground has to be a 'creation out of nothing' (Knitter, 2002, p. 230).

That question leads to another: is it really in the interests of all religions to insist on irreconcilable differences? Isn't it rather the case that all religions – or at least most living religions – make universal claims? In other words, what religions claim is not meant just for them but for all men and women. This is the case with

Christianity without doubt; but the same applies to others, too.

> 'Allah,' 'Brahman,' 'Nirvana'—as different as they are—are understood by their respective religions to embody the goal not just of one's own community but of all persons. In other words, it seems to be part of the experience and conviction of each religion that there is Something that can be meaningful for persons in all religions. (Knitter, 2002, pp. 230–31)

Denying that right for universal claims does not seem much different from what Heim critiques in other kinds of pluralisms: whereas Heim accuses conventional pluralisms of the imperialism of assuming the 'rough parity' among religions despite seeming differences, he himself is prone to be guilty of imperialism by insisting on radical differences against the intended universalistic orientation of religions. Ironic as this sounds, it is a serious challenge to Heim. He could – and probably would – respond that the imperialistic hetero-interpretation of other religions is avoided by linking the differences, not to some ideology (such as pluralism) but rather to the diversity in the triune God. For Christians that sounds good (if we leave aside the questions raised above as to the validity of Heim's reasoning), but what about the followers of other religions? An appeal to the triune God of the Christian faith, much as it is embraced by fellow Christians, leads Heim to yet another serious problem.

The problem I mean here is Heim's insistence on linking the salvation in Christianity and the religious ends in other religions to the triune God of the Bible. This raises the question of whether Heim's proposal is pluralistic at all. I doubt it. Let us take a closer look at this linkage which, of course, for Christian theology is an axiom. In his theology of religions, Heim takes for granted the idea of the Christian God and does not even question its relevance for the rest of religions and their religious ends, an inevitable conclusion of his interpretation being, for example, that the validity of *nirvana* for the Buddhist end is based on the triune God (see 2001, especially p. 179). But this claim is, of course, nothing other than a typical inclusivist reading of other religions, totally against their own self-understanding, thus making Heim's critique of the faults of other kinds of pluralisms begin to falter.

If one maintains (as Heim does as a Christian theologian) that all salvation and religious ends derive from God, one needs to posit a unified concept of God among world religions, a hypothesis not easily agreed upon by the followers of religions. What I am trying to highlight here is that Heim is not exempted from considering the concept of God if he is trying to build a theology of religious ends based on (the triune) God. The conception of the divine in Hinduism, Buddhism and other religions is, of course, very different from that of the Jewish-Christian faith. To tell Buddhists, Hindus and others that in fact their religious end is ultimately based on the Christian conception of God does not make a good pluralistic theology! At best, it is inclusivism in a new form. The question of God's identity is *the* crucial issue for Heim's system, and as long as he sticks with the idea of the trinitarian God – not in a generic sense like Panikkar but based on the salvation history of the Bible – not much room is left for raising the question of whether this is nothing other than imposing the Christian understanding of God on other religions. Dupuis, as we saw, tackled the issue of the identity of God (whether the Christian God can be identified with the gods of other theistic religions) and even if his solution leaves room for criticism, he at least tackles the issue. Pannenberg and D'Costa, wisely enough, leave it open whether, for example, an interreligious prayer addresses the one and same God or not. I will come back to the issue of 'how pluralistic' Heim's approach really is after I touch on some other issues.

The ambiguity about the God-concept has serious implications for the taxonomy of religious ends as exposited above. While it is true that there is a kind of 'absence' or 'emptiness' in the presence of God in God's creation, it is again a huge leap logically and theologically to say outright that this is to be identified with the idea of *moksha* or *nirvana*, and then take the still more questionable step of saying that therefore the *Buddhists*' vision of *nirvana/moksha* is a valid end from the perspective of Christian theology (even if not preferred for Christians, unless they move towards that end). Two serious challenges are interrelated here. On the one hand, if one is ready to say that the 'emptiness' in the Christian God can be correlated with the Buddhist idea of 'emptiness', it is simply a 'correlation', as there is a correlation between the triune nature of the Christian God and the threeness of *Brahma-Shiva-Vishnu*. In light of Christian revelation, an identification cannot be made, or it is just speculation. On the other hand, if it is argued that this 'dimension' (as Heim puts it) of the triune God is to be identified with the 'emptiness' of Hinduism, then that can only be said from the perspective of the self-understanding of Hinduism. And if Hindus say it, they do not say it on the basis of the biblical revelation of the triune God but in light of their sacred scriptures. And this takes us to the task (tackled in a preliminary way by Dupuis) of the relationship between 'revelation' in the Christian faith and in this case Hinduism. That task is not pursued by Heim, but it should be done in order to be able to make such an identification. Therefore, Heim goes too far in his presentation of the taxonomy of religious ends. What he can say on the basis of Christian tradition is that there might be parallels; to proceed from that to the idea of identification, and not only identification, but the validity of those ends, endorsed by the triune God, is clearly something unwarranted by any stretch of Christian trinitarian theology and, from the perspective of other religions, is nothing other than a typical inclusivist reading of them.

My final major questioning has to do with the implications of Heim's proposal for eschatology, a topic he himself deals with as presented above. From the perspective of biblical vision and Christian theological tradition, the idea of the validity and at least relative permanence of a number of religious ends – as 'second bests' – is problematic for the hope of the unity of humankind and the integrity of God's final victory. Heim does tackle the issue and notices that, apart from universalism, this is a burden for Christian theology in general.

Other challenges to Heim, who undoubtedly will continue working with his project, are the following: what is the relationship theologically between the presence of God in the incarnation (of the man Jesus of Nazareth) and in a general way in the world? In Christian theology, God is present in the incarnated Son in a way different from God's presence elsewhere in God's creation; of course, one does not have to posit a total discontinuity (and should not), but unless there is a distinction, the meaning of the incarnation hardly is preserved. And it is conducive both to Heim's own theology and Christian theology in general to hold to the uniqueness of the incarnation, even though that must not mean an exclusive claim to the presence of God.

My final conclusion is that Heim's proposal is not pluralistic but inclusivist, even if very novel; to be pluralistic in light of Heim's desire to hold on to varying ends, his trinitarianism should leave behind the particularity of the *Christian* trinitarianism. Either way, his trinitarian pluralism fails. The implications for interfaith dialogue are less than satisfactory. Holding on to the radical differences in ends, ironically, makes the dialogue fruitless; the possibility of a few individuals, or even a few groups, changing their allegiance is by far too meagre a goal for inter*religious* dialogue, the representatives of which come from particular religions claiming universal validity for their views.

Notes

1   Heim (1995, part 1) offers a critical dialogue with these theologians and their pluralisms.

2   Cf. the title for ch. 5 in Heim (1995, p. 129): 'Salvations: A more pluralistic hypothesis'.

3   Heim, as most other contemporary writers on the Trinity, makes use of and dialogues with the communion theology of the Eastern Orthodox John Zizioulas (1985). According to Zizioulas, God does not first 'exist' as one and is then perceived as Trinity; rather, to be God (in Zizioulas's terminology, also to be 'person') means being in communion. Communion is the proper and primary way God exists, and as any 'person'; personhood does not, as in our contemporary parlance, denote individuality as its basis, but being in relation, in communion.

4   For the dialogue with Panikkar, see Heim (2001, pp. 148–56); which also discusses the views of Ninian Smart and Steven Konstantine (1991, pp. 156–65).

5   Here Heim is echoing more the approach taken by Smart and Konstantine (1991), even though Heim differs from them in several significant points. See further, Heim (2001, pp. 164–5).

6   In Heim's earlier work three religious ends are envisioned: lostness, penultimate religious fulfilment and communion with the triune God (1995, p. 165).

7   This kind of vision is likely to be a target of two kinds of criticism. It is either criticized for being quasi-universalism or as a somewhat novel version of the standard judgment-and-division model, reserving salvation only to Christians. Heim responds that his trinitarian theology of religious ends does not necessarily side either with universalism or the more traditional view of dual ends; it can go with both (2001, p. 258).

8   This is less evident in a later work of Hick on Christology (1993), where he goes into a detailed dialogue with Christian theologians; yet the burden of the book is to show that much of what Christians have traditionally believed about Christ cannot be maintained in light of the latest findings of New Testament scholarship.

9   In Hick's and many other pluralists' case, an appeal to the Bible or doctrinal tradition is not only

irrelevant but partially counterproductive, since they either attempt to show that later theological tradition is a deviation from the biblical tradition (Hick) or that even if it were basically in line with the biblical tradition, it has to be reinterpreted to fit the pluralistic ethos (Panikkar) or be replaced in a way that puts priority on praxis rather than doctrine (Knitter).

Part IV
A Case Study in Trinitarian Theology of Religions

The Roman Catholic Church's Trinitarian Doctrine and the Monotheism of Islam

Trinitarian Theology in Christian–Muslim Encounters

Thus far our discussion has focused on expositing and critiquing the views of individual theologians from a wide variety of theological and ecumenical orientations regarding the relationship between the Trinity and other religions. The present chapter offers a case study to make our discussion more concrete and specific. Since the late 1970s, there has been a theological and pastoral dialogue in France between the Roman Catholic Church and a significantly large Islamic community. The documentation of that dialogue serves as the source for this case study; we are fortunate to have available a recent doctoral dissertation written by the Finnish theologian Risto Jukko, titled *Trinitarian Theology in Christian–Muslim Encounters* (2001).[1]

Significantly for our purposes, Jukko's main finding is that even though the dialogue process, conducted over the period of two decades and still going on, did not have an explicitly trinitarian purpose, its structure and themes have clearly been based on (Catholic) trinitarian doctrine. Thus it makes an ideal candidate for our case study.

The Muslim–Christian dialogue in France is significant in that France has by far the largest Muslim minority of all European countries, and the Catholic Church in France has a longer history of dialogue than other countries in the continent. Muslims who have migrated to France represent various North African Islamic countries and beyond and a large number of varying Islamic communities, thus making a quite representative sample. To respond to the growing religious challenges in 1973 the Roman Catholic Church founded the 'Secretariat for Relations with Islam' (*Secrétariat pour les Relations avec l'Islam*; hereafter S.R.I.) led by a bishop. The Catholic Church acknowledges that Islam represents a major religion in France and thus makes the dialogue a test laboratory, not only for Christian–Muslim relations but also others, concerning the theology of religions practice (pp. 9–16).

The sources utilized by Jukko are neither theological studies, official minutes nor proceedings from the dialogue itself. Rather they are occasional papers meant to assist both the leadership of the church and especially faithful Catholics in their dealings with Muslims. So even though there are occasional sections written by the

Muslim counterparts in the dialogue, the documentation is Catholic and has to be read as a Catholic interpretation of the dialogue. The nature of the sources as occasional opinions that still represent the official voice of the Roman Catholic Church also has to be kept in mind when assessing their significance. We are greatly helped by the detailed, meticulous work of Jukko. Furthermore, our task here is not to ascertain how accurately the documentation follows the official Catholic magisterium, but rather to reflect on the outcomes of this case study as a way of making our discussion more specific.

The approach to the dialogue with the Muslims was guided by central Roman Catholic orientations, fundamental theology and (Thomistic) anthropology, the latter of which teaches that human beings, created in the image of God and capable of self-determination, are oriented towards the transcendent, that is, God (often called teleology). The grace of God fulfils rather than destroys what is there in nature, as the basic Thomistic axiom affirms (p. 112).[2]

As already mentioned, even though there was no clear theological outline to begin with, very soon a trinitarian structure for the dialogue began to emerge. I will first look at the treatment of God in the dialogue, then focus on the Christological and pneumatological orientations, and finally on the significance of the kingdom of God. These trinitarian considerations help us paint a picture of the dialogue's theology of religions and approach. At the end of the chapter, I will offer some critical notes and point to further challenges.

Is the Christian God the Same as the Muslim God?

It is well known that Islam has no deity but Allah. God is absolutely one and unique. It is also a well-known fact that the Qur'an claims that Muslims and Christians have the same God, who is one (Sura 29:46). Yet Islam criticizes the Christian doctrine of the Trinity as a distortion (Sura 5:73 among others). For Muslims, the Trinity is nothing other than tritheism. Therefore, Christians are really not monotheists, but 'associators', having committed the sin of *shirk*, that is, associating other deities with God (Jukko, 2001, pp. 94–5).

According to Muslims, Christians and Muslims worship the same God. The Catholic side suffers no lack of recent pronouncements affirming that this is also the view of the Church. Pope John Paul II made the often-quoted statement, 'As I have often said in other meeting with Muslims, your God and ours is one and the same, and we are brothers and sisters in the faith of Abraham' (quoted in Kasimow, 1999, p. 19).

The dialogue partners jointly agreed that both Christianity and Islam affirm that there is one God who is creator and sustainer of the universe and humankind (Jukko, 2001, p. 79). The idea of God as the creator suits Christian dialogue with Islam especially well, because Islamic theology has not been subject to challenges from nontheological pressures as much as Christian theology has (p. 81).

On the basis of theological anthropology, humanity's creation in the image of God, the S.R.I. documentation underlines the fact that our common humanity makes Christians and Muslims share common responsibilities. It also orients them both towards transcendence, God who is the Creator and is One. Jukko summarizes with references to the documentation:

> As a matter of fact, interreligious dialogue takes place between believers, between religious men and women who seek God in their own traditions. In dialogue, both Christians and Muslims are believers in the creator God, and they speak to this one God and seek him. In a Muslim, one is to see first a believer (in one God), and then, after that, a Muslim. (p. 89; see also p. 84)

According to the S.R.I., thus, 'Every human ... represents a certain form of the relationship with the Creator of the mystery of the human condition' (p. 89). Muslims and Christians are said to be brothers in God and in humanity, thus making the encounter 'a dialogue of believers' (p. 90).

The belief in one God and the common origin of humankind has social implications. The combination of divine origin and common faith in one God should not leave Christians and Muslims inactive, but should lead them to work together to build up a better or a more human world, to foster 'social justice, moral values, peace, and freedom' (p. 84; quotation from *Nostra Aetate* # 3). Solidarity and justice in Christian–Muslim dialogue are thus linked to faith in one God, the Creator of the human being (Jukko, 2001, p. 86). In addition, efforts to secure peace in the world are linked to God and especially to prayer to the one God (p. 88).

This much is clear in the S.R.I. documentation. But questions arise when one poses the question of whether it is really possible to establish identity between the Christian God and the Muslim God. Do these two faiths have the same God? Here our sources become less than clear. On the one hand, it looks as if identity is assumed. On the other hand, there are critical remarks in the documentation: when Christians and Muslims say *God*, they do not say exactly the same thing. According to the documentation, God is the same, but yet it is asked at the same time, 'Who is this God?' Not much help is gained from the following statement: 'It is to the same God, to God unique and creator, that we talk, even if we do not know him in the same way' (p. 97). There is an honest desire to go as far as possible towards the affirmation of identity, yet among the Catholics there are questions that make this identification uncertain. What is clearer, however, is that the *doctrinal concept* of God is not identical in these two faiths (pp. 97–8).

One way to tackle the issue of the identity or lack of identity of the God(s) is to refer to both faiths (and Judaism) as 'Abrahamic faith'. Our sources affirm that Islam is an heir of Abraham and a receiver of his benediction through Hagar and Ishmael. Islam is viewed as a monotheistic religion that has integrated doctrinal elements from the Abrahamic tradition and participates in the Abrahamic promises

(p. 136).[3] Nevertheless, as is well known, the story of Abraham in the Qur'an is not identical with that of the Bible, a fact acknowledged by the S.R.I. (p. 138).

Jesus and the Spirit

An indispensable part of the Christian doctrine of the Trinity is a high Christology. How does that fare in the Muslim–Catholic dialogue? It is said that the central point in Christianity is the death of Christ and that the specificity of the Christian faith is linked to the confession of faith in the resurrection from the dead, that is, the paschal mystery (p. 140; see also p. 141). How does this distinctively Christian conviction relate to the monotheism of Islam? And how can we reconcile it with the view of the Qur'an according to which Jesus is only a prophet but not a god?

The S.R.I. documentation, acknowledging the tension – routinely mentioned in theologies of religions – between the universal saving will of God and the particularity of Jesus (see pp. 143–52), attempts to negotiate it in a way that sounds theologically quite questionable. It makes a distinction between Christ's act in the Church and in the world. It says that Christians have to learn not to confuse the universality of Christ as the unique mediator and the universality of Christianity as a historical religion. That distinction is assumed to avoid exclusivity (p. 147). But unless it is explained how that works (for example, what then is the role of the church?), it remains an abstract principle without much help to offer. Another way the S.R.I. documents negotiate this tension, equally unsatisfactory in my opinion, is the reference to 'mystery' concerning the uniqueness of the economy of salvation in Christ (p. 148). As soon as theology begins to appeal to mystery when encountering irreconcilable problems, one needs to be cautious: 'mystery' can mean so many different things to different interpreters. Again, no specific guidance is offered as to the meaning of the mystery.

What, then, is the role of the Spirit? The question asks how Christ's presence, acts and grace reach out to non-Christian religions if salvation in Jesus Christ is the universal destiny of all human beings, regardless of which religion they belong to. The answer says that it happens through the universal presence and ministry of the Holy Spirit. The S.R.I. quotes with approval the central passage from Vatican II's *Gaudium et Spes* (# 22):

> All this [the union with the dead and risen Christ] holds true not only for Christians, but for all men of good will in whose hearts grace works in an unseen way. For, since Christ died for all men, and since the ultimate vocation of man is in fact one, and divine, we ought to believe that the Holy Spirit in a manner known only to God offers to every man the possibility of being associated with this paschal mystery.

The documentation also cites other relevant passages to the same effect, for example the Pope's reference to authentic prayer as called forth by the Spirit (Jukko, 2001,

p. 157). In accordance with the Catholic teaching, it is assured that the Holy Spirit is working in non-Christian religions, in the hearts and consciences of people (p. 161). In sum, Jukko concludes that the S.R.I. documentation seems to agree with the Vatican pneumatological emphasis (p. 164).

If so, does this work of the Holy Spirit mean that Islam is a way of salvation? The S.R.I. documentation leaves the question open in the same way the mainstream interpretation of Vatican II does; it admits that Vatican II, especially *Nostra Aetate*, does not let us regard other faiths as salvific. Yet it seems to me that the S.R.I. answer can be read in more than one way: on the one hand, it is admitted that Islam is a way 'towards' God, and that on the level of religion, the Muslims are believers who come to God via another way than Christians. Islam is seen as a way to God and as a place of the Spirit. On the other hand, the sources say that even though Islam invites people to pray, it does not enable them to meet God or to have union with him, implying that if Muslims do not meet God in their devotional life, their religion is not adequate to save. The question here is: what does it mean for Muslims (like other non-Christians) to be related to the paschal mystery through the work of the Spirit? Perhaps the preposition *towards* was intentionally chosen to leave the impression that Islam goes a long way in the right direction but in itself is not fully salvific (pp. 166–8).

What about Islam's relation to the church and the kingdom? The view is that Muslims can be regarded as comembers in the kingdom of God. Thus, the documentation concludes, the mission of the church and the work of the Holy Spirit are given new dimensions when the children of the kingdom are to be recognized in the world (p. 194; see also pp. 193–7 especially). Therefore, both Christians and Muslims should participate in the building of the kingdom until it comes at the eschaton. They are not building the church, which is the task for Christians, but the kingdom, which is a wider concept. Here there is a close relationship between the kingdom and the Spirit; the building of the kingdom is seen as a sign of the work of the Spirit who acts and makes the messianic kingdom come (p. 195). What is also significant about the building of the kingdom is that the positive values of various religions (as well as, of course, the Christian faith) have their foundation in God: the consciousness of God, of justice, consideration of the poor, forgiveness, peace and so on (2001, p. 213).

One final question remains here before we take a summary look at the theological foundations of interfaith dialogue between Christians and Muslims, namely, what is the relationship between the Spirit and the church, ecclesiology and pneumatology? The documentation does not address this question adequately (pp. 208–9).

The Trinitarian Basis of Interfaith Dialogue

The dialogue process has revealed two foundational perspectives. First, the

Christian – in this case Roman Catholic – approach to other religions is trinitarian. Second, the dialogue process took notice of the fact that the trinitarian faith is not something on which both Islam and Christianity agree. For Christians it is clear that the trinitarian faith is monotheistic, but for Muslims it means blasphemy (p. 140).

The theological starting point for the interfaith dialogue, according to the S.R.I., is the nature of the triune God. Human beings as created in the image of God are 'obliged' to relate to others, equally created in the image of the same God (p. 83). God himself invites Christians to dialogue with others, and those others invite Christians as well. Even though this particular dialogue had a primarily pastoral orientation, significantly enough it was made clear that dialogue in itself is not a pastoral strategy but a theological attitude (p. 213). The theological description of the interfaith dialogue is explicitly trinitarian:

It must be:

● Bold in the power of the Holy Spirit and in the obedience to the command received from the Lord and Saviour.
● Respectful to the action of the Holy Spirit in the heart of men.
● Humble in acknowledging that Christian faith is a free gift of God.
● Incarnated in the culture of those to whom it is addressed. (pp. 213–14)

This theological basis is also stated in a slightly different, yet complementary way: 'The Church is committed to dialogue above all because of her faith in the trinitarian mystery of the one God. Christian revelation makes us catch sight of a life of fellowship and exchanges in God himself, source of all mission and all dialogue' (p. 214). It is said that the triune God is in dialogue within himself. Dialogue corresponds to the Being of the triune God, which Christ has revealed. The reason for dialogue is human beings' inherent teleological searching for God and God's universal grace operative through the active presence of the Holy Spirit in every person (pp. 214–15). Jukko summarizes in a helpful way the trinitarian foundation of the dialogue:

> The theological motive of S.R.I. dialogue is the triune God. It seems that only the concept of the trinitarian God can be the basis for fruitful interreligious Christian dialogue with non-Christians, in the case of the S.R.I. with Muslims. Even though the concept is an article of Christian theology and was not articulated by Jesus himself, it unites transcendence and immanence, creation and redemption in such a way that from the Christian standpoint dialogue becomes possible and meaningful. It is the hermeneutical key to interpret the religious experiences of non-Christians (as well as of Christians). (p. 221)

The documentation also says more specifically that it is the Holy Spirit who urges Christians to dialogue and makes Christians discover aspects of their faith that they have not yet known or recognized in Christ (p. 161). Furthermore, it says that the incarnation is the summit of dialogue in which God fully reveals himself. Dialogue corresponds to the way in which God meets human beings and enters into a covenant with them (pp. 215–16). Interfaith dialogue, the S.R.I. reminds us, is not only an exchange between individual believers or groups, but is also societal, 'incarnated in the culture'. Religion is at the heart of every culture, and that is why faith – and interfaith dialogue – must be inculturated (pp. 161, 217).

The end result of the dialogue is mutual enrichment of both parties' faith: 'Even if this seems paradoxical, the Christian–Muslim encounter can help, among Christians, to receive the revelation of God in Jesus Christ' (2001, p. 219).

Critical Reflections

As mentioned above, the nature of the documents being used here need to be taken into consideration when assessing the theological – especially trinitarian – coherence and integrity of the Muslim–Christian dialogue. Not too much theological accuracy and sophistication need be expected of documents meant to serve pastoral more than theological needs. In general, it is clear that the S.R.I. documentation follows the mainstream Catholic teaching on other religions, and is heavily dependent on Vatican II guidelines. The following critical remarks and questions are not meant to imply that the dialogue process itself has failed; the purpose of this final section is not to give a comprehensive appraisal of the dialogue itself. Rather, these comments are limited to assessing how trinitarian doctrine is maintained as the theological substratum.

The question of the identity of the Christian God with the God of Islam is an extremely challenging one. The dialogue process did not express itself clearly about that, perhaps for the obvious reason that the Catholic doctrine does not either. I am inclined to side with both the Catholic D'Costa and the Protestant Pannenberg in leaving open the question of the identity/nonidentity (even though I do not find it helpful to say as Pannenberg does that this is a question to be solved only by God; all theologians probably agree with that in principle, but theology, even as a human enterprise, should inquire into ways to know something more). The trinitarian doctrine affirms that the only way to know God is through Jesus Christ and that there is no decisive knowledge of God apart from this Mediator (even though there is a 'relative' knowledge of God in the world as a result of creation and the cosmic range of the Spirit of God). Therefore, without leaving trinitarian parameters, it is extremely difficult for a Christian theologian to affirm an identity between this trinitarian God and the God(s) of other religions. Regarding the Catholic Dupuis's desire to do so, I expressed my reservations above. True, Islam is a special case (as is the Jewish faith too, in an even more concrete way) for two reasons. First of all, it is not a problem for the Islamic faith to affirm the identity of the God in both traditions. Second, like Judaism, Islam is an uncompromising monotheism, making it far easier for Christian theology to find common ground. Yet, even with these qualifications, affirming the identity seems to go beyond trinitarian parameters.

A corollary question asks: if the identity can be affirmed, what then is the role of Christ and the Spirit? (This is of course an even more urgent question regarding Christian–Jewish relations.) Is the affirmation of the identity of 'God' between the Christian faith and Islam really possible theologically? What is the meaning of the term *God* for Christians who hold on to Trinity? Any kind of generic concept of the divine, without reference to the concrete form of the Christian God as Father, Son and Spirit, seems to be both too vague and logically inconsistent with the trinitarian doctrine. Jukko rightly notes that if Muslims and Christians share the same faith in the same God, what then is the meaning of the question, 'How to proclaim the Good News of Jesus Christ, while respecting the Muslim faith?' (p. 141). I raise these foundational questions here not to discredit the desire of Christians and Muslims to find a common ground but to highlight the task of the present study to inquire into the specific meaning of the doctrine of the Trinity to Christianity's relation with other faiths.

To a certain extent Christology did become a problem in the dialogue process. I have already expressed my reservations about the attempt to negotiate the role of Christ by means of the distinction between Christ's role in the church and in the world. The two roles can be distinguished, of course, but cannot – as the S.R.I. documentation in that context seemed to imply (p. 247) – be contrasted or separated. It is a dead end to 'soften' the uniqueness of Jesus Christ by creating an inner tension between his role as Mediator in the church and the world. Not only does that leave unclear the role of the church – a perspective not unimportant to Vatican II, which regards the church as 'necessary' for salvation – but the integrity of the Trinity is called into question. I find it much more helpful to follow the approach of the Catholic D'Costa, to whom the universal, cosmic sphere of the Spirit's ministry is not divorced from either the Son and the Father or from the church.

A question not tackled in a satisfactory way – and a question that has bearing on both the identity question and Christology – is the nature of religious language, particularly the use of the same term in different religions. Does a term such as 'god' or 'faith' have the same referent in different religions? The expression 'I believe in One God', confessed by both Muslims and Christians, seems to make the same affirmation, but that is the case only if the terms 'believe' and 'One God' refer to the same reality. Jukko raises this issue (p. 97), but does not delve into it.

With reference to Jukko's earlier comment about the confusion regarding the need to proclaim the gospel of Jesus Christ to Muslims if they really share the same faith, I share his wondering about whether there is an inherent tension between dialogue and mission in the documents (p. 141). This is yet another area that calls for more clarification.

In sum, it can be said – paradoxical as it may sound – that even though the proper theological foundation for the interfaith dialogue with Muslims is the Christian doctrine of the Trinity (of course, from the Christian perspective), the doctrine itself cannot be used in actual encounters with Muslims, since the Islamic faith denies it at the outset (p. 244). How this translates to the trinitarian conviction, shared by all

Christians, that the outer works of the Father, Son and Spirit cannot be separated (whatever the Father does in the world, the Son and Spirit are also involved) is one among the crucial theological questions to be pondered. Trinity pushes Christians to dialogue with other religions, especially with monotheistic 'cousins', yet at the same time it also sets rules for Christian talk about God. How this dilemma is being solved determines to a large extent the future of trinitarian interfaith dialogue for Christians.

This and many related topics will be reflected on critically in the last chapter of the book. It attempts not only to summarize the main findings of our inquiry but also to advance a theology of religions discourse from a Christian perspective by pointing to basic guidelines and orientations that we can draw from our critical reflection on the significance of the Trinity to Christian theology of religions and interfaith dialogue.

Notes

1   The study is based on the documentation produced by the *Secrétariat pour les Relations avec l'Islam*, originally in French. Though in principle the original sources are available to all interested readers, because most readers of the present book would only read English, I will give reference to Jukko's book, which, in the style of dissertations in the continental tradition, contains in the footnotes the full text of the most significant passages analysed in the main text. For the nature of sources and methodological considerations, see Jukko (2001, pp. 19–26). Unless otherwise indicated, all references in this chapter are to Jukko (2001).
2   In the background there is of course the heavy influence of Rahner's theology, especially his theological anthropology.
3   The name of the very first S.R.I. publication, which came out in 1980, is significant: *Tous fils d'Abraham* ('All sons of Abraham').

Conclusion: Toward a Trinitarian Theology of Religions

The purpose of this last chapter is to gather together the core orientations of my own understanding of a trinitarian theology of religions. In other words, I try to explicate the basis for my critical dialogue with the leading trinitarian theologies of religions discussed in this book. Some might have preferred that I had placed this chapter at the beginning of the book to let the reader see the perspective from which I have approached various proposals offered. On the other hand, placing it at the end makes more sense, I believe, since my own current understanding of the role of the Trinity in Christian theology of religions has been shaped by a sustained analysis of, and dialogue with, these theologians.

Systematic theology by its very nature is both critical and constructive. Even the critique of other positions always entails at least a tentative understanding of one's own position. At the same time, theological critique, based on a careful, patient listening to various proposals, is already the first step in constructing one's own view.

My aim here, however, is again limited. I do not wish to construct a full-scale trinitarian theology of religions – who could within the confines of one brief chapter? My goal, rather, is to raise the crucial issues as I see them, highlight their significance, and so point to the imminent tasks for the future. I am not repeating here the critiques I have expressed earlier in this book, neither am I trying to summarize them (for the obvious reason that my critiques of earlier proposals, while guided by more general theological convictions, have been case-specific, targeted on the viewpoints raised by my dialogue partners). I will constantly refer back to the previous discussion and I assume that my readers have read the book starting from the beginning; this final chapter does not purport to fulfil the expectations of a mystery novel reader who wants to know the real secret ahead of time! I reiterate my earlier comments only as required to develop my argumentation.

One could say that the goal of this last chapter is to offer, in light of the critical dialogue carried on with nine leading theologians and the insights from a case study between Catholics and Muslims, an outline of topics that need to be taken into consideration and dealt with on the way to a more coherent, satisfactory trinitarian theology of religions. As an outline, its function is heuristic and tentative, and I look forward to continuing work in this area. One of my longer-term writing projects is to try my hand at a full-scale trinitarian doctrine of Christian theology of religions in dialogue with ecumenical voices and learning from the existing dialogues between Christians and representatives of other religions. But this chapter only begins that endeavour.

The course of the discussion is as follows. I will begin by showing the role trinitarian doctrine serves in the criticism of existing pluralisms. Then I will highlight the significance of the pursuit of the truth of Christian doctrine as the backbone for an authentic trinitarian theology of religions. Next, I will ask what is distinctive about the Christian doctrine of the Trinity, to be followed by a discussion of the role of Christology and pneumatology, relating that discussion to the church and the kingdom of God. After that I will take up the critical issue, arising especially out of Heim's proposal, of the meaning of 'diversity' in a communion trinitarian theology. I will close this chapter by drawing conclusions from all of this for the understanding of the religious Other and interfaith dialogue.

Trinitarian Theology as a Critique of a 'Normative' Pluralism

With reference to thinkers such as Hick and Knitter, the Sri Lankan evangelical theologian Vinot Ramachandra takes up the challenge of 'normative and programmatic' pluralism that goes beyond the recognition of the variety of religions and enforces itself as the only plausible mindset (Ramachandra, 1996, p. ix). Many critics have rightly noted that ignoring the self-understanding of adherents of religions means nothing less than violating their religious rights. It has been dubbed 'elitistic', 'imperialistic' and even 'intellectual Stalinism'.[1] Panikkar, for whom all (Western) attempts to construct universal theories are doomed to fail, rightly regards a 'universal pluralism' to be a contradiction in terms. It fails to acknowledge the fact that each religion deals with ultimate questions, and thus its views cannot be freely modified, and also that the future may give birth to new kinds of religions. Instead of universal pluralism, Panikkar calls for deepening respect between religions in view of the existing real differences (1987b, pp. 120–25, 141). The critique by Gordon D. Kaufman (1993, pp. 102, 146), himself no stranger to pluralism, arises from a similar kind of concern. Philosophically it is highly suspicious to claim a higher knowledge about the perennial questions of life than what another religion itself claims. By doing so one ignores the real differences between religions.

Basically I agree with the criticism of pluralism expressed by D'Costa and Heim (the latter of whom, of course, advances a specific type of pluralism himself). The main problems of pluralisms according to these two authors can be summarized in these terms:

1   Pluralisms represent the tradition-specific project of the Enlightenment and are not, as they claim, honest 'brokers to disputing parties' (D'Costa, 2000, pp. 20). Failure to acknowledge the tradition-specificity of pluralisms distorts the pluralists' self-understanding and consequently also their understanding of other positions.
2   Pluralisms, thus, fail to redeem the promises of openness, tolerance and equality.

3 In granting a type of equality to all religions, they end up denying public truth
   to any or all of them.
4 Pluralisms also fail because they do not actually embrace plurality of religions
   but rather offer yet another 'right' answer, a kind of 'universal' religion,
   composed of items drawn from several religions, yet not identical with any of
   them. Thus they do not take seriously dialogue with the Other and are not
   willing to learn from them.

What then are alternative ways to advance the discussion on plurality of religions
in today's world? For starters, I propose that the following guidelines be taken into
consideration (based on Kärkkäinen, 2003b): first, the self-definition of each
religion has to be taken seriously. As Harold Netland (2001, p. 235) states, 'An
adequate theology of religions must accurately reflect the beliefs and practices of
the religious traditions'. Second, the quest of religions for ultimate truth has to be
honoured. An essential premise of religions is that there are competing truth claims.
Third, the nature of religious language and its relation to myth – however one
defines this much-debated concept – has to be studied much more carefully than it
has been in Hick's system. A related task is to analyse in much more detail the
nature of hermeneutical work with regard to the question of religious identities,
competing truth claims and understanding of the godhead. An appeal to the
'mythical' or to the nondualistic advaita, if it is only meant to foster tolerance and
avoid facing the competition among truth claims, is a dead end. Fourth, the very
idea of religious pluralism and its conditions has to be scrutinized critically and not
taken for granted as often seems to be the case, perhaps as a reaction to earlier
supposedly self-evident exclusivism. Even though exclusivism might not be a
viable option for many Christians in today's world, neither is an uncritical
pluralistic view. The main problem of the theology of religions in my view – not
only of a Christian theology but also those of other religions – is how to even begin
to think of pluralism without sacrificing the built-in tendency of each religion to
assume the finality of its own truth claims.

Christian trinitarian theology that takes seriously the Other and engages in a
meaningful dialogue, respecting the history and differences, has the potential of
moving beyond an exclusivism that says *no* to dialogue without engaging the
dialogue and beyond pluralisms that tend to deny the right of the Other to be
different. In order to advance a classical doctrine of the Trinity, the truth claims of
religions need to be given full hearing. Religions, Christianity included, by nature
issue truth claims with a universal orientation.

Religion as the Search for the Ultimate Truth

While religion plays various roles, such as identity-formation and culture-shaping,
it can be argued that the main function of religion is to advance the quest for the

ultimate truth. If religion is denied that function, as in atheistic societies, ideology takes that role. Religion by its very nature deals with the ultimate issues of life and death and it may not be meaningful to talk about religion at all without this component (see further Taliaferro, 1998, pp. 206, 236). Amnell notes this pointedly:

> Without [this] element of truth claim, the teachings of religions would not make sense, since the question of the truth is an essential aspect of religions. If a religion does not talk about the ultimate things, but rather talks about the more superficial, that religion most probably cannot be regarded as a genuine religion. For the perspective of metatheology, the conceptions of religions concerning the truth vary significantly, but still the right to present a truth claim is an irrevocable right for any religion. (1999, pp. 64–5; my translation from Finnish)

Even several Asian religions such as Buddhism and Hinduism, while they have been more tolerant and pluralistic than Christianity and Islam, still regard themselves as the true religions.[2] Tolerance and denial of the truth claims of one's religion are not identical questions, but Hick does not make a clear distinction between these two. Thus, H.J. Verweyen calls this aspect of Hick's programme 'the absolute denial of all absolute claims' (1996, p. 133), and Moltmann (1990) believes that most often this kind of relativism is just a mask for a new kind of absolutism.[3]

To argue, as do pluralists, that the truth claim for Christ only applies to those inside the Christian household is a self-contradictory notion: truth cannot be true only to some people. It either is true or is not. It does a disservice to Christian mission vis-à-vis other religions to try to soften the encounter by reference to a 'partial' truth. Moltmann (1990, p. 155) rightly notes that a 'religion which has given up claiming uniqueness ... is of no special interest. As a Marxist or as a Muslim, I believe I would have little interest in a Christianity that makes vital concessions before entering into conversation with me'.

One way to try to avoid the stumbling block of issuing truth claims with universal intention is to refer to 'many absolutes' as if there were many unique and universally powerful revelations of truths or, as in the case of Heim, legitimate religious ends. This sounds appealing but is another dead end. As the pluralist Knitter notes, 'many absolutes' may end up meaning 'no absolute'. To posit more than one 'absolute' is to stretch the limits of logic to the point of making it self-contradictory. I expressed my hesitations toward that kind of exercise in relation to Panikkar's advaitic philosophy (ch. 8).

A more helpful way to negotiate the tension between acknowledging the perspectival nature of our knowing and thus the particularity of any given position (contra typical pluralism) and refraining from any attempt to issue truth claims (as in relativism) is to follow in the footsteps of Newbigin and Polanyi, as briefly explained above in the context of Barth's theology (ch. 1). Even though there is no detached, 'neutral' point from which to view the world but only a diverse series of perspectives, according to 'critical realism', reality can be known by locating oneself in the places where reality makes itself known, by viewing it from certain standpoints rather than others. This is no arbitrary subjectivism but (as Polanyi has shown) the approach of even science and philosophy: certain 'plausibility structures' must be posited as the basis for advancing any kind of knowledge. That starting point cannot be posited with any absolute certainty, but it has to be presupposed as a kind of hypothesis. Pannenberg, in fact, treats theological statements as hypotheses to be tested with the help of argumentation and appeal to truth criteria.

In Christian trinitarian faith, appeal to history and eschatology, as Pannenberg most vocally has argued, are the arenas in which one hopes the truth question will be settled finally. The task of (systematic) theology is to advance the quest for the truth. Even though I basically agree with Pannenberg's approach in this regard, I find Newbigin/Polanyi's way of approaching the truth question more helpful. Without going into further exposition of Newbigin's position, the outline of which is well known,[4] I will highlight just the key concept: the gospel as 'public truth'. Resisting the modernist split between public facts and private values/beliefs, Newbigin maintains that all knowledge is always interested; it is always what he calls 'personal knowledge'. It is not legitimate to reduce faith primarily to the subjective arena any more than it is possible to regard the arena of facts as free from subjectivity (see Newbigin, 1991). This kind of knowledge is committed, yet not subjectivistic, since 'it is a commitment which has an objective reference'. In other words, it is a commitment 'with universal intent', as Newbigin puts it. It looks for confirmation by further experience. Therefore, it is something 'to be published, shared so that it may be questioned and checked by the experience of others' (Newbigin, 1991, p. 35). When a Christian says 'I believe', he or she is not merely describing an emotion or even a value statement, but affirming what he or she believes to be true, and 'therefore what is true for everyone' (1991, p. 22). In other words, since faith is more than personal, it has an objective reference point outside itself and is necessary to be brought into the public arena. This is what Christian witnessing is all about. Not only has Christianity every right to publicize its truth claims, more importantly, it forms a kind of distinctive 'truth community'. Appropriately, Newbigin titled one of his latest articles, a contribution to a symposium dealing with the Trinity and religions, 'The Trinity as public truth' (1997).

The truth of Christian trinitarian faith is an appeal to truth with universal intent. Following Pannenberg, we can say that its truth claim has been tentatively, 'proleptically' confirmed in the resurrection from the dead of Jesus Christ by the Father in the power of the Spirit. The final verdict is yet to come as Christian faith looks into the final eschatological victory of the triune God among the gods of religions. History and eschatology are thus the criteria to which Christian trinitarian faith appeals.[5] Doing so means that the doctrine of the Trinity in Christian theology and faith cannot be a generic view, but must be a particular view rooted in history and an expectation of future confirmation.

The Uniqueness of the Triune God of the Bible

For Barth, the doctrine of the Trinity served as a criterion for distinguishing the God of the Bible from other gods. This is the question of the criteria. Stephen Williams, in an important contribution titled 'The Trinity and "other religions"' (1997), lays out the significance of the criteriological question that must be answered: 'What enables something to count as a formulation of the doctrine of the Trinity?' (1997, p. 28). He refers to the well-known questions posed to trinitarian theologians by Michael Durrant (1973). Durrant took up the challenge posed by many concerning the incoherent nature of the doctrine of the Trinity. At the end of his argument, he came up with the obvious criticism that at most what he had shown was that specific formulations of Christian belief in God as Trinity can be shown to be incoherent; the doctrine itself was not under threat. Durrant, however, was not happy with this pseudo-answer, so he challenged the objector to identify the criteria for what exactly constitutes the essence of such belief apart from its formulation. There is no way to have a 'doctrine' of the Trinity apart from a specific formulation. Without criteria of any sort, a reformulation of the doctrine may end up being something else; that's why we need criteria. And Williams fears that reformulations of the doctrine of the Trinity by such leading pluralists as Panikkar and Smart and Konstantine[6] totally ignore the discussion of the criteria. Therefore, it 'may seem that such a challenge threatens to reduce discussion to the level of semantics and misses out on discussion of the substance and usefulness of the proposals in question' (Williams, 1997, p. 29).

Christian trinitarian theology, anchoring itself within the biblical and classical theological parameters, maintains that the talk about Father, Son and Spirit is the only possible way of identifying the God of the Bible. As already noted in the context of dialoguing with Pannenberg (ch. 5), this has enormous implications for theology of religions. That the only way to talk about God is to refer to the Father, Son and Spirit naturally resists the temptation of mythologizing the concept of God or changing it into generic talk about the 'Ultimate Reality' as in Hick. Furthermore, it both presupposes and establishes both Christological and pneumatological strictures. Christ's divinity follows from the doctrine of the Trinity and thus makes any kind of pluralistic 'theocentrism' a self-contradictory approach; not only Christ's divinity but also his incarnation is to be posited, unless trinitarian faith is to be divorced from 'real' history. Any kind of mythologization or 'generalization' of the incarnation that divorces the man Jesus of Nazareth from the incarnation resists trinitarian understanding (it is another issue to negotiate the possibility of God's presence 'outside' the incarnation). Trinitarian doctrine also integrally links the talk about the Spirit to the Father and Son and resists those kind of pneumatological theologies of religions in which the Spirit is made an itinerant, independent deputy.

In light of this, I have to agree with John Milbank that Panikkar's attempt to equate trinitarian and neo-Vedantic pluralism falls short of orthodox trinitarian theology (Milbank, 1990a, p. 188; Vanhoozer, 1997, p. 63, agrees) – because of the absence of criteria. I am not, of course, saying that we should shy away from using extrabiblical or extra-Christian vocabulary to express our faith in the trinitarian God of the Bible. What I am insisting is that whatever formulations are used, their adequacy and limits need to be assessed in light of some criteria. For classical Christian theology, biblical salvation history and the creedal tradition has served as a fence between what was considered a legitimate contextualization and what is not. It is important to note that indeed the main function of the creeds has been mainly that of drawing lines. The creeds do not express the contents of the biblical faith in a timeless, 'neutral' way since creeds themselves are already highly contextualized attempts to express the nucleus of the biblical traditions. Yet they do claim to be based on the biblical traditions and with all their limitations – and perhaps even some distortions – they have helped the church come to a fuller understanding of the essence of the trinitarian faith.

In the introductory chapter we observed that one of the emphases of the revived doctrine of the Trinity in contemporary theology is linking the Trinity to history. Three implications follow. First, the basis for discerning the emergence of the doctrine of the Trinity is to look at the biblical salvation history. Second and consequently, the trinitarian doctrine is not based on abstract speculations nor primarily on alleged similarities among religions. While pedagogically and heuristically it is appropriate – as Hick and especially Panikkar have done – to search for parallels to Trinity in the structure of reality or other religions, these observations are no more than parallels. Earlier on, I expressed my serious reservations about the adequacy of the logic of concluding from these parallels that the concept of a generic 'triune' God (or in Hick's case, Ultimate Reality) can be posited. This is a leap, theologically and philosophically unwarranted and in contradistinction to the salvation-history-based view of classical trinitarian faith. Third, what happens in the world, in history, has reference to God; Trinity and history are related, but inproportionately, since a symmetrical relationship would limit God's freedom. Thus the triune God is not divorced from history; on the contrary, history counts and is 'included' in the 'history of God' not only with regard to salvation history (incarnation, crucifixion, resurrection, ascension) but also creation and the rest of history. This reference to history is the clue to exploring the rise of the doctrine of the Trinity as a distinctively – and thus, particularly – Christian interpretation of God.

Methodologically we have to take the route of Pannenberg and others who ground the doctrine of the Trinity in revelation, in other words, in the way God reveals himself in salvation history. If the doctrine is based on God's self-revelation, it cannot be made an optional appendix but must remain the crux of the exposition of the Christian God. The clue to the doctrine of the Trinity is to discern how the three trinitarian persons come to appearance and relate to each other in the event of revelation as presented in the life and message of Jesus. It is only on the basis of this triune God that Christian statements about the one God and his distinctive 'nature' can be discussed. In the confines of this chapter, a detailed study of the emergence of the doctrine of the Trinity in the New Testament cannot, of course, be attempted. Suffice it to say that its basis is in the self-distinction of the Son from the Father. Jesus' differentiation from and service to the Father and the coming of the Father's kingdom forms the basis for a distinctively Christian doctrine of the Trinity. The Spirit is introduced by virtue of his involvement in God's presence in the work of Jesus and in the fellowship of the Son with the Father, as a constitutive element of the biblical concept of God.

Finally, trinitarian doctrine also rules out the kind of kingdom-centred approaches (of Knitter among others) in which the advancement of the kingdom is set in opposition to or divorced from the Father, Son and Spirit. It is the kingdom of the Father, the coming of which the Son serves as a humble Son in the power of the Spirit. Again, it is negotiable how much 'wider' is the sphere of the kingdom than the church. But however that relationship is defined, I see it as mistaken to divorce the two so much that the church becomes an obstacle to, rather than a God-willed agent that participates in, the kingdom's coming (a concern I expressed regarding Dupuis, while I welcomed his corrective to Knitter; see ch. 3).

If we follow the methodology outlined thus far, the crux of the trinitarian doctrine and its appeal to history centres on Christology with its claim to the incarnation of the Son of God in the man Jesus of Nazareth. But before delving into that central issue, a crucial topic needs to be taken up, namely, the relation of talk about the Christian triune God to god-talk in general. Traditionally, the question has asked what there is in common between the God of the Bible and the god of the philosophers. For Barth, there is no common point between these two discourses. Again, I would rather follow here in the footsteps of Pannenberg. As explained above (ch. 5), even though he insists on the particularity of the doctrine of the Trinity in Christian theology, based on the biblical revelation as it interprets salvation history, there needs to be some correlation between general god-talk and talk about the distinctively Christian trinitarian God. Taking his clue from the fact that in the Bible the term *god* not only serves as a proper name but also as a general designation, he argues that specifically Christian god-talk only makes sense in connection with terms for species. Therefore, to make God-talk intelligible, both in Christian theology and in relation to especially the Jewish faith but also to other (theistic) faiths, Christian theology would be better not to cut off ties to philosophical and religious discourse. This also guards Christian trinitarian talk from 'involuntarily regressing to a situation of a plurality of gods in which Christian talk about God has reference to the specific biblical God as one God among others' (Pannenberg, 1991, p. 69).

The Critical Role of Christology for the Doctrine of the Trinity

As mentioned, our trinitarian approach determines our view of the person and work of Christ and of the Spirit in the Trinity. In Christian theology in general and trinitarian theology in particular, Christology plays a criteriological function. According to Craig Evans's statement:

> Apart from the divine identity of Jesus as the Son there could not be a Trinity – at least not in the traditional Christian sense. The concept of Trinity expresses the idea that the three Persons that make it up are fully divine: God the Father, God the Son, and God the Holy Spirit. (Evans, 2001, p. 29)

Hick's theology of religions is a textbook example of the indispensable role of Christology to our view of the Trinity. Having left behind the biblical and theological parameters of classical Christian Christology, he himself admits to advancing a monistic, nontrinitarian view of God (see e.g. Hick, 1989, p. 271–2, and our discussion in ch. 7 above).

The doctrine of the Trinity cannot stand without a high Christology and a (more or less) classical view of the incarnation; conversely, the view of the Christian God as triune determines one's Christology and pneumatology. Is this a vicious circle where one establishes what one presupposes? No, it is a matter of mutual conditioning and it is based on a methodological choice, currently agreed by all (even though implications vary dramatically based on one's theological orientation). In opposition to 'Christology from above', the dominant approach of Christian theology until the time of the Enlightenment – an approach that presupposed what it sought to establish (i.e. the divinity of Christ) – contemporary scholarship takes the route of 'Christology from below'. That method studies the history of Jesus of Nazareth in the biblical testimonies and tries to discern to what extent interpretations (of the Christ of faith) arise intrinsically from this salvation history. It takes on the task of inquiring into and possibly defending the Christological traditions in which the man Jesus is seen as the Christ. Actually, Christological methodology does not make From Above or From Below an either–or choice, but acknowledges the primacy and criteriological function of the From Below method.[7] Therefore, while in theological research one cannot take for example the Christological titles such as 'Son of Man' or 'Messiah' at face value without inquiring into whether they correspond to the meaning given them by salvation history in the person and work of Jesus of Nazareth, nor can one arbitrarily recast them into new meanings as Hick especially does in his Christology (and as many other pluralists such as Samartha and Panikkar also do).

Again, history matters, since Christian trinitarian doctrine is necessarily based on the history of Jesus of Nazareth and the Old Testament revelation of Yahweh. The incarnation, crucifixion and resurrection, as part of salvation history, are historical events, indispensable parts of salvation history. Dismissing their particularity means dismissing the historical basis for a specifically Christian doctrine of God.

Outdated as it is in postmodern times to resort to a concept as problematic as 'history', I do not see any other way to guard the truth claims and uniqueness of Jesus Christ. I agree with Pannenberg that unless the resurrection can be shown to be a historical event, Christian theology has no court of appeal to determine whether or not Jesus' claims to being the Son of the Father were true.

In regards to incarnation, negotiating between two extremes, namely, Rahner's tendency to downplay the 'newness' of incarnation, the crucifixion and resurrection and Moltmann's desire to read history into the 'development' of God, thus threatening the freedom of God, I want to steer a middle course. Incarnation in Christian theology, based on the biblical salvation history, claims to be a particular event in human history and cannot be extended to mean any kind of divine inspiration (Hick, following D.E.F. Strauss and other Classical Liberals) or only one instance of the realization of the Christic principle (Panikkar). Here I want to go a long way with Heim. He, in contrast to other pluralists, is not willing to give up the historical ground for the emergence of the specifically Christian doctrine of the Trinity. Heim takes the biblical salvation history culminating in the incarnation of the Word as the crucial revelation and act of God, the key to distinguishing the triune God. According to Heim, Christians' belief in the incarnation affirms that in Jesus the trinitarian relations that constitute God's divinity and the external relations between God and humans participate in each other. This does not, of course, necessarily mean limiting God's presence in the world to the particular history of Jesus of Nazareth, but that the history of the man Jesus makes it constitutive and the criterion for discerning God's presence elsewhere. Heim's balanced judgment is worth quoting again:

> The Trinity teaches us that Jesus Christ cannot be an exhaustive or exclusive source for knowledge of God nor the exhaustive and exclusive act of God to save us. Yet the Trinity is unavoidably Christocentric in at least two senses. It is Christocentric in the empirical sense that the doctrine, the representation of God's triune nature, arose historically from faith in Jesus Christ. And it is so in the systematic sense that the personal character of God requires particularity as its deepest mode of revelation. (2001, p. 134)

The only question that needs to be raised concerning this paragraph is the somewhat ambiguous statement according to which Jesus Christ cannot be 'the exhaustive and exclusive act of God to save us'. I am not quite sure what Heim means here, but I fear this statement can be misinterpreted in the way typical pluralistic theologies do, regarding Jesus Christ as one of the saviour figures. Rather than seeing Christ as one saviour figure, biblical revelation and Christian theology can instead attribute salvation to Jesus Christ even when conscious personal faith may not be required to participate in its effects (postconciliar Catholic inclusivism being the most typical representative of this view).

Earlier, I criticized Panikkar's method of postulating a Christic-principle, which he then connects to the history of Jesus of Nazareth and other saviour figures, as an approach that is not methodologically adequate in that it works on the same premise as Christology From Above. It defines the meaning of Christ apart from historical contours and reads the narrative of the Gospels in light of this preconceived 'theology'. I wonder with Ramachandra if Panikkar has drained the word *Christ* of its historical significance in the radical distinction between the Christ of faith and the Jesus of history. While there is no need to 'worship history'[8] neither should we be content with discarding the history of Jesus. For Ramachandra it is

> in the wounds of Jesus that we encounter that which is ultimately real, and it is through his death and resurrection that we are not only led to affirm the value of all human history but brought into a radically new relationship with the ground and goal of that history. (Ramachandra, 1996, pp. 83–4)

Even though there is no need for Christians to have a monopoly on Christ – a Christ only for Christians would not be the Christ of the New Testament, Ramachandra notes – history and universality may not be set in opposition to each other as Panikkar seems to be doing (Ramachandra, 1996, p. 87). Wisely enough, Ramachandra also notes – in contrast to many of his evangelical colleagues – that the problem of particularity should not be confused with the problem of the ultimate status of those who are not Christians. 'The claim that God has revealed his truth in historical events does not entail, at least without further premises, that those who lack this revelation are excluded from the benefits of that revelation' (Ramachandra, 1996, p. 130). The question of the access to salvation, while not totally unrelated to this issue, is a separate issue and should not be made a criterion here.

Divesting Christ of salvation history has other disastrous effects, not only on trinitarian doctrine but also for the encounter between God and humanity. Again, with Ramachandra, I wonder if Panikkar's Christic Theandrism ends up with a nontrinitarian view of the deity. On the one hand, it divests Jesus Christ of full divinity, and on the other hand, it makes the Christian doctrine of the incarnation unintelligible. According to Ramachandra, this leads to the nondualism of Eastern religions in which there is no distinction between the divine and human, and consequently no 'encounter' is possible. Panikkar's nondualistic view of the deity seriously compromises the principle of freedom, both with regard to God and human beings. Even when a mutuality between the divine and human is affirmed, 'within that mutuality there must be room for that about God which is more than the mutual relation, and also room for that about man capable of denying and seeking to distance himself from that mutuality' (Ramachandra, 1996, p. 89).

So far we have been talking mainly about the impossibility of divorcing the Father and Son from each other. Much more could be said of the Father–Spirit and Son–Spirit relation along the same lines. However, rather than reiterating what I have already insisted in my discussion above (with reference to D'Costa and Pannenberg especially), I will rather connect my reflections on the Spirit to the Trinity–church relationship. As background I assume the kind of balanced Spirit-Christology presented by Pinnock (and also Pannenberg, even though he eschews that designation for fear of adoptionism; see chs 6 and 5, respectively).

The Church, the Kingdom and the Presence of the Triune God in the World

In my assessment, one of the greatest advantages of the trinitarian-pneumatological theology of religions of D'Costa is his insistence on the integral relationship between the presence of the Spirit and the Father and Son, which then translates into an integral relationship between the triune God and the church. Over against Dupuis, who tends to see the role of the church as an obstacle to – or at least something to be downplayed for the purposes of – the dialogue with the Other, D'Costa insists that the Holy Spirit's presence within other religions is both intrinsically trinitarian and ecclesiological. It is trinitarian in referring the Holy Spirit's activity to the paschal mystery of Christ, and ecclesial in referring the paschal event to the Spirit's constitutive community-creating force, under the guidance of the Spirit. In light of the wider New Testament teaching (apart from the Paraclete passages on which D'Costa focuses), it can also be said that church is generally described in trinitarian terms and most often in relation to the triune God: people of God, body of Christ, temple of the Spirit. D'Costa's insistence on the close correlation between the triune God and church does not, however, lead to a kind of 'ecclesiocentrism' that is blind to either the Spirit's presence everywhere in the world and creation as the principle of all life or to the Spirit's activity in society and history, peoples, cultures and religions. Yet to insist on the integral relation between the triune God, the church and also the kingdom (since as we noticed above, the kingdom is the kingdom of the triune God) makes one's theology of religions authentically trinitarian.

Two insights from Pannenberg, I believe, help support this trinitarian theology. First of all, Pannenberg, more vocally than any other theologian, has emphasized the principle of continuity between God's works in creation, in salvation, in forming the community of Christ and in eschatology. The one and same Spirit of God, who is the life-principle of all creation, raised Jesus from the dead, dwells as the Spirit of sonship in the hearts of believers, serves with Christ as the foundation of the church, makes possible the believers' participation in the life of the triune God, and acts as the agent of judgment and purification at the eschaton in the coming of the kingdom of God. Thus there is continuity between creation, the new life in faith, the forming of the community of Christ, and the eschaton, the completion of the creation.

The second and consequent insight from Pannenberg points out that the church is the anticipation of the kingdom of God. Therefore its essence is constituted by the kingdom, of which it is the sign. As such, both the kingdom and the church, which serves and participates in its coming, are directed beyond themselves to the unity of humankind under one God. The essential goal of the church is to be a sign and tool of the coming kingdom of God; the church has its end not in itself but in the future of a humanity that is reconciled to God and united by common praise of God in his kingdom (Pannenberg, 1998, p. 45). Pannenberg envisions that '[i]f Christians succeed in solving the problems of their own pluralism, they may be able to produce a model combining pluralism and the widest moral unity which will also be valid for political life' (1977, p. 138). The unity and peace between Christians and between them and their God is a proleptic sign of the renewed humanity. So Pannenberg's trinitarian ecclesiology provides a healthy warning against a typical Protestant view that sees the church primarily as a lifeboat to save individual souls. Interestingly, Pannenberg's vision of the centrality of the church as the instrument of the coming of the kingdom of God also does not make him 'ecclesiocentric' in terms of access to salvation. He represents an inclusivistic position akin to D'Costa and Vatican II. The possibility of salvation is not confined to the church even though Christ, as mentioned, is the norm.

Thus the church always points beyond itself to the eschaton, to the coming of God's kingdom and the unity of all people under one God. This eschatological orientation is also, in my opinion, a critical issue in dealing with the concerns raised by Heim as to whether diversity in the triune God speaks for diverse religious ends.

Communion, Unity and Difference

It is the consensus of contemporary trinitarian theology that communion is the key to understanding the concept of the triune God. This starting point, as our introductory chapter briefly explored, holds not only for Western theology but is also gaining significant support from outside, such as trinitarian theologies in Latin America (Boff, 1988) and Africa (Ogbonnaya, 1994). The triune God as a perichoretic communion is a helpful way to negotiate the dynamic and tension between one and many. Let me take a parallel from a recent African trinitarian theology and the way it negotiates the dynamic between many gods (polytheism) and one god (monotheism). In his work, titled *On Communitarian Divinity: An African Interpretation of the Trinity* (1994), A. Okechukwu Ogbonnaya, building on the foundations of Tertullian, the first (African) trinitarian church father, argues that 'communality is the essence of the gods' (Ogbonnaya, 1994, p. 13; quoting Ilogu, 1974, p. 201). This takes Ogbonnaya naturally to the heart of the debate concerning the understanding of God in African traditional religion: whether it is monotheistic or polytheistic. For Ogbonnaya, these two views are not the only options; he prefers the idea of the Divine conceived of as a community of gods. 'Divine Communalism is the position that the Divine is a community of gods who are fundamentally related to one another and ontologically equal while at the same time distinct from one another by their personhood and function' (1994, p. 23).[9] As part of being related, gods are connected with family, generativity and proliferation. Ogbonnaya summarizes: 'the concept of *the One* is present in African religions, but so also is the concept of *the Many*', and this cannot be called either monotheism or polytheism but communalism (ibid., p. 27).

Shifting this idea of Ogbonnaya to Christian theology of God, we may surmise that trinitarian persons, while ontologically equal,[10] are interrelated in such a way that in their going out to creation and humanity their works are united[11] and in their inner relations they are distinct. Father, Son and Holy Spirit are an interpersonal communion of the Godhead, a communion of love. As D'Costa, Dupuis, Heim and others have emphasized, the Trinity as communion gives room for both genuine diversity (otherwise we could not talk about the Trinity) and unity (otherwise we could not talk about one God).

What, then, are the implications of this communion theology for our theology of religions? Here I want to focus just on one crucial point raised up by Heim, since I see that as a paradigmatic case. In chapter 9 I criticized Heim's proposal of the legitimacy of various religious ends on the basis of diversity in the triune God as a mistaken interpretation of the Trinity. Here, I do not reiterate the problems I mentioned there regarding biblical teaching and theological tradition. I only want to focus my criticism on the understanding of God as communion and its relation to God's eschatological purposes in bringing about the new creation. It seems to me that the idea of diversity of religious ends is neither a legitimate nor desirable vision in a trinitarian theology of religions. In terms of logic, as I mentioned before, Heim's leap from the diversity in the godhead to the diversity in religious ends willed by God is far from obvious. I believe there is a more helpful way to account for the diversity-in-unity in the Trinity. But first, let me take an example from the doctrine of creation. That creation, according to Christian theology, is the work of the triune God, does not entail several 'origins' or 'goals' of creation, but one single origin and goal arising from the fact that outward works of the Trinity are undivided. I realize the example is limited and may be misleading, but it makes my point: diversity in the 'personhood' of God does not speak for the diversity of the ends.

Theologically, the leap is even more problematic, especially in terms of eschatology. Heim anticipated this objection and tried to respond to it, but I do not find his response satisfactory. It seems to me that positing more than one 'salvation' ends up either truncating the concept of salvation to the point that it never achieves its final goal (communion with God) or frustrates God's purposes, the biblical vision of God's people gathered together under one God. Keeping in mind what I mentioned about the role of the church as the sign of the kingdom, pointing to the unity of all humanity under one God based on Pannenberg's ecumenical theology-of-religions vision, let me refer to another ecclesiologist who takes his clue from eschatology. Miroslav Volf, in his trinitarian ecclesiology *After Our Likeness: The Church as the Image of the Trinity* (1998), connects the church to the coming of the kingdom and new creation. The future of the church in God's new creation is the mutual personal indwelling of the triune God and of his glorified people according to the vision of the apocalyptic seer in Revelation chapters 21 and 22. Echoing (but not giving any reference to) Pannenberg's principle of continuity in all God's work, especially when it comes to the Spirit of God, Volf envisions the future of the church in this way:

> Wherever the Spirit of Christ, which as the eschatological gift anticipates God's new creation in history (see Rom. 8:23; 2 Cor. 1:22; Col. 1:12–20), is present in

> its *ecclesially constitutive* activity, there is the church. The Spirit unites the
> gathered congregation with the triune God and integrates it into a history
> extending from Christ, indeed, from the Old Testament saints, to the
> eschatological new creation. This Spirit-mediated relationship with the triune
> God ... constitutes an assembly into a church. (1998, p. 129)

This vision of Volf and Pannenberg fits the idea of the triune God as communion,
drawing all into a perichoretic communion where identity is affirmed by the
participation in one divine life and differences embraced, reflecting the diversity-in-
unity in the triune godhead. That not all people will attain this eternal communion –
unless one is universalist, which neither Heim nor the majority of Christian
theologians are – is a fact to be reckoned with, and I am more than ready to admit
that it poses problems with which Christian eschatology has yet to struggle (such as
whether it is another kind of frustration of God's final goal if not all his creatures,
created in his image, will reach the goal). Yet – and here comes the crux of the matter
– it is one thing to say that not all will attain the goal of participating in the eternal
communion under one God and another to make that a theological programme. It is
here that I think Heim fails most dramatically. Even if one could legitimately
presuppose the possibility of a diversity of religious ends on the basis of the diversity
in the triune God (a view that I do not see founded), one should still ask if this is the
goal or ideal. Most theologians – and the whole Christian tradition – says 'no'.

Heim suggests that what makes his proposal viable is the (alleged) presence of
the triune God with people at various 'levels' of salvations. God's presence, as he
gathers from Dante and other sources, is not absent even from hell. This contains at
least three problems. First of all, I am not convinced that Dante's vision here is
biblically or theologically sound. My reading of biblical references to the afterlife,
especially from the Old Testament, gives exactly the opposite impression.[12] Second,
even if God's presence were found in other ends than the new creation, would it then
be a comforting, desirable presence? Wouldn't it be rather a threatening reminder of
the loss of eternal communion? Or, if one is the supporter of conditional immortality
(annihilationism), doesn't missing the communion with God naturally lead to the
'eternal death', loss of survival? Another problem, even if there were various levels
to salvations, an idea that is virtually unknown in Christian tradition, is that it would
seem to lead to an idea of 'temporal' solutions not unlike purgatory. Would those
other ends really be 'final'? If not, what then would be the final 'final'?

In sum, it seems to me that Heim's proposal, in many ways creative and helpful
(in that it elevates the biblical-theological doctrine of the Christian doctrine of the
Trinity to the centre of theology of religions), creates many more problems than it
solves and is therefore unacceptable.

What then, is the significance of unity-in-diversity for the triune communion to
Christian theology of religions? Rather than speaking for varying religious ends, it
speaks to the topic of how to relate to the Other. It then has implications for the
interfaith dialogue.

Trinity, Communion and the Religious Other

In the Christian West, the Other until the sixteenth century was 'pagan', during the Age of Reason 'unenlightened', in the nineteenth century 'primitive', in the twentieth century 'different' (McGrane, 1989). According to Vanhoozer (1997, p. 43), in our times, 'the Other is first and foremost a hermeneutical problem, an often intractable interpretive challenge that resists our faltering attempts to understand it'.

Barth was on the right track when he tied the knowledge of God to the self-revelation of the triune God to human beings. It is only when the triune God reveals himself, lets human beings, the Other, enter into a saving communion and thus draws human beings into his own self-knowledge, that the human person can know God. This opening up of communion serves as the paradigm for relating to the Other among human beings too. It is not about denying differences nor eliminating distinctions, but about encountering the Other in a mutually learning, yet challenging atmosphere. The Christian, coming from a particular perspective, is both encouraged and entitled to witness to the triune God of the Bible and his saving will, yet at the same time prepared to learn from the Other. This helps the Christian to get to know the Other and may also lead to the deepening of one's own faith. D'Costa's quotation is worth quoting again here: 'The other is always interesting in their difference and may be the possible face of God, or the face of violence, greed, and death. Furthermore, the other may teach Christians to know and worship their own trinitarian God more truthfully and richly'. D'Costa believes that trinitarian Catholic theology provides the 'context for a critical, reverent, and open engagement with otherness, without any predictable outcome' (D'Costa, 2000, p. 9).

I further agree with D'Costa that other religions are not salvific as such, but other religions are important for the Christian church in that they help the church to penetrate more deeply into the divine mystery. This is the essence of what D'Costa calls the Spirit's call to 'relational engagement'. The acknowledgment of the gifts of God in other religions by virtue of the presence of the Spirit – as well as the critical discernment of these gifts by the power of the same Spirit – means a real trinitarian basis to Christianity's openness towards other religions. It also ties the church to the dialogue with the Other: wherever the presence of the Spirit – and thus the presence of God – is to be found it is not unrelated to the church. Thus the discernment of the activity of the Holy Spirit within other religions must also bring the church more truthfully into the presence of the triune God. Again, citing D'Costa, 'if the Spirit is at work in the religions, then the gifts of the Spirit need to be discovered, fostered, and received into the church. If the church fails to be receptive, it may be unwittingly practicing cultural and religious idolatry' (D'Costa, 2000, p. 115). The church had better be ready for surprises since a priori, there is no knowing what beauty, truth, holiness and other 'gifts' may be waiting for the church (D'Costa, 2000, p. 133).

What about the highly valued virtue of tolerance? Quoting Alan Levine, according to whom toleration 'is one of the most attractive and widespread ideals of our day', Harold Netland (2001, p. 145) notes that in the popular consciousness, tolerance and pluralism are linked in the perception that particularism is inherently intolerant of other faiths whereas pluralism is appropriately tolerant. But this has a significant corollary. More recently the meaning of tolerance has changed so that to be tolerant of another religion is often regarded as a matter of not saying anything negative about that religion. In addition, scepticism about the possibility of determining truth in the midst of competing religious claims, the breakdown of traditional community life that had sustained common visions of the true and the good, rampant consumerism and individualism that feed upon pragmatism – all of this encourages an uncritical tolerance that refuses to make negative judgments about alternative beliefs and practices (Netland, 2001, pp. 142–5).

But appearances may be misleading. As D'Costa argues, tolerance does not mean ignoring differences or distinctions but taking seriously the challenge of difference, thus taking history seriously. It is good to keep in mind that the root meaning of the term 'tolerance' in Latin (*tollere*) denotes bearing a burden. Pluralisms do not require tolerance, since they have already made up their minds. Neither does exclusivism have much use for it. In contrast, those who work within the trinitarian unity-in-diversity paradigm need to listen patiently to the Other, discern where they are right and where they err, as well as their own truth and errors, and still affirm the Other even with their differences. Christians do not own the truth but, as Newbigin reminds us, are witness to the truth in the triune God. Witnessing is as much listening and sharing as speaking and invitation. It is tolerant in that it affirms the Other, and it is passionate in that it believes itself to be witnessing to truth with the universal intention that pertains to all men and women and hopes for a common destiny. This is, I believe, the way to approach interfaith dialogue from the perspective of a trinitarian theology.

Implications for Interfaith Dialogue

In my assessment of Barth's theology of religions with its potential for interfaith dialogue (ch. 2), I commended several things that Trevor Hart's incisive interpretation brought to light. While I leave it to Barth specialists to decide how much of these insights really come from Barth and how much they come from Hart's interpretation, coupled with his use of Newbigin and Polanyi, those guidelines are most helpful in light of the trinitarian outline of the theology of religions I am developing here. Even though knowledge of God, based on the self-revelation of the triune God, comes only from a certain perspective, it still has a universal intention and is to be shared with all. Rather than mythologizing or ignoring central tenets of Christian faith such as the Trinity, incarnation and resurrection, they are to be regarded as truths presented to people of other faiths in the spirit of a humble, yet confident witness. There is no room for arrogance or rejection of others, but rather only for humility and respect, since as Hart (1997, p. 139) paraphrases Barth, the person giving the witness is 'a sinner among sinners, who feels that his own glass home is rather too fragile for him to be throwing any stones'. Furthermore, the Christian knows that his or her own religion is under the judgment of religions and that he or she has the potential of learning more from the encounter with the Other.

The purpose of the dialogue is not only to learn and share but also to persuade the Other (contra Dupuis and pluralists), yet in ways that honour the Other and give him or her the right to make up his or her own mind. The Christian and followers of other religions come to the dialogue table with convictions, the truth of which they are convinced. They are witnesses to the answers to the ultimate questions, answers they believe to be true. In that sense, religious dialogue is more than what Pannenberg envisions, an exercise done by more or less 'neutral' researchers into the world religions' truth claims. It does not necessarily entail a sense of superiority, yet one can only persuade the Other to change his or her allegiance if one is convinced of being a witness to the truth with universal intention. Even then, as Pannenberg reminds us, with full conviction of the truth of the Christian message, anchored in the triune God, there is still the sense of provisionality. Even if the resurrection of the Son is *the* proleptic confirmation of the truth claims of Jesus of Nazareth, it is only at the eschaton that the God of the Bible will be all in all. The dialogue process becomes a real *process*, as noted above (ch. 5). The dialogue process may shape the understanding and conviction of the participants, or one may wonder if it is a true dialogue at all, but rather two or more monologues.

In the final analysis, trinitarian faith and the 'scandal of particularity' of Christian faith are not to be thought of as opposites. According to Ramachandra (1996, p. 233), this is 'a particularity that God takes seriously in his dealings with his creatures'. God chose a nation to be the bearer of the cosmic history to the rest, and one mediator to include all. Thus incarnation is geared toward universality. Particularity is for the purpose of universality, not exclusion. Therefore, the Christian faith has always been a missionary faith. Missionary urgency flows from the very logic of the incarnation, death and resurrection of the Messiah of all peoples (Ramachandra, 1996, ch. 7). As an Asian theologian, Ramachandra further argues that the normativeness of Jesus, inherent in trinitarian faith, rather than being something foreign imposed on Asian religions, in fact, 'safeguards some of the legitimate concerns of contemporary Asian theologians' (ibid., p. 216). Unlike the major Asian religions, Christianity, for example, takes seriously the cause of the poor, fully endorses the equality of all persons created in the image of God, and celebrates humility and self-sacrificial life and service, among other things. The 'gospel humanity' results in the creation of a new human community that celebrates plurality under one God.

Final Reflections

In this last chapter I have not been able to solve the riddle of the relationship between the doctrine of the Trinity and other religions. What I have tried to accomplish is to make more explicit the underlying convictions and understandings that have guided my critical dialogue with leading trinitarian theologians across the ecumenical, theological and cultural borders, as well as point to the tasks for future work in this area.

My all too brief outline has not only been very general in nature but also selective. For example, I have not even touched the question of salvation, not because I do not consider it a worthy question, but because I believe there is only one major divide theologically, and that is the one between pluralists and the rest. My general dissatisfaction with pluralism includes critique of their either too general view of salvation (the 'self-realization' of Hick) or too particularist (the eco-liberation of Knitter). I side with Pannenberg and others who argue that the transcendental aspects should not be dismissed from the biblical view of salvation and that there is one religious end with two destinies, however one sorts out the classical battles, say, between defenders of hell or annihilationism. Regarding access to salvation, it is clear that among the defenders of classical trinitarian faith two kinds of opinions can be maintained: the inclusivistic orientations of Vatican II, mainline Protestants or some evangelicals (Pinnock among others), on the one hand, and more exclusivistic views such as those of many evangelicals, even though a majority sides with the inclusivists. Universalism of various sorts from Barth to pluralists, as well as the idea of varying religious ends as God-willed, legitimate goals, work against Christian tradition and trinitarian faith that honour differences (even to the point of letting people say 'no' to God) but envision a unified goal, one people of God under one God.

Many tasks such as the following are left for the future: what exactly is the relationship between the Spirit and Jesus Christ in the outward works of the triune God in the world? Is a distinctively 'pneumatological' theology of religions needed as complementing the older, now much rejected 'Christological' or should we only aim at a trinitarian one?[13] Are there various forms of trinitarian theologies of religions that are biblical and theologically sound? If so, what are the essential criteria for their soundness (other than those discussed above)?

An appropriate conclusion to our study is offered by Vanhoozer in the book he recently edited, *The Trinity in a Pluralistic Age*:

> ... the Trinity is the Christian answer to the identity of God. The one creator God is Father, Son, and Spirit. This is an identification that is at once exclusivistic and pluralistic.[14] And because this God who is three-in-one has covenanted with what is other than himself—the creature—the identity of God is also inclusivistic. The Trinity, far from being a *skandalon* [stumbling block], is rather the transcendental condition for interreligious dialogue, the ontological condition that permits us to take the other in all seriousness, without fear, and without violence. (Vanhoozer, 1997, pp. 70–71)

Notes

1   Amnell (1999, p. 63) and McGrath (1996, pp. 200–209). Berger (1980, pp. 119–20) has raised the legitimate question: what gives the modern interpreter a superior knowledge concerning ancient religions? The Finnish theologian M.T. Amnell (1999, pp. 57–60), in his critical work on Hick's pluralism, rightly notes that the question relates directly to the sensitive issue of interpretation. Interpretation always begins with some kind of preunderstanding (H.-G. Gadamer) that is then being corrected in light of further experiences and insights. The Enlightenment dream of presuppositionless interpretation is just a dream; Hick's presumptuous reinterpretation of world religions, over against their own self-understanding, does not in fact represent a pluralism of freedom but borders on hegemony. In other words, it shows that the self-understanding of religions is 'wrong' and has to be corrected by the 'right' understanding of the modern interpreter. This of course violates the very principle of pluralism. Jenson (1995, p. 25) similarly notes that the type of pluralism advocated by Hick ends up becoming a normative rule of what is and is not acceptable in various religions.

2   See further D'Costa (2000, part I), in which he dialogues with Jewish, neo-Hindu and Tibetan Buddhist pluralists and shows that all of these pluralisms, with all their seemingly tolerant mindsets, have a built-in tendency to regard their own religion as *the* religion.

3   Risto Saarinen (1995, pp. 150–56) has similarly noted that Hick's two-level model in which the surface level consists of unimportant differences and the deeper level of a unified core is problematic both epistemologically and phenomenologically. How do we know that there really is something below the 'surface'? In addition, religions by their very nature are not only theories about life and death, but also 'supertheories' that make assumptions about something absolute, something true. There is no going beyond these supertheories in the way Hick has wanted to do.

4   For a brief exposition of Newbigin's position, see Kärkkäinen (2003a, ch. 25). Newbigin's main ideas are expressed in the collection of essays titled *The Gospel in a Pluralist Society* (1989).

5   Is the view that I am advancing here a typical form of foundationalism, believed to be left behind with the advent of postmodernity? (The term *foundationalism* as a technical philosophical term simply denotes the belief that there must be universal and common foundations for anything claimed to be valid. Two kinds of foundationalisms are usually identified: rationalistic, owing to the heritage of Descartes, which requires that all truth claims must base themselves on universally agreed conceptual foundations, and empiricist, which bases its certainty on some form of data of experience – difficult as the whole concept in itself is philosophically).

It has become fashionable to identify oneself as nonfoundationalist, as if foundationalism in itself must be totally unacceptable to a thinker living in postmodernity. An appealing way to claim to avoid foundationalism is to appeal to narrative theology like that of Ronald Thiemann's widely discussed book with a telling subtitle, *Revelation and Theology: The Gospel as Narrated Promise* (1987). This detour, however, is not as adequate as one might expect. I agree with the late Colin Gunton (1997, p. 90) that to base a theology in narrative is to preclude any discussion of the grounds for preferring one narrative to another. In order to prefer one narrative as something with a claim to 'universal' truth, one needs to appeal to some 'foundations', yet one can do so without being a naïve foundationalist either in its rationalistic or empiricist form. Christian trinitarian faith, in my understanding, seeks to find outside the human person the grounds for preferring one narrative over another, that is, in the biblical salvation-history which narrates the history of the triune God in sending the Son in the power of the Spirit to save the world and bring it into an eternal communion. If that is foundationalism, so be it. At the same time, no religious claim, certainly no form of pluralism, is void of 'foundations' in the sense that all kinds of truth claims, even those that claim to be nontruth claims, are perspectival and come from a particular viewpoint.

6   In this study, we have not discussed the novel idea of the Trinity by Smart and Konstantine (1991). Suffice it to say that it is an attempt to bring together elements from various religions combined with quite idiosyncratic new concepts created by the two authors.

7   As stalwart a defender of the critical-historical method and the From Below approach as
     Pannenberg, in his mature thinking, argues for the necessity of combining these two approaches, yet
     giving priority and primacy to the From Below (see further, Pannenberg, 1994, pp. 278–9).
8   This is a reference to Panikkar's concern according to which classical theology and Christology
     From Below 'worship history'.
9   For the consideration of monotheistic and polytheistic views, see Ogbonnaya (1994, pp. 14–23).
10   There is, of course, a debate between Eastern Orthodox theologies with their idea of the Father as
     the monarchy and source of the Trinity, and theology espousing the social doctrine of the Trinity,
     whose most vocal proponent recently has been Moltmann, who eschews any idea of the primacy of
     the Father. This debate, which we cannot enter here, does not in my opinion determine the views
     taken in theology of religions as far as our discussion is concerned.
11   This is the essence of the classical rule, attributed to St Augustine, according to which outward
     works of the Trinity are undivided.
12   For starters, see the balanced, careful treatment of biblical materials related to eschatology in
     Schwarz (2000, pp. 31–96).
13   See further, Yong (2003) for a distinctively pneumatological theology of religions.
14   Here I do not find the term *pluralistic* helpful for the simple reason that the term is already used in
     such a variety of ways that adding one more, in this case Vanhoozer's quite idiosyncratic definition,
     only adds to the confusion. A term like *inclusivistic*, even though that term is also widely used, may
     better serve the purposes of this quotation; in fact, that is the way Vanhoozer defines his term
     'pluralistic' in what follows in the same quotation.

Bibliography

Ahlstrand, K. (1993), *Fundamental Openness: An Enquiry into Raimundo Panikkar's Theological Vision and its Presuppositions*, Studia Missionalia Upsaliensia LVII, Uppsala: Uppsala University.

Amnell, M.T. (1999), *Uskontojen Universumi: John Hickin uskonnollisen pluralismin haaste ja siitä käyty keskustelu*, Vammala: Suomalaisen Teologisen Kirjallisuusseuran julkaisuja 217 [*The Universe of Faiths: The challenge of John Hick's religious pluralism, and the debate it has inspired*, University of Helsinki].

Anderson, G.A. & Stransky, T.F. (eds) (1975), *Mission Trends No. 2: Evangelization*, New York: Paulist.

Anderson, N. (1984), *Christianity and World Religions: The Challenge of Pluralism*, Downers Grove, Ill.: InterVarsity Press.

Badcock, G. (1997), 'Karl Rahner, the Trinity, and pluralism', in Vanhoozer, K.J. (ed.), *The Trinity in a Pluralistic Age: Theological Essays on Culture and Religion*, Grand Rapids, Mich.: Eerdmans, pp. 143–54.

Balthasar, H.U. von (1979), *The Theology of Karl Barth*, New York: Holt, Rinehart & Winston.

Barth, K. (1956–75), *Church Dogmatics*, edited and translated by G. Bromiley and T.F. Torrance, Edinburgh: T. & T. Clark.

Berger, P.L. (1980), *The Heretical Imperative*, London: Collins.

Boff, L. (1988), *Trinity and Society*, Maryknoll, NY: Orbis/Wellwood; London: Burns & Oates.

Boyd, G.A. (2000), *God of the Possible: A Biblical Introduction to the Open View of God*, Grand Rapids, Mich.: Baker Academic Books.

Braaten, C.E. (1988), 'The place of Christianity among the world religions: Wolfhart Pannenberg's theology of religion and the history of religions', in Braaten, C.E. & Clayton, P. (eds), *The Theology of Wolfhart Pannenberg: Twelve American Critiques with an Autobiographical Response*, Minneapolis: Augsburg, pp. 287–312.

—— (1992), *No Other Gospel? Christianity Among the World's Religions*, Minneapolis: Augsburg Fortress.

Bracken, Joseph A. & Suchocki, Marjorie Hewitt (eds) (1997), *Trinity in Process: A Relational Theology of God*, New York: Continuum.

Brunner, E. (1949), *The Christian Doctrine of God*, London: Lutterworth.

Bunyan, J. (1962), *Grace Abounding to the Chief of Sinners*, ed. Robert Sharrock, New York: Oxford University Press.

Chung, P.S. (2002), *Martin Luther and Buddhism: Aesthetics of Suffering*, Eugene, Ore.: Wipf & Stock.

Clendenin, D.B. (1995), *Many Gods, Many Lords*, Grand Rapids, Mich.: Baker.

Cobb, J.B., Jr. (1996), 'Metaphysical pluralism', in Prabhu, J. (ed.), *The Intercultural Challenge of Raimon Panikkar*, Maryknoll, NY: Orbis, pp. 46–57.

Cousins, E.H. (1996), 'Panikkar's Advaitic Trinitarianism', in Prabhu, J. (ed.), *The Intercultural Challenge of Raimon Panikkar*, Maryknoll, NY: Orbis, pp. 119–30.

Davis, S.T. (1999), 'John Hick on incarnation and Trinity', in Davis, S.T., Kendall, D. & O'Collins, G. (eds), *The Trinity*, Oxford: Oxford University Press, pp. 251–72.

Dayton, D.W. (1990), Karl Barth and wider ecumenism', in Phan, P. (ed.), *Christianity and the Wider Ecumenism*, New York: Paragon House, pp. 181–90.

D'Costa, G. (1986), *Theology and Religious Pluralism: The Challenge of Other Religions*, Oxford: Basil Blackwell.

—— (1993), 'Christian theology of religions: An evaluation of John Hick and Paul Knitter', *Studia Missionalia* **42**, pp. 161–78.

—— (2000), *The Meeting of Religions and the Trinity*, Maryknoll, NY: Orbis.

Dunn, J.D.G. (1980), *Christology in the Making*, Philadelphia: Westminster Press.

Dupuis, J. (1991), *Jesus Christ at the Encounter of World Religions*, Maryknoll, NY: Orbis.

—— (1994), *Who Do You Say I Am? Introduction to Christology*, Maryknoll, NY: Orbis.

—— (1997), *Toward a Christian Theology of Religious Pluralism*, Maryknoll, NY: Orbis.

—— (1999), '"The truth will make you free": The theology of religious pluralism revisited', *Louvain Studies* **24**, pp. 211–63.

Durrant, M. (1973), *Theology and Intelligibility*, London: Routledge & Kegan Paul.

Evans, Craig A. (2001), 'Jesus' self-designation "the Son of Man" and the recognition of his divinity', in Davis, S.T., Kendall, D. & O'Collins, G. (eds), *The Trinity*, Oxford: Oxford University Press, pp. 29–47.

Fulljames, P. (1993), *God and Creation in Intercultural Perspective: Dialogue between the Theologies of Barth, Dickson, Pobee, Nyamiti and Pannenberg*, Frankfurt: Peter Lang.

Geivett, D.R. & Phillips, W.G. (1995), 'A particularist view: An evidentialist approach', in Ockholm, D.L. & Phillips, T.R. (eds), *More Than One Way: Four Views on Salvation in a Pluralistic World*, Grand Rapids, Mich.: Zondervan, pp. 211–45.

Glasser, A. (1981), 'A paradigm shift? Evangelicals and interreligious dialogue', *Missiology* **9**, pp. 392–408.

Grenz, S.J. (1989), 'Commitment and dialogue: Pannenberg on Christianity and the religions', *Journal of Ecumenical Studies* **26** (1), pp. 196–234.

—— (1990), *Reason for Hope: The Systematic Theology of Wolfhart Pannenberg*, New York: Oxford University Press.

—— (1994), 'Toward an evangelical theology of the religions', *Journal of Ecumenical Studies* **31**, pp. 49–65.

—— (2001), *The Social God and the Relational Self: A Trinitarian Theology of the Imago Dei*, Louisville, Ky: Westminster John Knox Press.

Grenz, S.J. & Olson, R.E. (1992) *Twentieth Century Theology: God and the World in a Transitional Age*, Downers Grove, Ill.: InterVarsity Press.

Griffiths Paul J. (1990), 'The uniqueness of Christian doctrine defended', in D'Costa, G. (ed.), *Christian Uniqueness Reconsidered: The Myth of a Pluralistic Theology of Religions*, Maryknoll, NY: Orbis, pp. 157–73.

Gunton, Colin (1997), 'The Trinity, natural theology and a theology of nature', in Vanhoozer, K.J. (ed.) *The Trinity in a Pluralistic Age: Theological Essays on Culture and Religion*, Grand Rapids, Mich.: Eerdmans, pp. 88–103.

Hart, T. (1997), 'Karl Barth, the Trinity, and pluralism', in Vanhoozer, K. (ed.), *The Trinity in a Pluralistic Age: Theological Essays on Culture and Religion*, Grand Rapids, Mich.: Eerdmans, pp. 124–42.

Heim, S.M. (1995), *Salvations: Truth and Difference in Religion*, Maryknoll, NY: Orbis.

—— (2001), *The Depth of the Riches: A Trinitarian Theology of Religious Ends*, Grand Rapids, Mich.: Eerdmans.

Hick, J. (1970), 'The reconstruction of Christian belief for today and tomorrow: 1 and 2', *Theology* **73**, pp. 339–45, 399–405.

—— (1973), *God and the Universe of Faiths: Essays in the Philosophy of Religion*, London: Macmillan (2nd edn 1977).

—— (1980), *God Has Many Names: Britain's New Religious Pluralism*, London: Macmillan; Philadelphia: Westminster.

—— (1983), Hick, *The Second Christianity* (3rd enl. edn of *Christianity at the Centre*), London: SCM Press.

—— (1987), 'The non-absoluteness of Christianity', in Hick, J. & Knitter, P.F. (eds), *The Myth of Christian Uniqueness: Toward a Pluralistic Theology of Religions*, Maryknoll, NY: Orbis, pp. 16–36.

—— (1988), *Problems of Religious Pluralism*, London: Macmillan.

—— (1989), *An Interpretation of Religion: Human Response to the Transcendent, Gifford Lectures 1986–87*, London: Macmillan.

—— (1990), 'Rethinking Christian doctrine in the light of religious pluralism', in Phan, P.C. (ed.), *Christianity and the Wider Ecumenism*, New York: Paragon House, pp. 89–102.

—— (1993), *The Metaphor of God Incarnate: Christ and Christology in a Pluralistic Age*, London: SCM Press.

—— (1995), *The Rainbow of Faiths: Critical Dialogues on Religious Pluralism*, London: SCM Press; American edition: *Christian Theology of Religious Pluralism*, Louisville, Ky: Westminster.

—— (1997), 'The possibility of religious pluralism: A reply to Gavin D'Costa', *Religious Studies* **33**, pp. 161–6.

Hunsinger, G. (1991), *How to Read Karl Barth: The Shape of His Theology*, New York: Oxford University Press.

Ilogu, Edmund (1974), *Christianity and Igbo Culture*, New York: NOK Press.

Jenson, R.W. (1995), 'The God-wars', in Braaten, C.E. & Jenson, R. (eds), *Either/Or: The Gospel or Neopaganism*, Grand Rapids, Mich.: Eerdmans, pp. 23–36.

John Paul II (1991), *Redemptoris Missio: On the Permanent Validity of the Church's Missionary Mandate*, Chicago, US Catholic Conference.

——— (1994), *Crossing the Threshold of Hope*, London: Jonathan Cape.

Jukko, R. (2001), *Trinitarian Theology in Christian–Muslim Encounters: Theological Foundations of the Work of the French Roman Catholic Church's Secretariat for Relations with Islam Trinitarian Theology in Christian–Muslim Encounters*, Helsinki: Luther-Agricola-Society.

Kärkkäinen, V.-M. (2002), *Pneumatology: The Holy Spirit in Ecumenical, International, and Contextual Perspectives*, Grand Rapids, Mich.: Baker Academic Books.

——— (2003a), *An Introduction to Theology of Religions: Biblical, Historical, and Contemporary Perspectives*, Grand Rapids, Mich.: Baker Academic Books.

——— (2003b), '"The universe of faiths": The theological challenges of John Hick's religious pluralism', *Dharma Deepika* January–June, pp. 5–16.

Kasimow, H. (1999), 'Introduction: John Paul II and interreligious dialogue: An overview', in Shelwin, Byron L. & Kasimow, H. (eds), *John Paul II and Interreligious Dialogue*, Maryknoll, NY: Orbis, pp. 1–23.

Kasper, W. (1984), *The God of Jesus Christ*, New York: Crossroad.

Kaufmann, G.D. (1993), 'Religious diversity and religious truth', in Sharma, A. (ed.), *Religious Diversity and Religious Truth: Festschrift to John Hick*, New York: St. Martin's Press.

Knitter, P.F. (1977), *Toward a Protestant Theology of Religions: A Critical Survey of Christian Attitudes Toward the World Religions*, Maryknoll, NY: Orbis.

——— (1985), *No Other Name? A Critical Survey of Christian Attitudes Toward the World Religions*, Maryknoll, NY: Orbis.

——— (1995), *One Earth, Many Religions: Multifaith Dialogue and Global Responsibility*, Maryknoll, NY: Orbis.

——— (1996a), 'Cosmic confidence or preferential option?', in Prabhu, J. (ed.), *The Intercultural Challenge of Raimon Panikkar*, Maryknoll, NY: Orbis, pp. 177–91.

——— (1996b), *Jesus and the Other Names: Christian Mission and Global Responsibility*, Maryknoll, NY: Orbis.

——— (2002), *Introducing Theologies of Religions*, Maryknoll, NY: Orbis.

Kraemer, H. (1938), *The Christian Message in a Non-Christian World*, London: Edinburgh House Press; New York: Harper & Row.

Kreiner, A. (1996), 'Philosophische Probleme der pluralistischen Religionstheologie', in Schwager, Raymund (ed.), *Die Streit um die pluralistische Religionstheologie*, Freiburg in Bresgau: Herder, pp. 118–31.

Krieger, D.J. (1996), 'Methodological foundations for interreligious dialogue', in Prabhu, J. (ed.), *The Intercultural Challenge of Raimon Panikkar*, Maryknoll, NY: Orbis, pp. 201–23.

LaCugna, C.M. (1992), *God For Us: The Trinity and Christian Life*, San Francisco: HarperSanFrancisco.

Lanzetta, B.J. (1996), 'The mystical basis of Panikkar's thought', in Prabhu, J. (ed.), *The Intercultural Challenge of Raimon Panikkar*, Maryknoll, NY: Orbis, pp. 91–105.

Larson, G.J. (1996), 'Contra pluralism', in Prabhu, J. (ed.), *The Intercultural Challenge of Raimon Panikkar*, Maryknoll, NY: Orbis, pp. 71–87.

MacIntyre, A. (1981), *After Virtue: A Study in Moral Theory*, Notre Dame, Ind.: University of Notre Dame (London: Duckworth, 1985).

—— (1988), *Whose Justice? Which Rationality?* Notre Dame, Ind.: University of Notre Dame; London: Duckworth.

McGrane, B. (1989), *Beyond Anthropology: Society and the Other*, New York: Columbia University Press.

McGrath, A. (1996), 'Conclusion', in Okholm, D.L. & Phillips, T.R. (eds), *Four Views on Salvation in a Pluralistic World*, Grand Rapids, Mich.: Zondervan, pp. 200–209.

Milbank, J. (1990a), 'The end of dialogue', in D'Costa, G. (ed.), *Christian Uniqueness Reconsidered: The Myth of a Pluralistic Theology of Religions*, Maryknoll, NY: Orbis, pp. 174–91.

—— (1990b), *Theology and Social Theory*, Oxford: Blackwell.

Miller, E.D. & Grenz, S.J. (1998), *Fortress Introduction to Contemporary Theologies*, Minneapolis: Fortress.

Moltmann, J. (1981), *The Trinity and the Kingdom of God: The Doctrine of God*, London: SCM Press.

—— (1990), 'Is "pluralistic theology" useful for the dialogue of world religions', in D'Costa (ed.), *Christian Uniqueness Reconsidered: The Myth of a Pluralistic Theology of Religions*, Maryknoll, NY: Orbis, pp. 149–56.

Moule, C.F.D (1977), *The Origin of Christology*, Cambridge, UK: Cambridge University Press.

Netland, Harold (2001), *Encountering Religious Pluralism: The Challenge to Christian Faith & Mission*, Downers Grove, Ill.: InterVarsity Press.

Newbigin, L. (1989), *The Gospel in a Pluralist Society*, Geneva: WCC; Grand Rapids, Mich.: Eerdmans.

—— (1991), *Truth to Tell: The Gospel as Public Truth*, Grand Rapids, Mich.: Eerdmans.

—— (1997), 'Trinity as public truth', in Vanhoozer, K.J. (ed.), *The Trinity in a Pluralistic Age: Theological Essays on Culture and Religion*, Grand Rapids, Mich.: Eerdmans, pp. 1–8.

O'Collins, G. (1983), *Interpreting Jesus*, Mahwah, NJ: Paulist Press.

Ogbonnaya, A.O. (1994), *On Communitarian Divinity: An African Interpretation of the Trinity*, New York: Paragon House.

Olson, R.E. & Hall, C.A. (2002), *The Trinity*, Grand Rapids, Mich.: Eerdmans.

Panikkar, R. (1964), *The Unknown Christ of Hinduism*, Darton, Longman & Todd.

—— (1973), *The Trinity and the Religious Experience of Man: Icon-Person-Mystery*, Maryknoll, NY: Orbis Books; London: Darton, Longman & Todd (also known as *The Trinity and the World Religions*).

—— (1975), 'Verstehen als Uberzeugtsein', in Gadamer, H.-G. & Vogler, P. (eds), *Neue Anthropologie*, Philosophische Anthropologie 7, Stuttgart: Thieme, pp. 132–67.

—— (1977), '*Colligite Fragmenta*: For an integration of reality', in F.A. Eigo and S.E. Fittipaldi (eds.), *From Alienation to At-Oneness*, Villanova, PA: Villanova University Press.

—— (1978), *The Intrareligious Dialogue*, New York: Paulist Press.

—— (1979), 'The myth of pluralism: The tower of Babel—A meditation on non-violence', *Cross Currents* **29** (2), pp. 197–230.

—— (1981), *The Unknown Christ of Hinduism*, rev. edn, Maryknoll, NY: Orbis.

—— (1987a), 'The Jordan, the Tiber and the Ganges. Three kairological moments of Christic self-consciousness', in Hick, J. & Knitter, P.F. (eds), *The Myth of Christian Uniqueness: Toward a Pluralistic Theology of Religions*, Maryknoll, NY: Orbis, pp. 89–116.

—— (1987b), 'Invisible harmony: A universal theory of religion or a cosmic confidence in reality?', in L. Swidler (ed.), *Toward a Universal Theory of Religion*, Maryknoll, NY: Orbis, pp. 118–53.

—— (1993), *The Cosmotheandric Experience: Emerging Religious Consciousness*, edited with introduction by Scott Eastham, Maryknoll, NY: Orbis.

—— (1996), 'Modern science and technology are neither neutral nor universal', in *Europe-Asia: Science and Technology for Their Future*, Zurich: Forum Engelberg.

Panikkar, R. & Barr, R.R. (1989), *The Silence of God: An Answer of the Buddha*, Maryknoll, NY: Orbis.

Pannenberg, W. (1970), 'The working of the Spirit in the creation and in the people of God', in Pannenberg, W., Dulles, A. & Braaten, C.E. (eds), *Spirit, Faith, and Church*, Philadelphia: Westminster Press, pp. 13–31.

—— (1971), 'Toward a theology of the history of religions', in Pannenberg, W. (ed.), *Basic Questions in Theology*, Philadelphia: Fortress Press, pp. 65–118.

—— (1972), *The Apostles' Creed in the Light of Today's Questions*, Philadelphia: Westminster Press.

—— (1976), *Theology and the Philosophy of Science*, Philadelphia: Westminster Press.

—— (1977), 'Christian morality and political issues', in Pannenberg, W. (ed.), *Faith and Reality*, Philadelphia: Westminster Press, pp. 123–38.

—— (1984), 'Constructive and critical functions of Christian eschatology', *Harvard Theological Review* **77**, April, pp. 119–39.

—— (1985), *Anthropology in Theological Perspective*, Philadelphia: Westminster Press.

—— (1990), 'Religious pluralism and conflicting truth claims: The problem of a theology of the world religions', in D'Costa, G. (ed.), *Christian Uniqueness Reconsidered: The Myth of a Pluralistic Theology of Religions*, Maryknoll, NY: Orbis, pp. 96–106.

—— (1991), *Systematic Theology*, vol. 1, trans. G. Bromiley, Grand Rapids, Mich.: Eerdmans.

—— (1994), *Systematic Theology*, vol. 2, trans. G. Bromiley, Grand Rapids, Mich.: Eerdmans.

—— (1997), 'The doctrine of the Spirit and the task of a theology of nature' in Albright, C.R. & Haugen, J. (eds), *Beginning with the End: God, Science, and Wolfhart Pannenberg*, Chicago: Open Court, pp. 65–79.

—— (1998), *Systematic Theology*, vol. 3, trans. G. Bromiley, Grand Rapids, Mich.: Eerdmans.

Peters, T. (1993), *God as Trinity: Relationality and Temporality in Divine Life*, Louisville, Ky: Westminster John Knox.

Pinnock, C.H. (1984), *The Scripture Principle*, San Francisco: Harper & Row.

—— (1992), *A Wideness in God's Mercy: The Finality of Jesus Christ in a World of Religions*, Grand Rapids, Mich.: Zondervan.

—— (1996), *Flame of Love: A Theology of the Holy Spirit*, Downers Grove, Ill.: InterVarsity Press.

—— (2001), *Most Moved Mover: A Theology of God's Openness*, Grand Rapids, Mich.: Baker Academic Books.

Pinnock, C.H., Rice, R. & Sanders, J. (eds) (1994), *The Openness of God: A Biblical Challenge to the Traditional Understanding of God*, Downers Grove, Ill.: InterVarsity Press.

Prabhu, J. (ed.) (1996), *The Intercultural Challenge of Raimon Panikkar*, Maryknoll, NY: Orbis.

Race, A. (1982), *Christians and Religious Pluralism: Patterns in the Christian Theology of Religions*, Maryknoll, NY: Orbis.

Rahner, K. (1965), *Theological Investigations*, vol. 1, London: Darton, Longman & Todd.

—— (1966a), *Theological Investigations*, vol. 4, London: Darton, Longman & Todd.

—— (1966b), *Theological Investigations*, vol. 5, London: Darton, Longman & Todd.

—— (1969), *Theological Investigations*, vol. 6, Baltimore, Md: Helicon.

—— (1974), *Theological Investigations*, vol. 12, New York: Seabury.

—— (1975), *Theological Investigations*, vol. 13, New York: Seabury.

—— (1976), *Theological Investigations*, vol. 14, London: Darton, Longman & Todd.

—— (1981), *Theological Investigations*, vol. 17, New York: Crossroad.

—— (1982), *Foundations of Christian Faith: An Introduction to the Idea of Christianity*, New York: Crossroad.

—— (1983), *Theological Investigations*, vol. 18, London: Darton, Longman & Todd.

—— (1988), *Theological Investigations*, vol. 21, London: Darton, Longman & Todd.

—— (1997 [orig. 1970]), *The Trinity*, New York: Seabury.

Raj, A.S. (1998), *A New Hermeneutic of Reality: Raimon Panikkar's Cosmotheandric Vision*, Bern: Peter Lang.

Ramachandra, V. (1996), *The Recovery of Mission*, Carlisle, UK: Paternoster Press.

Rescher N. (1985), *The Strife of Systems*, Pittsburgh: Pittsburgh University Press.

Rice, R. (1985), *God's Foreknowledge and Man's Free Will*, Bloomington, Minn.: Bethany House.

Ruokanen, M. (1992), *The Catholic Doctrine on Non-Christian Religions According to the Second Vatican Council*, Leiden: E.J. Brill.

Saarinen, R. (1995), 'Eri uskonnot—sama Jumala? Jumalakuva uskontojen välisessä dialogissa' [Different religions—same God? Our perception of God in interfaith dialogue], in Ahonen, R. & Kvist, H.O. (eds), *Jumalan kasvot: Jumala ihmisen todellisuudessa* [*God's face: God in human reality*], Tampere, Finland: Kirkon Tutkimuskeskus, pp. 150–56.

Sachs, J.R. (1996), '"Do not stifle the Spirit": Karl Rahner, the legacy of Vatican II, and its urgency for theology today', in Dreyer, E. (ed.), *Catholic Theological Society Proceedings 51*, Chicago: American Catholic Theological Society, pp. 15–38.

Samartha, S.J. (ed.) (1974), *The Living Faiths and Ultimate Goals*, Maryknoll, NY: Orbis.

Sanders, J. (1995), *No Other Name: An Investigation into the Destiny of the Unevangelized*, Downers Grove, Ill.: InterVarsity Press.

Schwarz, Hans (2000), *Eschatology*, Grand Rapids, Mich.: Eerdmans.

Shults, F.L. (1999), *The Postfoundationalist Task of Theology*, Grand Rapids, Mich.: Eerdmans.

Smart, N. & Konstantine, S. (1991), *Christian Systematic Theology in a World Context*, Minneapolis: Fortress.

Taliaferro, C. (1998), *Contemporary Philosophy of Religion*, Malden, Mass.: Blackwell.

Thiemann, R. (1987), *Revelation and Theology: The Gospel as Narrated Promise*, Notre Dame, Ind.: University of Notre Dame Press.

Tidball, D.J. (1994), *Who Are the Evangelicals? Tracing the Roots of Today's Movement*, London: Marshall Pickering.

Vanhoozer, K.J. (ed.) (1997), *The Trinity in a Pluralistic Age: Theological Essays on Culture and Religion*, Grand Rapids, Mich.: Eerdmans.

Veliath, D. (1988), *Theological Approach and Understanding of Religions: Jean Danielou and Raimundo Panikkar: A Study in Contrast*, Bangalore: Kristu Jyoti College.

Verweyen, W.J. (1996), 'Pluralismus als Fundamentalismusverstärker', in Schwager, R. (ed.), *Christus allein? Der Streit um die pluralistische Religionstheologie*, Freiburg: Herder, pp. 132–9.

Volf, M. (1998), *After Our Likeness: The Church as the Image of the Trinity*, Grand Rapids, Mich.: Eerdmans.

Welch, C. (1952), *In This Name: The Doctrine of the Trinity in Contemporary Theology*, New York: Charles Scribner's Sons.

Williams, S. (1997), 'The Trinity and "other religions"', in Vanhoozer, K. (ed.), *The Trinity in a Pluralistic Age: Theological Essays on Culture and Religion*, Grand Rapids, Mich.: Eerdmans, pp. 26–40.

Wong, J.H. (1994), 'Anonymous Christians: Karl Rahner's pneuma-christocentrism and an East-West dialogue', *Theological Studies* **55**, pp. 609–37.

World Council of Churches (1975), 'Towards world community: Resources and responsibilities for living together', Memorandum of the World Council of Churches multilateral dialogue between Hindus, Buddhists, Jews, Christians and Muslims on 'Towards World Community – Resources and Responsibilities for Living Together'. April 1974, Colombo, Sri Lanka. Geneva: WCC.

Yong, A. (2000), *Discerning the Spirits: A Pentecostal-Charismatic Contribution to Christian Theology of Religions*, Sheffield: Sheffield Academic Press.

——— (2003), *Beyond the Impasse: Toward a Pneumatological Theology of Religions*, Grand Rapids, Mich.: Baker Academic Books.

Zizioulas, J. (1985), *Being and Communion: Studies in the Personhood and Church*, New York: St. Vladimir's Seminary Press.

Index